C000260841

About the author

Debut author, Matt Simkin, has travelled extensively across the world, fuelling his love for travel by working in the food and entertainment industry. Currently living in London, he continues to travel and write about his experiences.

@mattsimkin

FOOD, CULTURE, LATIN AMERICA

Matt Simkin

FOOD, CULTURE, LATIN AMERICA

Vanguard Press

VANGUARD PAPERBACK

© Copyright 2019
Matt Simkin

The right of Matt Simkin to be identified as author of
this work has been asserted by him in accordance with the
Copyright, Designs and Patents Act 1988.

All Rights Reserved

No reproduction, copy or transmission of this publication
may be made without written permission.
No paragraph of this publication may be reproduced,
copied or transmitted save with the written permission of the publisher,
or in accordance with the provisions
of the Copyright Act 1956 (as amended).

Any person who commits any unauthorised act in relation to
this publication may be liable to criminal
prosecution and civil claims for damages.

A CIP catalogue record for this title is
available from the British Library.

ISBN 978 1 784654 21 4

Vanguard Press is an imprint of
Pegasus Elliot MacKenzie Publishers Ltd.
www.pegasuspublishers.com

First Published in 2019

Vanguard Press
Sheraton House Castle Park
Cambridge England

Printed & Bound in Great Britain

For LJC

Foreword 26.12.15

Every time I come back from travelling, I return home with the regret that I have to come back to a life I'd much rather leave behind. It's as if I know that there's something to face up to the moment the wheels hit the runway. That 'something' is reality, and the desire to remain in my own bubble is never more urgent than in those last few moments before landing. The dream, like many, has always been to travel, and when I'm not travelling or feel distanced from being able to pack up and go again, the feeling of losing grip on my dream is confusing. I started this book years before I left as part of my own version of therapy to help deal with not going travelling.

Whilst looking for a job, people would always say, 'there is a job for that'. This is true, and what I've learnt is that there's always a story behind everything: the story of who wrote this book, who printed it, and who is reading it. Sometimes you think you know everything about someone when you don't at all; that is one of the beauties of travel. Of course you never know who you may meet and what they can tell you about something you don't know anything about.

Travelling around the UK and abroad, I've met some of the most interesting people when talking about food. From placing an order at a bar, a shack or even in a restaurant, I love to hear each individual's stories. Whether the food I'm to be served is reared from their own farm, or shipped in from abroad, I'm always curious to know how food and cultural stories of a place can blend into each other. After years of anguish on a wage at a job that I thought gave me comfort, freedom and happiness, I realised that two things – food and travel – interested me more than anything else. Small adventures and weekends away offered a slice of the life I craved, but they weren't appetising enough, so the money I had sensibly saved to buy a house went to a travel agent instead. I poured my savings into flights to Latin America, drinks at work-leaving parties, and raised some extra cash through selling as many of my possessions as I possibly could, things I never wanted and never needed. After all, I'm a middle-class bloke born in Watford, I'm hardly Che Guevara, and this book isn't about him, nor does it intend to change the world.

I broke my foot with four weeks to go until I flew, and met a girl who I was almost reluctant to leave behind. It wasn't a great start to my trip – hauling around a backpack with a set of crutches and resigning myself in the months prior to leaving, that the girl I knew and was with in London, would soon become the Girl Back Home (GBH). It is an emotional and mental assault that would stay with me and that gave me a reason to stay, but I couldn't silence the voice in the back of my mind asking: 'what if I never do this?'

Not prepared to take the gamble, I trust my instinct and head to the airport with nothing but hesitation, a backpack, notepad, my passport and – of course – a moon boot attached to my swollen foot. Leaving the dejected GBH in London, I board my flight to Mexico. I knew there would be times I'll love, and times that I hate, but as long as it's better than what I was doing, I didn't care.

Belize

Belize – best served eating lobster:
- 1 Whole lobster
- Garlic butter
- A portion of coconut rice
- Side salad

Fresh out of the lobster trap, behead and cut the lobster in half with a machete and toss it flesh side down over a wood fire grill. Leave for 5 minutes and spread garlic butter over it to melt into the meat until it's white and tender. Eaten on a bench in Caye Caulker out of a polystyrene box with pre-cooked rice and a salad, looking out to the beach.

To Belize – best served with a cocktail 28.12.15.

Preparing for the start of a journey is a strange feeling. The first time I embarked upon a long trip, doubt crept in. My whole life I'd wanted to travel, yet as my departure date grew nearer, uncertain nerves developed. It's the same every time: "Just get on the plane and deal with it later, Matt." With this in mind, I travelled from London Heathrow to Toronto, and then onto Cancun.

It's tiring and it's hot. Really hot. I had planned to head straight to Belize, having hated Cancun on a previous trip, but the bus I needed sold out. I head to downtown Cancun, the only place in Mexico I had ever felt unsafe, to kill a few hours until the Chetumal bus arrives.

Arriving in Chetumal, it's 3.45 a.m. and I'm greeted by aggressive taxi drivers waiting outside the bus terminal, berating me to get in. It seems that the only logical option is to sleep in the bus terminal; suddenly sleeping on a plane doesn't feel so difficult any more. After an hour's broken sleep, the rattling of the bus's engine wakes me; it's time to figure out how to get into Belize. I'm tired and disorientated, cold but trying to cross a border; I'm not sure where it is.

Upon meeting two older travellers, each wearing a full-page outfit from a retired travellers' magazine retailer with Birkenstock, it becomes apparent that it's more economical to share a taxi between us. Now here's a life lesson: unless you're tired to the point where you just don't care, never get into a car with strangers. Things started to go wrong when the taxi driver took myself and (as I discover within five minutes) the two recently single sixty-five-year-old women to the wrong ferry terminal. They went from bad to worse when my taxi companions, while standing in a small hut at the border with nothing for miles but open waste land and armed military, decide to refuse to pay the $25 exit fee that's necessary for overland exits from Mexico. A standard procedure fee to pay, and a Mexican border control team are not the best people to pick an argument with. It's a lose-lose situation as our taxi fare continues to rise, but eventually the female travel companions agree to pay the exit fee and we are on our way to the correct ferry terminal.

Before this trip I was looking forward to meeting travellers; some I'd rather never see again.

I wanted to go to the island of Caye Caulker, but with no boat until the afternoon I made my way there via San Pedro on a speedboat as I approached the thirtieth hour of travel since leaving London. Spontaneity is fun, but when you're tired and asked if you love every minute of travelling, the answer is a firm 'no'. Yet as soon as I arrive in Mexico, where people stumble over language barriers and point me in three different directions for the same boat, I start to feel excited. The confusion of what's going on and the feeling of acute alienation is all part of the thrill of travelling.

Docking into San Pedro, the small sandy beach has shops and stalls all the way along. The tourism boom has made San Pedro a popular stop for travellers and prices are inflated for that very reason. The sun's now up so naturally it's time for a piña colada. After a few hours of practice drinking cocktails on the beach in San Pedro in my awkward position of being sat in the sand in a foot brace and sweaty jeans, I'm now very unbalanced. I can't be bothered to get changed – my discomfort seems fitting for the moment, as I know that a more relaxed island awaits me.

The guy who makes the cocktail inadvertently reassures me that Caye Caulker is much more my speed, as he slags the island off for being what San Pedro used to be twenty years ago: less travelled, cheaper, quieter, and more relaxed. This is perfect – all trips should start on a beach to clear the head and relax. I wobble to the boat as the bartender mocks my tired legs and wishes me well, telling me to 'go slow'.

Caye Caulker – best served closer to Paradise 2.1.16.

Now this was more like it! I'm not greeted by loud Tiesto music from bars competing for punters like in San Pedro; instead a dusty sand road stretches out in front of me. No cars are allowed here, and it's the only main road on the whole island. Buggies drive up and down, up and down with not quite the intensity of rush hour traffic but… but there's a hammock on the beach with my name on it.

I get to my hammock and first things first. I drop my bag and sleep. Relief that I've finally got to my first destination gives me a sense of pleasure. Back home, while I sat behind a desk at work, this was exactly what I wanted to be doing. Just as I doze off, Justin Beiber blasts out from the speakers above my head; I guess this wasn't much more chilled than San Pedro after all. I'm all for a party, but I can't be bothered to play 'The Gringo' and cringy tourist just yet; before anything, I need my first taste of Caribbean waters. This moment was what I worked towards on those cold, wet days during London's winter, how miserable they are. There are always so many moments along the way that I think people back home would like to hear about, and travelling alone I almost imagine what those conversations would be like. I can't record them or even describe the smells, the colours or the people with the accurate conviction they deserve, recalling stories never do them justice.

I spend the first night with some dark rum in the hostel as I battle my jetlag. Rum will be a good ally here, but I should make a lukewarm attempt at being sociable so I introduce myself to an older guy at the bar who spends an hour telling me about his wealth. I couldn't care less. I later find out that he was a billionaire and owner of the hostel, and that he splits his time between Caye Caulker with his right-hand man, Benedict (who, incidentally, is in the Belize football hall of fame), and home in Texas with his third wife, who is twenty-five years old. This onslaught of random information was another reminder that you meet all kinds of random characters travelling.

Drinking rum and relaxing is my path for Caye Caulker. Despite my foot injury I was optimistic that it could hold out for snorkelling, so I joined a small tour group. The environmental chairman of the island takes us for a three-part dive onto one of the most famous corals in the world. As stingrays and sharks swim around us I feel as far from home as ever, and remind myself, while taking the number of wildlife around me for granted, that this moment needs to be cherished. The sharks, however, would probably disagree, as I manage to give one a swift kick in the face as I climbed back into the boat.

I feel less guilty when the tour guide, who upon first conversation seemed an environmental enthusiast, talked about the damage that his boat fumes cause the coral and the damage tours do. Such contradiction stains the experience. I am all too aware how the tourism factor can be a double-edged sword, providing jobs whilst ruining a landscape. The construction of a man-made beach on Caye Caulker causes further damage to the land, as sand is pumped underground from one side of the island to the other. It's so ugly and unnatural, yet the locals are in favour as it'll bring in more tourists. They live off the tourism trade and visitors aren't content to sit on the dock of the island and soak up the sun; apparently, they need a bigger beach.

The fishermen here seem to have it figured out for the simple life. Boats go out to catch conches and lobsters, which are grilled on the beaches and sold to tourists. Straight from the lobster traps, they're pulled out alive – heads off with a machete and thrown on the grill, wriggling around, holding their last breath. They're delicious. Caye Caulkers is best known for its lobster and coconut rice dinners – the best value dish you can buy on the island.

Amidst a break from burning my skin in the sun, I enjoyed a drink with the chef of the hostel, Jason. Moving to Caye Caulker from Belize City, he moved not to jump on the tourism boom (although that's where he now works) but to get away from the dangers of the capital city where his favourite pastime was shooting people. He assured me that 'people are too nice here to shoot anyone; having a gun's pointless and that suits me', so I continue to drink. Jason learned to cook from his wife and this new passion gave him a lease of life that seemed unimaginable in his old life. With lobster being the staple dish of the island, he invited me to cook dinner with him. I taught him some English dishes as he taught me his fried lobster fritters specialty. We drank beers before the local rum was passed around and we raised a toast to the imminent New Year.

I was here for New Year's Eve and there was, as always, too much fuss and build up for the most pointless party of the year. It's one of those events I always make plans for at the last minute, and this year was no different.

The day started early with beers, again with Jason and some other backpackers, (I'm still trying to avoid being a gringo on day 3), and as the fireworks went off amidst all the fun and laughs, I felt no different. As I tried to dance with hundreds of people I'd never seen before and would never see again, it felt like a pretty standard New Year's Eve. Then I looked out ahead of me. As far as New Years go, drinking beer on a tiny natural island just a two-minute boat ride from Caye Caulker wasn't a bad way to start off 2016.

I needed to crush the guilt of leaving the abandoned GBH and actually make the most of this year. It was very much in my hands. I was on my little island with welcoming Jamaican-Latinos and people from all over the world. In my ignorant bubble, no longer feeling how my life at home sucked the enthusiasm out of me, that energy was coming back now and it felt good.

Guatemala

Guatemala – best served eating tacos:
- 1 flat taco
- Pulled pork
- Crumbled white farmers cheese
- Sliced beetroot, cabbage
- Pickled carrots and jalapenos
- Xela street market tacos

Fry the taco in the pulled pork's hot oil. Once the taco is crunchy, pile the rest of the ingredients on top of the pork over the taco. Eaten on a park stool in Xela's central park, freezing cold, sipping mescal.

Xela – best served aimlessly wandering with fried chicken 9.1.16.

In my mind, the journey to get from one place to another in Central America is taken by foot, boat, bus, van and more. Last time I was travelling I felt rushed; this time around I am going to take a leisurely approach, travel slower and soak in my environment. It's so tempting to rush and squeeze everything in, but I accept that – as with everything – you can't do it all. I'm spending months in Central America if my 'plans' are anything to go by, though I feel as though it would take as many months to thoroughly explore Ecuador.

I left Belize with three other travellers I'd met in the hostel and travelled with them as far as Flores in the north of Guatemala. Border controls are like airports; you want to get through them as quickly as possible because they are awkward and uncomfortable, so naturally there's a two hour wait. Nobody seemed to know the reason, and despite being momentarily amused by a stray herd of bulls meandering past the bus, I felt anxious as a result of the boredom. Sat almost stationary with a dance remix of the Tetris soundtrack on loop, we then bounced along unpaved roads at an agonisingly slow pace, falling into potholes and surging out of the other side. It's so continuous, so disruptive and bad it's funny.

The delay arriving into Flores buys me little time for my connection, and as my first-world problems begin to stack up, my bank card that 'can be used anywhere in the world' is, essentially, useless as it appears unusable with the ATMs in Guatemala. The Guatemalans laugh off my cash problem and tell me not to worry, offering me a 'worry doll' toy to carry, which is a symbol to prevent their anxieties. With this surprising act of kindness, I realise that even after a few days on Caye Caulker the rat race of London is still in my system. The humbling gesture which I intend to heed, makes me feel a little freer as I continue on to Xela, in southwest Guatemala, alone.

Arriving in Xela, it is neither unpleasant nor picturesque. Then again, I've never arrived at a bus terminal anywhere in the world and thought 'this bus terminal is beautiful'. I pull into the main square and it's perfect: a small church in the square surrounded by dozens of street food vendors. I've signed up to a language school for a few weeks so that I can get by with the locals, and as I'm yet to see a tourist, it seems I'll need the lessons if I'm going to understand anything here.

I think it's important to have some basic pleasantries in a country – at least 'travelling language': how to get a room, a bus, order food, etc. My ambition is to become more advanced with the language, to be able to converse and learn more about where I am travelling. I still hate the rat race imbedded in me for thinking that would be an achievement; it adds a sense of distain to doing this.

The first week of classes are fun but intense. Sat opposite each other for five hours a day over an old school desk, my teacher speaks no English at all, so we often found it tough, or nearly impossible, to understand each other. I'm not sure awkward silences are a good thing in my language classes. A whiteboard was used to scribble words, vowels and adjectives – it's like a scene from the movie *Good Will Hunting* – two geniuses working together to tackle two of the easiest languages in the world and failing miserably with a sentence as apparently simple as 'what are you doing later today?'

I used the learning app, Duolingo, for six months prior to my trip, and this helped me get some footing. Google Translate was my saving grace: both a blessing and a frustration to realise just how necessary it is to travel with a smartphone. It has never before been so easy to research travel, but being so accessible with communication can be a burden when trying to take in the present situation without unnecessary phone distractions, more notably trying to move on from the GBH.

It is great to be in Xela, the Miguel de Cervantes School, which is also my home for the next few weeks. There are a few English speakers here, but we all try and speak Spanish to each other for practice. Guatemala is incredibly cheap and private one-to-one lessons are incredible value for five hours a day. I make friends with other students while sitting on the kerbs in the main square, munching on delicious $1 taco dinners, where eating the utensil you use to eat with, in the form of a corn taco or wrap, is the communal routine here. Being in one place and a country for an extended period of time makes you feel comfortable. So comfortable, that I often get lost on the snaking streets and end up somewhere I never intended to go.

On one occasion I stumbled into an old warehouse that had been converted into a local workers' lunch canteen – a style called 'comedores'. Noticing me straight away, the locals instantly invited me to sit down with them, and amidst the steaming pots and pans of stews and beans behind the dinner ladies which echo and reverberate in the loud room, a feast of fried chicken awaits. The guy sitting next to me encourages me to try it, and with my new understanding of the language, I find it easy, and myself at ease to accept. The workers' dinner of rice and refried black beans was not the most adventurous of meals, but the genuine smiles on the cooks' faces endeared me to them further. Knowing that someone who doesn't usually eat Guatemalan food enjoyed one of their favourite dishes, which they serve for their working regulars each day led them to look after me that bit more. They went out of their way to look after me and welcome me to their daily routine, something that tourists don't often experience. Making an effort with slowly spoken, broken Spanish aided one of the nicest episodes in the working life of the Xela people I have had, as they shared their excitement for their favourite meal and me being there with them, compared with their usual visitors and occurrence who seemingly return daily.

My 'go-to' free activity in a new place is aimlessly ambling: a great way to discover new places and learn about local customs. Even if three hours around Xela doesn't offer much, it's nice to feel comfortable exploring, and to be content.

The transportation around here and Guatemala can be described as 'second-hand' at best. Big yellow school buses, donations by the USA, have been Latinized with bumper stickers and food market crates strung to the roof with rope. The first world is helping the third world; perhaps my faith in humanity is being restored by seeing somewhere new after all!

Xela – best served eating a taco trying to learn the language 16.1.16.

My first lessons in language school – the arrogance of English speakers to assume everyone else speaks the same language and that it'll be OK. I did French for ten years at school and I couldn't buy a bus ticket in France now to save my life. Learning Spanish is a way to prevent that repeating itself.

Living in the highlands of Xela, I woke daily to cold mornings, and freezing showers to match. It was a brutal wake up call for the five hours of lessons a day that I'd signed up for, but a great distraction from the GBH. It felt like an easy day's work in comparison to the drain of working in London, although signing up for this number of hours every day for two weeks was exhausting, my teacher, Danny, was my hero. He made the language fun and taught me conversational chatter instead of focusing on phrases such as 'where is the toilet?' Going through exercise books in the class room, he also took me food shopping at the local market, learning vocab for foods that we bought. We'd have a beer together in a bar and get to know each other, all in Spanish. Despite being corrected ninety per cent of the time, a natural learning experience was exciting. I understand why travellers come here to learn as opposed to other touristic places in Guatemala.

The school also runs communal Guatemalan cooking classes, where everyone brings a homemade dish – a tradition in Guatemala when visiting other homes. Salsa classes are also organised. I consider myself to have an element of rhythm, which is why, when it was my turn to practise with a diminutive Guatemalan, I didn't focus on the difficulty or my embarrassment. Trying to reassure onlookers that I was not trying to butcher one of their favourite pastimes with my one-legged attempts at spinning my dance partner the wrong way, I somehow managed to scratch my partner's arm and add in a couple of awkward moments. I could probably do with salsa lessons too, best start those in English.

Before my trip, I was determined to hike around Guatemala as much as possible. In reality, my foot injury meant that I couldn't, so I missed out on hiking up volcano Santa Maria to see an eruption. Accepting disappointment and finding new things to look forward to, takes an unexpected amount of energy and effort as well as crushing the theory of 'loving every minute of travelling' when these disappointments come up. Despite intensive language classes, the communication barrier is still there and a lot of the time I haven't a clue what's going on but I'm happy to be ignorant on some things. I am starting to feel engrossed in Xela and the idea of going back to more touristy places or 'the gringo trail', as it's known, is a bit 'cringy'. I am a tourist myself, of course, and like anyone I am drawn to popular destinations to meet likeminded travellers and see the worthwhile attractions in those areas, but the purpose of my trip is to fully immerse myself in Guatemalan life, as opposed to vomiting in a party hostel to a Tiesto soundtrack – a tacky, fake inauthentic experience – 'the Tiesto effect'.

Being in a school that you voluntarily sign up for implements a routine that as a result brings the Friday feeling after the classroom, and therefore socialising at the end of the week with other students is something I look forward to. I met James and Carly on the bus to Xela, and we celebrated our first week of classes by watching the local football team, Xelaju FC, play in a stadium where kids are encouraged to set off fireworks to improve the atmosphere and to distract them from begging or selling sweets for cash. The same children sell the legendary Xela tacos outside the stadium with their mothers. The women are still traditionally the kitchen workers, whilst their fathers sell beers from their vans. The food vending culture of selling beers and tacos is a family affair here. It's my round to buy a beer, and it's all a bit suspect as groups of friends who are fathers to the kids hand beer and cash to each other with what seems like no order or coordination.

As I get to the front of the queue there is, suspiciously, no more beer left. I figure that they're running low and want to keep it for themselves, until one of the fathers, swaying drunkenly, approaches me with a stern look and shouts Spanish in my face. I don't have time to 'Google Translate' it – and this would be too awkward – but his friends laugh as his teenage daughter, who is standing in the crowd, screams. An English-speaking local tells me that the man has just announced that I will marry his daughter in exchange for beer. Lifting my hands above our heads he heralds me as his new son, and insists I have photographs with him and his mortified sober daughter in exchange for beers. I willingly agreed, and leave his daughter on the brink of tears, joining James and Carly with a new round of freshly poured beers as Xelaju lose 3-1.

The night ends in a tiny one-room-sized local mescal bar, getting to know James more and drinking too much mescal to top off a fun evening. The next morning, I begin a gentle climb to the spiritual ceremonial spot, Laguna Chicabal (a volcanic lake), with the other students, a colonial ritual that feels far away from city life in Xela, a good test for my foot, while dealing with a hangover that I blame the altitude for, and I am now able to tick 'climbed a volcano' off my bucket list. An accomplishment with regard to the 'things I would never do if I'd decided to stay miserable in London' list, Xela has been an interesting place and is serving me well.

Leaving Xela – learning about 'Gringos' 21.1.16.

I have now been here for three weeks and feel that I have a decent intermediate standard of Spanish. It's been a lot of hard work with homework each day, but now my sister, Sarah, is coming to visit so I'm heading off to see more of Guatemala.

For my last evening in Xela I go out to dinner with Danny and some friends from the school. It's Danny's birthday, and we went to a small restaurant, but the mood changed from jovial to non-conversational when a group of American students sit on the table behind us. 'Stupid gringos', Danny muttered under his breath. The group were loud and obnoxious for a small place, but I asked him what the difference is between these 'gringos', and the way that I am seen as a 'gringo'. Danny's answer is that it's in the way that you conduct yourself and what you want to get out of travelling. Although it is his job and Danny respects our desire to learn the language and engross ourselves with locals, an honest opinion considering his exposure to different travellers through his job. But what kind of gringo am I, then? 'Gringo' is always used to sound aggressive to me, as if the identified person is being intrusive, a dirty representative of travellers based on the definition coming from locals telling foreigners to leave – 'green-eyes – go' – abbreviated to 'gringo'. Having sat with Danny in the square eating street food, a spot I'd come to get a break from class during the day, I'm not sure whether I look like a gringo or not to outsiders... perhaps the level of respect is the difference to make it clear whether those in the square who I make company with want me there, or whether they want me to go.

Looking to the next place, I'm curious and nervous to be out of my bubble again and head to the country's most touristy city, Antigua. The 'Tiesto effect', the gringos that Danny despises, the crowds of people… still, they're not the worst problems to have. To feel overexcited about exploring again cements for me that looking back on my lack of happiness at home, I am beginning to understand how important it is to be content with what you have. Just having that mindset is the is the challenge.

Antigua – best served with marshmallows up a volcano 26.1.16.

As Sarah is meeting me in Antigua, I rode the old American school bus, which cost less for the four-hour journey than my taxi ride to the bus terminal. With the bus ride, a theme is developing: bumping the whole way, sandwiched between two large women while my bag rolled from side to side on the roof rack, I was ready for out. Everyone seemed to know when to jump on or off the bus, and as soon as the bus approached cobbled paths and colonial buildings I intuitively knew that I'd arrived in quaint Antigua and jumped off. Unfortunately, I was then told that I was still an hour's walk away from the centre. It was boiling hot but I had no other option than to walk, with my bag and limping foot, towards the large church turret I could see in the distance – a beacon with a backdrop of beautiful volcanoes.

With plenty of museums, restaurants and shops, Antigua caters to tourists yet retains a laid-back atmosphere. The volcano hike up Acatenango is the most popular excursion, yet a step too far for my foot after its recent test. The city is an international food haven and, with that, in comparison to Xela, the prices are comfortably three times more and the city is much more touristy – excellent food, but this is my first reminder that I'm back on the gringo trail. Eating out for Guatemalans is not a regular occurrence. They stick to the workers' markets as a treat, while here, to eat in a restaurant, often with laid out cutlery as opposed to the relaxed commodore approach, is the most lavish of pleasures.

Acatenango, the active volcano, was one of the hikes I had desperately wanted to do, but instead I settled for the volcano, Pacaya. A guide is a necessity for these kinds of hikes due to bandits who rob tourists en route, so Sarah and I joined a group. Hiking up a volcano is an inspiring and peaceful experience as you scale up mounds of molten rock, but being in a group with tourists who complain about the uphill ascent is far from peaceful. Of course it's uphill – it's a volcano! At this point in my trip, the GBH and I have agreed to cut each other off, as opposed to dragging this out long-distance, and the added negativity on this climb isn't doing me any favours. I don't want to hate doing tours as they're often the convenient way to see certain places and are a great way of meeting new people, but I found myself walking away from the group at the summit for a moment to myself. The ground was steaming; heat from the lava rose from beneath my feet, cue to pull out some marshmallows to cook against the molten earth. Enjoying this experience with my sister was great, but sometimes I need to be on my own. It's one of those days when I hate other travellers and I was hating myself over the GBH. Home was still in my head, even though I'm so glad not to be there. It was holding onto me in a cruel way.

Lake Atitlan – best served with hippies 29.1.16.

Lake Atitlan is the postcard of Guatemala. Dotted with colourful Mayan villages around its vast shore, we chose to spend our first night in Pana, one of the largest towns on the lake. Slowly driving down hairpin roads to the lake, the mountains around us were as impressive as the lake itself. Pana is the busiest town and I wasn't keen to get involved in the tacky touristy restaurants on the strip. My trip was still in its early days and avoiding being another gringo is paramount. Being beside the water was so peaceful, yet I missed the friendly family-run businesses that I'd seen so far in Guatemala.

From Pana we hopped onto a small boat which drenched me the whole way as I swallowed far more dirty lake water than I anticipated, something that was to come up again later in the evening. Saint Marcos is a chilled out hippy village with picturesque views of the lake. As paths wind in-between hostels, trees and shrubs, hippies serenely lie abandoned on the streets. This was, without a doubt, the hippiest place that I have ever been to. With nothing to do but relax on the rocks, this was the perfect place to catch up with my sister and take the time to slow down again.

Still fresh from a rigid and boring job, I find that this hippy culture misses any Guatemalan influence; more ironic and hypocritical. Overhearing conversations of a free world, of how their paths have led them here from a crystal reading, and how the local Guatemalans deserve equality, the hippies interrupt themselves to get cash out of their American bank, which they spend on acid to take in their five-star hotel, where the local staff are paid less a week than they are an hour. Fair play, enjoy yourself and your moment, but their ignorance is nauseating. The hippies work in the fields for 'escapism', yet they know that they are soon returning to a reality that they preach against, just as I do. These hippies preach about equality as they have a whip-round for money to buy drugs off an eight-year-old drug dealer, and I ask myself: 'where's this equality and free world you want?' Preach all you like but fuelling the fire of such issues by buying drugs off someone in a desperate situation who has probably never sat in a restaurant before as you are doing, is insincere and hypocritical. Still, it was entertaining to listen to their nonsense. I don't feel bad if they're happy, but they should take some more responsibility; the gringo tag I have in my head is how I imagine Latinos judge other travellers by.

The 27 Club – best served with a view 30.1.16.

I've reached that infamous age of twenty-seven, the age for famous people to die. I try not to dwell on that fact, and instead feel optimistic that this could be my best year yet. With it being my birthday, we had strategically decided to visit the livelier side of the lake, San Pedro, one of the cheapest places on the tourist trail. As you arrive, you're greeted by American-Irish pubs and a strip of UV-lit bars that are more like the Khao San Road in Bangkok than anything remotely Latino. These types of places can no doubt be enjoyable, but having come from San Marcos to be inundated with noise and tackiness, it felt awkward. I took advice from a friend about where to stay, but I soon realised that I should have taken into account that this friend and I have very different tastes. Upon arrival, it became apparent that Sarah and I wouldn't be spending too much time in the hostel.

I didn't know much about the lake before arriving. I thought it would be a boat ride, not a 35km circumference with multiple villages and things to do. We ventured to San Juan, a settlement with weavers and painters sprawled out on the pathway leading up to the mountains. Within the peaks themselves, which being so high and dry are the perfect climate to grow coffee, plantations overlook the numerous shops serving up the best brew around. The weavers' skills are fascinating, their intricate works take weeks to complete, weave by weave. The painters spend up to four days working on a piece the size of an A4 page, and only receive ten US dollars when they make a sale. As a day job goes, it's of little surprise that most took the initiative to build up the tacky western restaurants in San Pedro and make the most of the growing tourism.

The artistry of the country seems so undervalued. Although that benefits me as a tourist, it makes me feel guilty about being 'skint' in London earning £20,000 a year. It felt a lot of money at the time, which it was, but my greed in wanting more, wanting the next best thing with the impatience that I developed, is laughable in comparison now. The comparison is thought provoking, but the terms, 'first world' and 'third world', carries weight here – we are worlds apart. Although Guatemala is more developed than I expected, it's still one of the poorest countries in the world. The locals' pride in their work and their talent is incredibly endearing. It's so refreshing that they're delighted to sell me a piece to simply 'enjoy'. The 'first world' price of art is so unattainable for me that I wouldn't even bother to stop and see the beauty in it. Once again I'm humbled by the artistic expression from those who have very little share.

The highlight of my birthday, however, was waking at 3.30 a.m. for a hike to a place called 'Indian Nose'. We were fortunate to discover that a £10 tourist bus was not necessary, so we took the local route via chicken buses for a tiny fee. The hour or so bus ride out of San Pedro felt like it would be arduous, but having never had a birthday abroad or at the top of a mountain, the appeal outweighed tired limbs. The hike in the dark was a little jittery, following footprints in sandy paths from previous days with no idea of the surroundings. The only light from a lantern at the top of the summit, or 'the nose'.

Arriving at the top through a fence, we see street lights from the villages below; no longer brightly coloured but glowing yellow lights are scattered around the rim of the lake. As the dark blue lines of the horizon rise slowly and a yellow-golden-orange sunrise forms in front of us, clouds cover the dark lake. They looked like soft pillows in the forefront of a night-blackened sky. The light changes are intense, therapeutic and well worth the wake-up call, there's few better entries to 'the 27 Club'.

As the sun continued to rise, a small Guatemalan man emerges and demands an extortionate entrance fee in order to reach the very tip of the nose. There's a toll booth at the bottom of the mountain that we didn't know about, and he is insistent we pay... in addition to a fee for us climbing the mountain without a guide. Our choices were to pay or leave, and as the sun had now risen, we chose the latter. We turned to head back down the mountain, but instead were locked in a pen (masquerading as a fence) that we had originally walked through. Now our only option was to stay, so we dragged out our time there, took more photos and after more haggling – whilst being held hostage – we paid the guy, the gate was unlocked and we were allowed to leave.

Now this was a time where I wished I'd had a tour guide, although the fact that we'd just been taken hostage at the top of a mountain whilst being fleeced didn't give me much hope for how legitimate they can be. The other benefit of being with a tour is there's no need to wait around for an hour and a half for a chicken bus to get back to San Pedro. The bus arrived, the whole town appears and a ruckus develops out of nowhere to board the chicken bus. Keen to return to San Pedro, we weren't willing to wait for the next. With the driver's help we climbed onto the roof of the bus and helped to hoist up an array of bags. These would become our seats. The sun was out, the road was covered with pot-holes and my seat is a 40kg bag of avocados that are on their way to the markets in the villages around the lake. Going in-between hairpin bends with a beautiful backdrop as the girls screamed with fear and held on for dear life, I was totally content to have had such a unique morning in a beautiful place.

Back in town, I spend the rest of the day exploring backstreets as a small group develops of myself, Sarah, James, Carly and Megan. In an overdeveloped part of the lake, some live music winds down along with poorly connected phone calls, food and tequila. It was time to part ways with James and Carly. Perhaps as I'm travelling solo and feel I can meet people more easily, I've noticed a lot of couples have been good company in comparison to previous trips. Perhaps it's because I'm missing the GBH and I want that kind of company here with me. It would be nice to have someone to share the experiences with. Sarah is a great travel companion, and spending close time with family is nice; something I wouldn't often say when I'm at home, but it's just not the same.

Tikal – best served with termites 2.2.16.

On the way to Tikal, and the city of Isla Flores is a stopping-off point about an hour away from my destination. There is little to see or do, but I watch groups of friends come together by the riverside to eat, drink and have a good time. Partying is seen as a rare indulgence to many whilst eating is a necessity, so this is a time when most get together and share each other's company. The street vendors bring enormous pots and pans straight onto the street from the kitchens, and there are no limitations on who can sit and eat as people sprawl over the streets before we continue onto Tikal.

Tikal National Park is older than Christ, from its old pronunciation of 'Tika-a-a-l', which translates as 'The Whispering City'. With no understanding of Mayan history to date, Sarah and I buy a guide to show us around the ruins in this enormous, humid jungle of a park. The acoustics between the ruins engulf everything in the park to make you feel how big and grand it really is, a Mayan amphitheatre. We were surrounded by enormous trees with animals scattering beneath our feet. In the distance we heard the echo between the mating calls of the national bird, the quetzal.

Guatemalans are notoriously short, and thousands of years ago when these enormous stone structures were built, the Mayans were even smaller. Plenty of locals nonchalantly carry enormous amounts of weight in wood and stone for constructing their homes across the country, and that's impressive for their body ratio. But looking at these towering structures around me and knowing that they were built years ago, so far from any civilisation and on difficult jungle terrain, is mind-blowing beyond recognition. Perhaps the termite nests which sit in the trees are what keep the Guatemalans going; they taste like carrots and are, apparently, full of nutrients. This was one of the more peculiar things I have eaten. Although Guatemalans don't have a staple dish to their name, Mayans' use of corn for their food and their use of corn tacos as a utensil, make corn the most frequently used ingredient to this day across the country. The humidity from the jungle and the limestone flooring means that climbing the monuments to gaze over the empire is possibly the hardest, yet most satisfying, way to cool down.

Once the morning crowds have died down, the animals take over. Birds and howler monkeys scream at each other on what feels like a negatron, completely hidden to the eye as coatis and peacocks graze the walkways around the monuments which we explore. The chance to be close to the animals for the first time at the UNESCO heritage site is exhilarating having not been close to animals on land on this trip, and certainly never in London. I would have loved to stay a night, camping in tents or cabins, but my budget has already taken quite a hit, and some things you have to miss out on, however much I thought I'd do everything. To be able to see the sunrise here and be around such an intense soundtrack of wildlife would have been a real experience, and I hope others are able to do this.

I feel aggrieved at the moronic nature of the human race at times. The tag of a being a 'traveller' and 'tourist' can be easy to throw around negatively, but when I learnt that archaeologists have only exposed twenty per cent of the ruins to protect them from vandals, I found it both logical yet infuriating. Who would vandalise this? People have engraved their names or marked their tag into the ruins. The names 'Dave', 'Jose' or 'Jules' are not Mayan or inspiring in any shape or form to be remembered for thousands of years to come. Areas of the park are receiving maintenance work, which is good to preserve the site, but to close sections indefinitely for this damage is maddening. When things have taken thousands of years to build and are being kept in good condition for generations to come, I hope people can be as conscientious as those working to preserve it now. The excitement from this negativity, however, is that where I am currently sat writing, there are underground tunnels. Like a Mayan highway system still yet to be discovered, there's still another part of the Mayan world in Tikal to be explored.

Semuc Champey – best served by a child 5.2.16.

Seven hours rattling from side to side in a stuffy van off road, driving hundreds of miles through mountains with no sight of civilisation. From any direction in Guatemala, the drive to the closest point of life to Semuc Champey is the beaten-up town of Lankin, with kids running riot in their football shirts, screaming frantically as tuk tuk bikes drive around, yet amongst the remoteness I felt very relaxed.

From Lankin, our hostel was another half-hour drive rattling around through darkness in the boot of a pickup truck to our ecolodge, Utopia Hostel. We arrived in the middle of the night to the sound of river rapids down the hill from our chicken-fence built cabin. The wooden frame bends in the slightest breeze as insects crawled on the outside of our mosquito nets. With no wifi or security, yet knowing it was so remote and safe, it was worth the long drive.

Clusters of civilisation make up the dispersed population located in waste lands so remote they make me wonder how they were ever founded in the first place, perhaps only possible by mistake. The river that we could hear at night is the main attraction of Semuc Champey, which has a short hill climb with a view over the turquoise lagoons below, flowing into each other in a staircase formation. As it's scorching hot, a swim in the therapeutic waters accompanied by fish harmlessly nibbling away at me, is a good way to spend a day.

This is a beautiful area with plenty to do in a welcomed, unforced manner. I explored caves and waded through high waters, climbing sharp rocks in pitch black tunnels with nothing but a hand-held candle. The lack of oxygen meant that your voice seemed so silent in the tunnels adding a sense of mystery to the unknown dark path. With the hostel ordering me to sign a waiver upon arrival, it basically outlined: 'we are so far from civilisation that if anything happens to you, it takes a day to get to the hospital. You may die. It's not our fault', there was little I could do.

Walking between each nearby attraction, local children run up to us selling beers from their coolers. The children are illiterate and all introduce themselves as Ronaldo. A language they do understand however, is that of bartering, and from the age of five these children make their first foray into working life. Some, I imagine, will be doing this their whole lives. They make their living from tourist groups, when people come along like us, we pay a small fee, enabling their family to live for the week. The first and third worlds have never felt so far apart.

Goodbye Guatemala – Best served craving the American dream. 6.2.16.

Guatemala is not typically known for its cuisine. Being one of the poorest countries in the world, most locals live on two of the world's most accessible commodities, rice and corn. Rice comes with every meal, but the different areas of Guatemala have their own character, and each state accompanies its beloved rice with its own variation of black beans to go alongside it. It's basic, it's cheap, but every area is a pleasant surprise. The variations of rice dishes reflect how the communities represent themselves. Each community congregates to eat food together with their homemade utensil – their beloved tacos – at the markets, or a home cooked meal (cooked by the wife, of course). The notion that a male would take a cookery class or not be the main earner in a household is laughable. Eating together, being together is important; the culture of sitting around the table in the home outweighs the lavish eating-out lifestyle that I perhaps took for granted in London.

Although the country is growing, it's too limited and underdeveloped. The American influence can't be ignored. America is recognised as the land of prosperity. If you make it there, you've truly made it. It's such a hard thing to achieve, as typical Guatemalans won't spend twenty dollars on a vacation. Their life is their family and earning money to live. The idea of getting beyond that is but a dream. They love the American buses, they love fried chicken (which they have adopted and is sold by each street vendor) almost in homage.

Being geographically so accessible from America and Mexico, the inevitable tourism boom is taking place and bringing a global cuisine demand with it. They even try to make the best of the bad American-Mexican beer they've inherited and tried to vary it by adding soya sauce-soaked lime wedges to improve the flavour and give it their own Guatemalan stamp. The American influence goes back to the 1800s, when larger fruit suppliers in the States would use Guatemalan land and labour as a cheaper alternative for growing their empires as they ship it back to America. Owning forty per cent of arable land in Guatemala, their dominance grew to become what it is today, and won't be changing any time soon.

My time here was dominated in my mind by my own reintroduction to education, something that Danny would hammer into me each day; yet education also seems to be the country's greatest downfall. Teaching is one of the most respected professions in the country, yet so many children are without formal education. They're learning and improving, but with no structural support, the confusion of American acceptance and the anti-gringo idealism means Guatemala's path to their own 'American Dream' is by interacting with the visitors, their tourism or local cuisine openings.

El Salvador

El Salvador – best served eating pupusas.

- 2 cups ground flour
- Pinch of salt
- 1.5 cups warm water
- 1 cup grated cheese

Mix the ground flour and salt together adding the water little by little, then roll into a flat circle. Fold the mixture to be stuffed with cheese, roll till it's smooth and circled. Then press onto a hot stove and flip when golden. Eaten while pretending I'm part of the surf culture in El Tunco.

El Tunco – best served (not) surfing 10.2.16.

"Don't go there," they said. Well now, I'm obviously going to go there aren't I. It won't be as bad as everyone says…

El Salvador is the smallest country on my route, so I'll spend the shortest amount of my travel time here. Parting ways with Sarah after a busy few weeks moving around, it was time to slow down and head to the more relaxed part of a notoriously dangerous country. The fear of travelling for some people comes from thoughts on what seem and sound like a dangerous place, it's a downer that you never want to hear. It's an opinion often based around little knowledge or understanding, but going to El Salvador it was justified. It's dangerous, but all you can do is sit on the bus and enter the country. Just like every other bus ride, it goes fine. Should there ever be an issue here, one of the most likely places to encounter trouble would be at a border, so I had no reason to be anxious travelling here.

I headed to the coastal town of El Tunco to try my hand at surfing in this famous surf spot – the Pacific coastline of the continent is popular for the sport. As I weigh up prices for renting a board, I manage to nick my foot and lose my balance on the pebbled beach. I decide that it's still too soon for my foot to surf now without its boot, especially as my balance on land (let alone on water) leaves a lot to be desired. The idea of surfing looks and sounds great, the reality – not happening.

The town has no glamorous frills – easy-going with enough to do, beach babies can get stuck here and surf morning and night. While the realisation that the surf culture would not be for me at this time, sitting on the beach and drinking beers at night to pass the time, suits me – no problem. The bittersweet curse is that this heat is no ordinary heat. Reaching 35 Celsius by 8 a.m., with little breeze, it's impossible to do anything come midday as all pores are dripping with sweat. Cooling down in the shallow ocean, enormous waves struck the beach like a wave pool at an amusement park. The physical struggle of flirting with the threat of drowning and sitting on the quiet beach with a beer always leads to good conversation with surfers and other 'wannabe' surfers, like myself. Starting and ending the day by having a swim in the world's largest pool, the Pacific Ocean, is an easy way of bringing a smile to anyone's face. Looking out and seeing nothing but the most incredibly intense orange sunset through the rock formation and the front of the beach, with blue ocean going for miles and miles with nothing else to see, thinking 'Fuck you, office job that I hated.'– a moment when I can laugh over any doubts that I had for travelling.

Beers on the beach escalates, I had a night out hopping from surf bar to surf bar in the small town which can be walked around in five minutes. On the weekend it was especially busy, even for a tourist destination, as El Salvadorans come down from neighbouring cities for a weekend away. The fiery Latino oomph on the dance floor gave every bar a lift and an understanding as to why they want to come here – because it's the prize of the country. Visiting here is a pleasure for them, the place to be and enjoy the great things of El Salvador – the food, party and beach.

San Salvador's murderous gang culture has led to a new

breakthrough for the government, and they're now able to clean up its act. The police can now arrest members of the named '18' and '13' gangs on the spot without a warrant as part of a plea for them to stay out of the way. "Fight amongst yourselves, not with the innocent," was the basic philosophy, with murder being the biggest crime associated with drug culture.

El Salvadorans are great people, and not just in spite of their criminal history. A pair of them, unprompted, introduced themselves to me at the bar in perfect English and offered to buy me a beer to beat the queue. I've never heard people speak so passionately about their home, despite the gang troubles that have tainted the reputation of the country. They explained to me the 'El Salvador Dream', of how they left the capital and moved to El Tunco with friends as a collective effort to try and get the country back on the world map and make it a destination again. I notice that Latinos I've met often need a hero to look up to, a motivation to aspire to; they're acting out of duty for their country's will to improve itself which is commendable in comparison to the self-entitlement that the world often holds for itself. A progressive culture derived from the Americans, this 'El Salvador Dream', is to make the little country a destination in Central America.

The conversations I have with the locals whilst eating their classic pupusa dish on the street, confirmed every thought I'd had since entering the country. There's no hiding the issues this country has. It's rough in El Salvador, which is why I chose not to travel too far off the beaten track. Copycat gangs have had run-ins with tourists, something that seems unthinkable whilst I've been eating street food and chatting away with locals passing by.

Similar to Guatemala, the staple dishes that they live off are based on what is most accessible, there's no opportunity to be more expansive, pupusa street stalls are a trade mark recurrence here on almost every road. A pupusa is a street snack that's basically a stuffed tortilla with meat and cheese, thought to have been first created two thousand years ago. Their habit of sticking with what they've got and have access to doesn't change. Compared to their neighbours though, they are smarter at using the ocean to their advantage with their fishing importation. They 'eat, live and breathe the ocean' for both food and work.

A daytrip goes to nearby La Libertad, a small fishing village with a seafood market that runs the length of its pier. All of the traders are selling a variety of fresh delicious fish, which is the staple protein for locals here. Everyone seems happy and friendly – from the group of travellers I'd met at a local restaurant to the bus driver – and it's a shame their reputation is one they don't deserve. It's a testament to how, whatever life throws at you, the way you conduct yourself can make those around you feel better. The glass of life being half full on this account is the best attitude, and one I hope I can take with me.

The country has issues, but for a tourist, they're all so utterly complicated and intertwined in decades of political confusion that I'm not here for long enough to even begin to get my head around it all, nor do I need to when the culture of this town doesn't want to either. If you had no idea there were issues here, you wouldn't notice and you'd just appreciate that this is a very untravelled gem of a country. The government has invested in new highway systems and roads to help with transportation across the country, which has improved the exportation routes. Economically they're getting stronger, while the beaches alone from what I've seen are worth the trip. There is a lot of police presence. This would be the only thing to make you think there may be something wrong, yet it's comforting to feel they'll protect you should an unknown issue arise – the ignorance of not knowing the issue is bliss.

The Travel Companion – best served solo?

When travelling solo, people worry about it being dangerous or lonely. This can happen, of course, but it's no different to home, which can also be all of those things. Out here, the way to meet people is to be outgoing and sociable. Here it's a normal and an enjoyable way to share the enjoyment of the food.

For a trip I've invested so many emotions in before I left, this is a selfish mission. I meet people who need to move on from a place and don't because they want to stay (or feel they have to) with their travel companions. My pragmatic approach to making friends while away is that, with this being a solo trip for me, I'm not prepared to let other people get in the way of doing what I want to do or where I want to go, especially when I've only just met them. I'm not someone to claim that, after one day of hanging out with someone, they've become my new best mate and that they're my new perfect travel companion, or travel family. The reality is, you probably won't see this person ever again (and seeing them on Facebook doesn't count).

I left having drilled into myself that I have always been a nomad, albeit having plenty of friends and family. This was my solo trip – a one-way ticket alone. Feel free to come visit, but if when and where doesn't fit for me, you probably won't see me. Sarah knew this and took the initiative to jump on board at the start, knowing that I was planning to sign up to a language school and explore afterwards. We had a great time together, and being related we have similar traits both good and bad, but when I'm in physical pain (the foot) or emotional pain (the GBH), she can be sympathetic and understanding whilst having the energy to go and do something positive and take advantage of being away. That, for me, is a good travel companion.

Spending time with people when I'm away is similar to what you need back home: common ground. In Xela I was with people who wanted to learn a language, but was not restricted to expanding on that. Travelling solo is where I feel most comfortable. As a traveller it's easier and I don't have to rely or keep an eye on anyone else. Being the only person to experience certain things is just as appealing in a selfish way.

Honduras

Driving through – Best served with an iguana.

I once worked with UNICEF, who had Honduras down as one of the worst three countries in the world. The tourist attractions here are safe and spectacular, although I didn't take the time to stop off and see them.

An uneventful, boring and slow journey as we weave between small clusters of houses every twenty minutes or so in a battered rusty minivan, and somehow a passenger knows when to jump off through no communication with the driver and they'd jump out and walk into the wilderness. The minibus would halt briefly and the one-legged driver would top up fuel from kids selling coke bottles filled with petrol on the side of the road which would provide something to look at curiously amid the uncomfortable, unbearably hot journey during the day.

At one stop, a passenger assisted the driver with his disability to climb up on the roof of the minibus and help him pull the luggage off. As the bus wobbles with every movement of the unbalanced weight above us, I am distracted by the group of kids next to our van selling fuel who have cruelly tied up three large iguanas by their tails. Heckling the driver with language I couldn't understand, within a flash the child flipped one iguana up by the stiff tail into his hand, and gutted it with a machete in front of our stationary minibus, which is now only filled with western tourists. The bus erupts with girls screeching as the blade saws into the stomach of the live creature, which squirms as its guts hang out. I watch in disbelief as more guts are ripped out of the iguana two yards in front of my face.

The suspension of the bus has a bounce as the one-legged driver jumps back into his seat and revs the engine, carrying on as if nothing had happened. At the border he tells me that iguanas are endangered as they're sold for soup stocks, which are apparently good for a hangover cure. I wasn't hungover, more nauseous having watched that brutal butchering. Maybe I'll try it some other time.

Nicaragua

Nicaragua – best served eating plantain.
- Peel long lengths of plantain
- Grill them gently on each side until they're crunchy.

Served on a disposable plate. Offer with tobacco sauce and a pickled mixed salad of cabbage, carrot, onion and diced habaneros with a side of fried chicken. Eaten leaning through a bus window to the jungle.

Crossing over 10.2.16

When I was at home, it was the unknown of Central America that appealed to me. A part of the world that isn't talked about as fervently as other destinations. I didn't know much about Nicaragua, but that alone made it all the more enticing as I sat in my box-sized-room in London.

I crossed the border after another stuffy long eight-hour rattily ride, this time in a minibus. It was warm and humid as I stood waiting at passport control, and I didn't have the correct currency to buy a bottle of water in what would have been some kind of redemption of the situation for me. After my passport was checked and stamped, I headed back to the minibus to carry on the journey. It's slow and the dragged-out manner of the journey makes it tediously stressful. The rat race back home could be as equally uncomfortable, but at least you knew it got you where you need to go. In Central America, I can't say the same and I love that. I'm always thinking 'How the hell did we get here alive?' Yesterday I was on a bus driving at full pelt when the driver's wingman climbed over me, out of the window and onto the roof with a sack of potatoes on his back. There was no room inside the bus, but there's always room on the roof.

As the dust from the road starts to filter through the wheezy air con, I take in the scenery. Mountains upon mountains stretch out from each side of the road, and it's at this moment when I realise how great this journey is, and how lucky I am to be here.

Perfection isn't always easy to come by. You have ideas about the place you're going to, but the truth is that when you're hot, tired and in an unfamiliar environment, these grand visions can melt into the landscape. You feel uncomfortable and nauseous for the most part. I find that I get past these feelings once I truly start to reflect on where I am, in this moment. At the end of the day, all you really have is a bag, a passport and yourself.

Leon – La Revolution – best served at a Fratanga Grill 10.2.16.

Arriving in Leon after an eleven-hour journey, this wasn't the start of spending the time here I had planned, but that familiar feeling of being lost somewhere I've never been before smothers that. My Spanish has marginally improved since Xela so taking directions is my only hope, yet one that comes with no guarantee of me getting anywhere fast. After what feels like a hundred wrong turns later, I find my hostel just as it starts to get dark. The hostel staff refuse to speak Spanish to me, as it's not their native tongue, allowing me yet another excuse as to why my Spanish isn't improving, not that I'm expecting to be some kind of Latino by now. Practising Spanish on the tourist trail is hard with other tourists around as so many don't bother to learn the language, but hospitality staff also want to practise their English as the country starts to develop more and more of a tourism industry.

Walking around Leon, it feels like a relative of urban Cuba. The Nicaraguan Revolution for independence from America was during the 1980s and Leon was instrumental during that period; it shows on the dusty cobbled side streets, Latino music booming out from beaten-up juke-boxes, and the crumbling buildings covered in street art. The city's almost intimidating in the crowded heat – this is the brilliant intimidation that Latin America flirts with. In shaded dirty corners huddles of people sit on barrels to escape the suffocating heat, sipping on drinks that clink with ice. Varieties of fresh juices (Jugo Nica) fill the hands of passers-by. As I sit enjoying my juice, a tall, hardened Latino guy orders a fattening corn milk alternative drink to my fresh juice called pozol con leche. With a menacing look on his face, he gulps down his heavy drink in a few gulps, grins like an innocent child and turns to head back into the shade looking like a kid drinking a Nesquik. His aesthetics tell me he has a story or two to tell.

A lot of goodwill has been shown to Americans so far on my trip, but around the corner from my hostel, sprayed on the walls of the Revolution Museum, are the words 'Bush Genosida'. The American government's influence here still stirs powerful emotions, so meeting an American photographer living in the city gave me an insight. He will always be 'the American gringo' to locals. As Danny in Xela told me, having more cultural awareness and respect for your surroundings means you'll avoid trouble with locals. Making an effort to integrate and meet locals is a great way to learn about a country, and there's no better way to do that than by eating food!

Behind the national landmark cathedral in the main square of Leon is a Fritanga grill stand, a grill vendor with the method of 'pay for how much you eat'. The cathedral is lit up at night, and I sit behind in a seating area of plastic seats. The smell of coals waft over me, multiple different cuts of meat sizzle on the grill above the burning flames. Caramelised plantain chips are the different take on the staple accompaniment dish of Latin America. Along with a beer, I dig in with my hands. The cooks who served and greeted me, were so excited to meet a gringo, they invited me to try a new improved take on eating rice every day, a dish called gallo pinto. A cheap variant to plain rice by mixing in kidney beans and onion was most welcome as the basic rice had started to become mundane even after a short space of time.

Waking up the next morning to the stuffy heat of Leon, it's time to explore a city that was the heart of the revolution. With the grand Revolution Museum around the corner from me, an old man sat on the steps wearing a veteran beret on his head. He welcomed me in and offered me a tour in Spanish; trying to improve my language skills I take him up on it, albeit doubting my ability to benefit from the offer. Fortunately, the museum was mostly comprised of old weapons (my guide recreated a bazooka movement towards my face and held the weapon on his shoulder to explain how it worked, complete with over-the-top noise recreations to help me understand) and photos, timelining the key incidents that took place. Being able to read some of the newspaper articles on display helped, but my language skills were definitely not good enough for this and I understood about half of what was going on.

The guide seemed to appreciate my language efforts and inquisitive nature. Rewardingly he invited me onto the roof of the building for a panoramic view of Leon to take photographs. Whilst scaling down off the roof, he stopped to show me more photographs from newspapers, one of which was himself as a seventeen-year-old revolutionist. He joined in campaigning for his country's independence from America when he was fourteen. The authorities killed civilians who expressed their rights. His description conjured a picture of an unimaginable childhood. Latinos have a reputation for fighting for their beliefs and for their resilience – it's clear from this as to why. Their Independence Day is a day of pride, yet for many people – including my guide – families who didn't know when or how their loved ones were killed, Independence Day is a bitter-sweet celebration and a communal anniversary of the mass deaths.

I begin to head back to my hostel and on the way make a new friend. A pint-sized Nicaraguan man (who is so battered and torn that he looks as though he's just come through his own revolution) asks if I speak English, and whether he could walk with me to practice. After my own struggle with language today trying to learn things I was underqualified to do in Spanish, I welcome him to practice with me. I speak to him in Spanish and he responds in English. He explains how, with Nicaragua's growing tourism trade, he is teaching himself to speak English in the hope of getting a better job. My level of Spanish means that it's basic conversation around the theme of me. He's such a nice guy, which reminds me how genuine Guatemalans are; I'm getting my hopes up that Nicaraguans are the same.

With warm thoughts and wishes to my new friend, I arrived at my hostel. I suddenly became very aware that I'd found some random guy on the street and walked him back to where I was staying... the small talk had been nice, but I wasn't inviting him in. He expressed disappointment at not having an invite in, and pulled a dusty notebook from his satchel and asks if we can become pen pals. He doesn't have e-mail, and as I have no postal address the offer was a sticking point that resulted in more rejection for him. He came up with a simple solution: I could give him money to buy a computer! I dropped him the final dose of rejection, but to my surprise he gave me a huge, breathtakingly tight hug. As his head met my chest, he slowly rubbed his face and beard against me and begins to kiss my chest. He squeezed his wrapped arms even tighter around me, and we stood like long-lost lovers in the street. With my arms rigid against my sides, I twisted my body in an attempt to manoeuvre out of this one-way hug whilst he moves his hand down to my balls and exclaimed 'I love you, you're my favourite. I prefer you to the others.'

For someone who doesn't speak much English, he knows how to chat up a bloke half his age in the middle of a busy street. With a firm 'no' and a gentle shove away, I say goodbye as politely as possible. Here's to meeting the locals.

A different side to Leon – best served next to a landmark 11.2.16.

After a day of being cultural with a side of sexual harassment, I go back to the Fritanga grill behind the cathedral in the square. The chance to try all the different food at a fritanga suits me to a tee. Pulling up a seat on the plastic stools as my favourite smell of grilled food wafts through, I notice a painter sat opposite me, covered from head to toe in paint. He acknowledges me sitting opposite him with a nod and a slow smile.

As my food arrives I accept the offer of a drink, and before I can say anything else the painter screams 'por favor' at me in a hysterically loud voice. He repeats the phrase in front of everyone, over and over again. The waitress assured me that it isn't an issue and no offence is taken, but as I eat my food I hear the occasional slur from the painter which are impossible to ignore across the table we share. I think the painter has come straight from work, had a bite to eat and one too many drinks. Or maybe he's just had a really bad day? I continue to eat my food whilst he pulls used paint canisters from his battered satchel, takes the nozzles off and inhales the gas as paint squirts over him. He isn't a painter.

After a few mouthfuls into my food with one of the most iconic backdrops in Nicaragua in the foreground, I realise I never will really have a clue what it's like to be a Nicaraguan, or a Latino. To know what this guy is thinking, or what the hundreds of thousands here and across the world have been through in a country like Nicaragua, is unfathomable. Homelessness and drug problems are all over the world, but it's so easy for them to be hidden in your own bubble of ignorance, only to think about what you actually want to see.

The waitress snaps me out of my daze when she throws a Ziploc bag of gallo pinto over my shoulder. It lands in front of the 'painter', she shoos him away with her hand before she walks away back to the grill. He laughs hysterically and inhales again as his eyes roll back into his head. Slumped in his chair, with no intention of moving, his face wrinkles up. There's a reason we are ignorant about problems like this: it's because it's horrible to see and we don't want to see or accept it. This is just a battered old paint canister to tide him over because he has no money.

Losing my appetite, I push my plate to him as I go to leave, which is discouraged by the staff. He glares at the food unconsciously before diving his paint-covered mouth into the plate. The rice on my plate turns black as the paint from his face mixes with the warm grains on my almost-untouched dinner.

I stand up to leave and turn to look at the beautiful cathedral in front of me, but hear a harrowing scream of agony that I'd never quite heard before, which I can't describe or explain. The waitress had taken the plate away from the painter and I watched him slump back in his chair, arms collapsed either side of him with exasperation and agony. Everyone around him carried on with their meal and lives, in a jovial manner – how the fritanga stands usually are.

After a day of being a tourist, the abrupt reality about this side of the city which is deliberately ignored, highlighted next to an iconic cathedral makes it all the more potent.

Cerro Negro – best served with a mouthful of grit 13.2.16.

Still excited by the novelty of volcanos surrounding Leon, I start to learn about new ways in which volcanos can be tackled. Arriving at Leon and learning of a new volcano forty-five minutes away is nothing new to me. However, this is a unique one as it's made of black sand and ash, after an eruption in 1999. You can see which buildings in Leon were damaged by their crumbling walls from the volcano and war, portraying how powerful a volcano is to be able to travel so far.

Approaching the volcano in a 4x4, we drove through a black desert of dead trees. The lava and sweltering heat of the sun have scorched everything in sight as the sand is incredibly hot. My friend from Belize, Nick, joined me for the trip to Cerro Negro and we learn that one option of getting down from the volcano is to descend on a homemade sledge in hand-knitted overalls as protection from the dust and dirt flying around in the wind.

It all sounds good but climbing up the volcano with a sore foot and extreme altitude was laborious. The wind picked up and the wooden sledge became an obstacle to carry as it catches the wind. With a painful foot I keep trying to catch up with Nick and make small talk with others on the walk, which is a big enough obstacle in itself. This is now becoming a fun ordeal. The heat of the sun is no longer a factor and as we get higher and higher the wind is now blowing everyone from side to side as their feet chase them up the hot dusty path. People start to fall over in the wind and loose path, as Nick achieves to my amusement. If you're going to cut your knee open, do it on an active volcano.

After a 'tutorial' on how to 'steer' the board, I felt pretty confident. Part of me wished that the volcano would rumble, just to have the notion that I was sledging for speed to avoid a volcanic eruption, having missed out on Acatenango.

The journey down was more fun than I anticipated for an attraction which are often over-hyped, despite ash constantly flying into your mouth. I crash at the bottom in a tumble of rocks and spit out volcanic dirt. The randomness and surreal feeling of climbing a volcano with a sledge isn't something I can say I do every day but sledging in the snow will take some beating after this.

Here I am in Camp Granada 14.2.16.

Nick and I had been sucked into a tourist trail recently, so I was determined to save the huge amount in equivalence to the area of fifteen dollars, although it required taking a longer, more uncomfortable route on a chicken bus to Granada. The most underrated and under-used tourist transport makes this uncomfortable method extremely cheap in comparison to tourist shuttles. Chicken buses are easily available and always more fun, enabling you to meet new people hopping on and off in the middle of nowhere, as the wingman of the driver knows where to stop each time, unprompted. As passengers are crushed into the bus and into your face, this leaves no other choice but to try and make small talk.

So here I am in Camp Granada, hit by what appears to be a smaller and busier Antigua. It's nice, but nothing new. I have found it healthier to keep in touch from time to time with friends back home and a phone call last night with the GBH made me doubt what I was doing on this trip. I'm not sure what's going on with me and the GBH other than intermittent contact, she's the girl back home, I'm the guy travelling and don't know if or when I'll be back. It's not like there's nothing in London for me, but I just don't want to be there. Keeping in contact seems right, but probably isn't. I ignore my doubts and press on and sign up to stay with a local family here whilst doing another week in a language school.

Nick booked us into a hostel for one night upon arrival, and whilst we stood in the quaint crumbling building as the incapable owner checked us in, my enthusiasm for this one-night stay plummeted. The Tiesto effect kicks in with the backpackers around us as I'm nagged to go on a bar crawl. I choose to be miserable and catch some sleep in my three-tier, 16-man sweaty dorm room. First impressions of Granada after a long day are underwhelming.

Granada – best served with family & beans 21.2.16.

Joining a language school is a little laborious with the routine of being 'back to school' but living with a family shows me more about the Nicaraguan way of life. With food and accommodation coming at a welcome price, economically it made sense too as a bonus to improve my average Spanish.

Knowing that I wouldn't speak any or much English here was daunting. Jumping in a taxi from the quaint cobbled square of Granada, the romantic polished postcard image of the city, within ten blocks to the home stay, turns to makeshift tin roofs on crumbling buildings. The recommendation to get a taxi wasn't made lightly, the atmosphere was instantly aggressive compared to the frenzy of floral horse and carriages in Granada's centre. Families viciously scream at their neighbours across the street, forming a series of slanging matches as I pulled into the street I was to call home.

The family is great. Three kids all under the age of five greet me with the housewife, Fatima, and I even get the luxury of my own bedroom for the week. Having shared dorm rooms with others for so long, my own space and peace is welcome. Unpacking in my room, I find a four-year-old who has somehow crept in is now sat at my feet. With a big smile he starts to tap away on my boots like a drum as his little brother brings in a puzzle wanting me to play with him. I quickly realise, while having conversation with them as we play for an hour or so, that their Spanish is on a level with mine which is a nice ego boost. Children want to talk about basic pleasures and words that are not complex such as animals, things they like and food. The innocence of small talk with kids isn't taken for granted in comparison to normal conversation about the horrors of the real world. For the family, my rent is a nice way to get a second income for them too.

Juan Carlos, the father of the family, is the entrepreneurial brains behind this idea. He encourages his family to speak Spanish slowly to be considerate to guests. He comes from a family of three brothers all called a variety of Juan and his good sense of humour breaks up awkward silences that learning a language brings. The dining experience for the family is a team effort. The kids help bring the food out for Mum to cook the region's take on refried beans. Each region of Nicaragua seems so different, from mountains to cities, jungles to beaches, and each area having its own take on the staple dish goes hand in hand! I help cook, and ask questions to try and work on my Spanish, whilst Dad sets the tone on how the evening will take place, eating all of our meals together and then conversing for the evening afterwards. The family environment feels a far cry from the trouble and crime that this city (and country) has so much of, a nice bubble to be in for a short while.

After half a day in the home stay, I could see the neighbours have a love-hate relationship with each other. One is the local shop owner, whilst the other is the charismatic and loud party organiser for the neighbourhood. The kids give each other stick over their day-long baseball and football matches, just how I used to do with my friends back home. Things are never as they seem upon a first impression, and I was glad to be around to see the day-to-day lives of this neighbourhood.

With their trustworthy local knowledge, the family are also

able to recommend transport routes to help make my time in Nicaragua easier. They want to show off their country and for me to see as much as possible. The financial limitations of being able to take a ten-dollar transport ride to the other side of the country is a wild fantasy to them, a fee that seems so little to the first world. Nicaraguans work almost three hundred and sixty-five days a year, so the opportunity and time to explore elsewhere isn't readily available, even if they did have the money. I don't pry into the finer details of their life on that matter, but Juan makes clear that although they have no money, they have no debt. I still have a large loan debt which I'll be paying for years to come and my net worth is in the minus. The western world's standard of living is significantly higher, but with more civilian debt. How is it that western materialism decides who is wealthier? As great as it is to stop and bond and spend time together, our worlds are entirely different.

Rio San Juan, San Carlos – best served on a bus 22.2.16.

Into the depths of Nicaragua's district of Rio San Juan, the untraveled rainforest jungle is complicated to get to as a lack of rain has meant that the lake waters are too shallow to take a boat from Granada across to Rio San Juan. Public bus routes across Latin America have food traders who jump on the bus at stops along the way in various directions, for hours at a time, to sell food to passengers. Their story of where they've travelled from to make money as they hop on and off triggers a world of imagination. Mothers and children are the sellers displaying their desperate situation for needing the money. They'll all cook together every night ahead of the next day's bus trips. They make plantain crisps, fried at home, and sell them to passersby on the buses. This is their basic day-to-day work in order to feed the whole family. The norm of families selling food is replaced by a more tragic tone of disabled children and the elderly, begging on each bus route all day, every day, in a desperate manner.

San Carlos is a stop-off city, there's little information in guide books and only one bus a week from Granada, such is the lack of interest in the area. It becomes clear that 'stop-off city' translates to 'there is nothing here worth seeing for the complicated journey that's required', in what can usually be done by boat directly from Granada were it not for the drought in the lake. The next step will be a two-hour boat ride to the jungle village of El Castillo, which means that I'll be even further away from the gringo trail. At last.

A short walk around San Carlos reconfirmed that there's nothing to see here as I stopped for a beer in a bar next to a park by the water. Back home, I used to long for this adventure, and now it was finally about to happen. I aimlessly stare out over the water with a beer in excited anticipation of what was ahead. Before I can leave my table, three young Nicaraguan men join me with a crate of beer and begin pleasantries. This was an improved, although not entirely different, version of life at home with small talk in a pub after work with colleagues, although this feels a lot less forced, and something that I actually wanted to do.

My new compadre's seem to be struggling to handle their beer, but it's good fun nonetheless as they hospitably call over musician buskers to our table to entertain us. Apparently, this is a trick in these parts to annoy restaurant and bar management as they choose to sing raucously along with them, holding a good balance of drunk enough to know what was going on, but sober enough to look detached from the hyena cackles and wolf whistles which accompany the performers. All of a sudden it goes too far and the three friends spray their beers all over the bar and onto the performers. It's awkward to be sat in between it all but hilarious to see. I stand up to settle my tab once more, still recognised as the soberer one who had little to do with the incident. Fines are paid by the group to the musicians and bar management, as the group disperse in a wet, drunken haze.

El Castillo is recognized as the original pirates of the Caribbean; these guys would be classified as middle-class pirates with their drinking habits but it's fun to imagine how the real pirates of the Caribbean once would have been with their debauchery. The unbelievable recreations in movies are always from legitimate grounds, there's always a story and legacy behind a myth

El Castillo – best served in isolation 23.2.16.

The boatyard has a departure timetable to El Castillo, but the term 'timetable' is to be used rather loosely as it simply goes once it's full. I arrived just before the boat departed so I took the last seat. With the bags piled on top of me, I'm able to just about, with my neck crooked, see the first tourist that I've seen for three days on the other side of the narrow boat. I exchanged pleasantries with the American as I learn his name, Wesley, but don't get a word in edgeways. A two-hour boat ride of being obnoxiously talked at loudly over a rusty motor boat engine about his extremist and negative views, this journey to a very remote area meant that I wouldn't be able to cut loose from this guy easily. There was only one place he was going, as were all the passengers on this tiny boat. I was going to be stuck with him.

Recommended in my home stay to 'find a guy called Juan Ardillo' (translated as John Squirrel), he would be the best person to show me around in the jungle to the most remote parts of Rio San Juan. Pulling into El Castillo, I quickly left to avoid Wesley who had talked me to death; this was my only chance. Stepping off the boat, I understand how small El Castillo is straight away, as there is only a single path along the river with houses scattered loosely behind the path. Wesley took the initiative to follow me in his clingy nature, albeit easily done with there only being one walkway. I was stuck with him, as he continued to talk at me about everything I didn't want to hear and how sorry his life is travelling alone. By chance I find a beach hut-sized porch with a wooden plank above it saying 'Juan Ardillo's house'. I have no idea who or what is inside, but I'm sold as soon as I see Juan in his fish-stained overalls and his bucket hat and he talks about how his father's father taught him everything about the area, and that he's never left; Juan will know the area better than most. He offered me a trip on his boat further into the jungle with some walking and excursions to leave early in the morning. I was buzzing with excitement, albeit knowing that Wesley will now inevitably prevent my isolation by joining the two of us.

The river ride was beautiful as the river banks roll into jungle to explore tiny El Castillo, which is more of a village than its self-labelled city, because of its pirate's fort at the top of the mound. From my conversation with Juan he made it clear this would be more about jungle and wildlife than pirates, with it being the twenty-first century. It's a fair reality check, but I couldn't be more excited.

To the Jungle – best served with fish 26.2.16.

At seven a.m. our narrow boat pulls away for a full day of exploring. Wesley and I watch the water plateau out behind our motor, whilst Juan takes great pride in pointing to the specific tree that divides the National Park between Nicaragua and Costa Rica. With no love lost between the countries, he brags how the river is a 'Nica' (slang for a Nicaraguan), and most definitely not Costa Rica's.

We docked next to a reed-thatched hut which has four armed personnel ready to open fire on poachers. Juan takes the opportunity to make it clear to never leave his side and not to touch any wildlife or fauna in case it's poisonous. The briefing ends, and as we are walking he raises his hand to signal 'stop'. I have followed him in silence (even Wesley has managed to stay quiet for a minute) step by step as we followed animal prints through thick mud (in a country that's currently having a drought). Juan points to a small sprig of bamboo where a luminous and poisonous (yet beautiful) green frog is sat. Do I back up to avoid being attacked? No, I lean and take photos, it's free and relaxed in its habitat so I have nothing to be afraid of, unless it wants to poison me of course. The frog hops around Juan as if he's Dr Dolittle. We are completely in the wild now, in the trust of a man who is a third-generation tour guide. The silence is broken as we walk, with Juan sharing anecdotes of himself as a kid smoking the local plants, when his grandfather gave him the jungle equivalent of magic mushrooms. He talks freely whilst his machete hacks through trees and branches to make our route. Pouring iodine out from a tree bark to peeling a leaf stem to use as a numbing anesthetic, this is a lesson on sustainable medicine whilst Juan continues to spot birds, boars and monkeys all around us.

When driving through or past remote places, I wonder what goes on somewhere which seems so abandoned and isolated. People, and not just animals, are living there, and like Juan they have found ways of being completely self-sufficient and content with their lives. Whilst Juan has been opening up about his livelihood, I ask him about the government's plans to compete with the Panama Canal along this river as part of a Chinese investment, which is to connect the Pacific and Caribbean coasts of the country. The manmade canal would alter the direction of Rio San Juan and completely destroy everything in-between, including most of this beautiful and inspiring area. Juan is obviously completely against the development, dumbfounded as to why it's been a proposition over the last ten years. The Nicaraguan consensus is that they hope it never develops, as it doesn't seem utterly essential for the country against the amount that is at stake.

Exploring in the jungle, every step is beyond ordinary. The transport, the heat, the density of your surroundings and the intense time spent alone with Juan and Wesley, it falls into a comfort zone of being so far from the norm that it feels right. We fish for our lunch off the boat with a reel and hook and a 'catch what you eat policy'. As a rookie fisherman against Wesley who is a self-proclaimed yet unsuccessful professional fisherman, and Juan who quickly caught three fish whilst I hadn't caught any, Juan reassured me I wouldn't starve as we oar the boat into the shrubbery to cook what he had caught. With Juan doing these tours more frequently, he has built himself a small thatched shack in the jungle where, with some pre-cooked rice from his wife, he lights a fire and we fry the fish in an inch of oil over the coals. As basic a cooking method as you can get in this surrounding, he's never known any different and the simplicity is refreshing. Juan tells us that the coco loco – coconut milk and rum – is his favourite drink as we make a dent in the afternoon to celebrate the surroundings and the simplicity of life.

I feel very fortunate to have taken a tour with such an experienced guide when it could easily have been an awkward few days. When paying for a guide who disappoints is always a letdown. As Juan points things out to us on the boat that are too far for the untrained eye, he passes a pair of binoculars while we cruise along in the sunshine. An abnormal skill that he's developed over his lifetime is that he still seems as enthusiastic as a child would be when he'd have learnt all about it. The idea that a canal could be built here, where an oil tanker would come steaming through, is depressing.

To finish the day, we pull up on the riverbank one last time as Juan has started to use an abandoned house as a base to pitch hammocks for the evening. The area is almost un-policed as it's so remote, another idyllic surrounding on the peaceful river. The previous owner died and didn't leave the house to anyone, so as a consequence the government couldn't take the land for canal construction work.

After some more fried fish for dinner, Juan wanted to show us the caimans at night, so once more we board our little narrow boat with nothing but a flashlight, crawling through the still waters. Juan cut the engine and the boat comes to a halt. He slowly lifts himself down into the water, with no lights at all; all we hear is a heavy thrashing – what is going on? The thrashing continues as Juan disappeared behind the shrubs to a deathly silence. The outline of his body then climbs into the boat as we point our lights onto him – he's caught a caiman with his bare hands. Looking comfortable enough, Juan clearly cares for the creatures here and he slips him back into the water. We cruise back to sleep under the stars to a soundtrack of howler monkey screams and chirping frogs.

As I finally get some rest from Wesley's persistent moaning

and rambling, I think of everyone else I'd rather be here instead of him. The GBH always comes to mind, but I think of how distant I am from a lot of people, especially those I'm close to, as I know they'd hate such an experience that I've enjoyed so much. The reality is, the GBH has never felt further away. She'd have loved this and I'm gutted that there's no one here who I would enjoy sharing this with. Instead it's Wesley who brings me down, but that's my problem and my problem only, the miserable prick.

The morning is slow and relaxed as we eat some fruit from the jungle whilst the thin mist over the river slowly rises in front of us, like an epic dawn awakening. Having had a full day of non-eventful fishing, no one is too bothered about doing any more; the consensus is we'd rather go and cruise the river, in Juan's boat. As Juan suggests a ride on his boat, he tells us he needs to go and run an errand first. Quite where, we aren't exactly sure as we are so remote with nothing around, it's all a bit bizarre as we wait around for him. Twenty minutes later, he calls us to the dock while he pulls in; he has returned with a six-foot tarpon fish with a plank of wood through its throat. Juan had seen a fish to catch and didn't have a fishing line so improvised. Having felt guilty over our lack of success fishing, he has gone over the top and gone to catch the biggest fish I could imagine or have ever seen. This is closer to a shark. Not knowing whether or not to burst out laughing at how he'd caught it, I'm still in shock as we help him hurl the fish onto the dock. Juan promptly offers us a helping for breakfast as he pulls his machete out, suggesting he'll do it straight away, but as it's a fish that's bigger and heavier than I am, it can feed his family three meals a day for two weeks and we offered it back to him.

The need to be economical is crucial and that one catch is a good day's work on what it returns! An area of the country that seems to have ample resources with an opportunity for more with the canal, I hope development doesn't mean destruction for the area but a better life. An unmistakable enthusiasm for tourism in El Castillo, locals constantly want to practice English, but they are well aware of how development may not bring what they want. I hope exploitation doesn't follow suit when this wonderful area does become more popular.

San Juan Del Sur – best served drinking rum on the beach 6.3.16.

I was craving the beach, after some family time in Granada and Rio San Juan, there's no better introduction back onto the tourist trail than the most gringo-friendly spot in Nicaragua. Although there are no McDonalds or skyscrapers here, there's a price mark-up on food and the Tiesto effect is in full swing in the surf haven of Central America. The town of San Juan itself has a nice, albeit windy, beach but it's not the best place to learn to surf. The all-day happy hour drink offers in the bars that stretch around the bay are friendly on my wallet, although those acclimatized here know how to make money from travelers.

A Canadian entrepreneur teamed up with four local hostels to create a pool-party-bar-crawl – 'Sunday Funday'. For thirty dollars you get a vest, and entry into the hostels, which are usually free entry. Extortionate in this part of the world as the hostels make a killing from inflated drink prices, and tourists who come here on a short break have cash to burn, it seems. The guy makes hundreds of thousands a year from this easy to run, one day a week event in a relatively unknown location that has grown. Fair play to him, a quick easy earner that was thought of ahead of the curve.

Having perfected the art of the all-day happy hour on the beach, I join a group whom I met in my hostel on the first night and begrudgingly sign up for Sunday Funday. The gringo cringe factor of being surrounded by people who think it's the best day of their lives means that within a few hours, I was done. I enjoy the all-day drinking, but I couldn't stand the tank top, steroid-pumped, obnoxious, ignorant, wealthy, brattish travelers that come with the event. Perhaps I was bitter about not understanding the fuss, but I think I'd been spoilt with seeing a different side to Nicaragua. This was a tacky side that I didn't want to be involved with, a side which every country has. Some are avoidable, some aren't.

Nursing what became a hangover from Sunday Funday, learning to surf seemed like a great idea. I was recommended by surfers in a bar to take a short jeep ride up the coast to Maderas beach. I meet a typically chilled-out surfer who offers to take me for a lesson. I hire a board from him and go out to start my first surf lesson, at a bargain price which also isn't a fraction of the cost of a vest at Sunday Funday.

The beach is spectacularly long and wide with two small bamboo-thatched hut-bars on it that serve quick food – Latin American food such as burritos. Quiet and remote with gentle reggae music being drowned out by waves breaking all the way along the golden cove. This is what I needed, what I wanted, and for less cringe than yesterday's bar crawl. As I start to become more hungover, I realised picking up the board, that surfing could actually be quite hard, and I've no idea how to do it. The first half hour is spent lying on a surfboard on a beach melting in the heat and convincing myself that I've taken something in from the teacher whilst I drown my hangover. Like a toddler, learning to stand up on my own again, with the addition of a language barrier. Lo and behold, as I go into the ocean with the instructor, he's a miracle worker and I manage to stand up and ride a few small waves at what feels like 100mph (it's more like 5mph). After a couple of huge wipeouts onto the shallow rock-hard sandbank within the lesson, floating on water whilst standing and having the therapeutic noise of the ocean around me with a beach as a place to rest, it's an exhausting but addictive hobby to take up.

The surf lifestyle is right up my street. Wake up, swim and surf in the sun, eat street food or fruit (usually covered in sand) on the beach, drink rum. Part of the need to get drunk all day and have a surf lesson to cure the hangover is to avoid the Tiesto effect; yet part of it is maybe to crush any agony I had for not being at home as things with the GBH became hard. Maderas was everything I wanted when I first saw it. Instead I got stuck somehow in San Juan town as it was easy with a nice group of friends, something I never said I'd do and I did. After a few weeks of enjoying being a solo traveler but feeling lonely, it was nice to be with people again who I manage to congregate with as an Anti-Tiesto party on the beach, surfing in an easy, simple town.

On to Ometepe – best served organic 13.3.16.

In a small-sized country, I'm convinced that everything should be adjusted to being small. Small people, small prices, and small distances all seem appropriate.

I arrived on the island of Ometepe, which has two volcanoes either end of the 250km square island which are enormous. Any island with two volcanoes on it shouldn't be classified as a 'small island'. A boat ride to Ometepe is required, which is a terrifying idea in the third world to many, although I preferred in this instance to translate 'fear' into 'experience'.

In true Nicaraguan style, the boat leaves overcrowded from the port without an inch to spare for any additional people or cargo on board. Chugging away in a struggle past the buoys, the turbulence suggests that the waves will be coming aboard too on the overweight boat, but I'm distracted by the beautiful landscape in front of me. Whilst absorbing the boredom of desk life where I allowed my boring job to get under my skin, Ometepe was one of the destinations that kept me going and motivated to do something that would make me happy again. Heading to an island with two volcanos on it in a unique little old fishing boat was that special moment I hoped I'd experience behind my desk.

I started to think of all the things I wanted to do, but I'm interrupted by panic behind me as people started to scream and scramble on top of each other as if a bag of snakes has just been set loose. As the Nicas roar with laughter, the tourists on this congested boat began to panic more as the corner of the boat clears whilst people clutch to the boat's beams on the ceiling. The corner of the boat has water gushing in at a steady rate and the back of the boat is sinking. Whilst the Nicas now begin to accept that this is a larger intake of water than normal after only just leaving the dock, I take heed of their advice to relax and accept the situation of either drowning or that it'll turn out OK as they pass beers around. I accept my fate that should the boat sink I'll probably lose my bag, but I remain hopeful that we will probably be found. After all, the country isn't *that* big, right?

Arriving alive in Ometepe at a heavily lifted and lopsided angle and only a bit wet, a group of us who shared intense breathing space together head to one of the smaller villages, San Carlos, for a tranquil experience in an eco-lodge. A week of less booze and some healthy, organic eating would do me good.

We arrived at an environmentally friendly hostel. The walls were built with cement and plastic or glass bottles as brick replacements. There is no official recycling system in Nicaragua, just the idea of nothing going to waste here is taken on board as all the infrastructure, which pops up throughout the farm's woodland, is made with recycled materials. Nicaragua doesn't have much of a waste management system. It's a dirty country with no education on recycling. The owners of the hostel are trying to change that. With no electricity in the rooms, the hostel had an organic farm where they sell their produce to avoid extortionate importation fees.

The practical way of exploring an island is on pushbikes or scooters as opposed to relying on the buses, which come and go as they please. Four of us on the sinking boat ended up coincidently sharing a dorm together, it's the most intimate way of getting to know someone by having your personal space completely intruded upon. We rented scooters together as some form of poor man's gringo Hells Angels. My partner on the back of my bike was a Dutch girl who seemed to have little interest in either the bikes or conversation, but seemed grateful that the bikes were limited in ability to go fast. I thought it was great to be able to take in the surroundings in the sunshine on what was a new mode of transport. Breaking to visit various beaches and Lagoon d'Apoyo for a drink and food stop, I can understand why people find bikes a great way to explore.

On our last venture of the day, we decided to go around the smaller one of the two volcanoes on the island. Underestimating that volcanoes' surrounding areas consist of dust, rubble, rocks and more dust, as well as volcanoes usually being enormous, a two-hour circuit around it turned out to be less fun than it first sounded and made the morning's exploring on smoothed roads and interesting layby stop-offs a more enjoyable, distant memory. The sun starts to go down and we still have a long way to go. Everybody is tired as we chunter along on the rusty hire bikes, when suddenly the bike buckles in the debris and we skid and fall. Shocked and in pain, although not surprised, I wiggle out with dusty cuts of blood all over me and fear the worst, although I'm not sure what the worst is. I am still able to move, albeit in pain, but the Dutch girl is carved up by the rocky road. I feel guilty as I was driving and I hardly know this shy, petite girl who is quick to make it clear, despite hysterical sobbing in her agony, that it was no one's fault.

Still not knowing what to say, I sit her down by the side of the road. We haven't passed people or villages for a while and I needed her out of my way to think clearly about what to do. Having met someone recently who was charged five hundred dollars for bike damage on a rental, I feared the worst for my wallet as I lifted the bike up to find damage all over – good times riding bikes! With the girl refusing to get back on the broken bike that's traumatised her, we had a long walk ahead and our two biker friends were now well and truly ahead of us on their faster bike. Flagging down anyone who was passing by with my bike helmet, without which I would be dead as it looks like it's gone through a blender, we learn that no one on the island has a car. Everyone is on bikes. It's a two hour walk back, which the Dutch girl is insistent on doing as opposed to getting on the bike. I can't leave her as she's insistent that someone will come to help despite there being no other option than to get on a bike. She reiterates it's nobody's fault, so I brace myself for the long walk back in bleeding agony. The enjoyment of the day has well and truly crashed.

The walk is awkward, broken with small talk on the best

method that she can help me push the bike. Claiming she's too sore to help push the bike uphill, my mood deteriorates to now having no patience with her. I'm physically broken and worrying what I'll have to pay in damages and she's pathetic. I don't even know her and I'm stuck with her behind a volcano in pitch black. Fuck this day, it's like Boxing Day, when you've had enough of your family after Christmas and you want rid, I need a miracle. Through the dark, a small torchlight approaches as our two biker friends have turned around to find us. I don't know if there's a biker code for 'never leave a man behind' but I couldn't be more grateful, as a day of having so much fun has deteriorated to an annoying day and now to gratitude to two people I met on a sinking boat.

With the help of the other two bikers, the Dutch girl finally accepts walking is a bad choice. Splitting up the driving, I remain on the damaged bike as it jumps and jolts back to the owners we met on the street by our hostel where we'd hired the bikes. I had to accept when pulling up to the bike owners that I was over a barrel in terms of what they wanted to charge me. I took the one hundred and fifty dollars damage fee I was charged as an expensive day out, but it could have been worse. I tried to navigate out of this arguing in Spanish with two henchmen who called their mates for physical support for their bike-hiring business; they circled us for two hours after the incident in which the rocks in my torn skin now began to gel. When people say 'I love every minute of travelling', I can assure you – they are liars. This is a situation many have been in and will be in again and I can say with confidence I hated it. With the cash the Dutch girl and I had on us, it wasn't enough, there came more joy as I limped up to the rear end of the farm where my dorm was, that didn't have electricity, to try and find more cash in my bag that I couldn't find in the room without any lights. The eco-friendly lodge I had taken to heart is now a nuisance, as I am harassed further by the bike owners who try and follow me up to my room in the dark. I am loving this day.

Heavily out of pocket, now isn't the time to ask the Dutch girl for money as she continues to sob, although I'm immune and uninterested as to what about. I go to check on her before I try and clean myself up. The 'hippy' vibe of the eco-hostel means that the owners are now wanting some of my newly adopted 'open wallet' policy as they insist on charging six dollars for using their first aid kit. I am happy to pay this to shut the Dutch girl up. A girl I'd barely spoken to has said more over the last three hours of sobbing than I'd ever wanted to hear. The price to shut her up I can deal with, but to pay for health care in a community where 'peace and love' is painted on the recycled wall, and where equality is rammed down my throat shows the hypocritic lifestyle that I disliked in San Marcos. I empathise with someone running a business but the owner, I've learnt, is a retired millionaire with a passion for eco-environmentalism. Congratulations on your money, but don't give a load of crap on how to be kind and loving and charge six dollars for a few bandages and wipes out of a child's first aid kit. Perhaps their passion for the environment and ecosystem doesn't stretch to human beings in this instance; their appearances and behaviour appear to be fake. Fortunately, the compassion shown by other travelers in the hostel as they help with injuries restores a bit of hope.

I calmed down with the acceptance that the outcome of this event could have been a lot worse for the Dutch girl and for me. I'm no longer able to go the beach or sea in case my wounds get infected, but this is the perfect place for some rest and recuperation in a hammock with a book. I had moved on, right up until the Dutch girl – who at first insisted that she would share damage costs with me – appears to have no more money. Limping around the farm to showcase her wounds, I hold firm, to get my share of the cash. I don't feel sorry for her now; I'm just as injured and my time spent alone is perhaps now less self-meditation and more self-assertion. I'm branded the bad guy around the hostel, exploiting an injured girl for cash she promised, but fuck her and fuck this fake hippy crap.

The animosity to Americans from Nicaraguans doesn't come unfairly from the history of the revolution. However, while enjoying my own company in the aftermath of the bike incident, I begin to spend time with Americans, whose company and positivity was refreshing, having become frustrated by the unraveling's in Ometepe. Negativity isn't an option for them, and that's just the kind of people I need to be around right now after being lured into perhaps a false community spirit in this hostel. I spend most of the remainder of my time with them: reading, relaxing and gently exploring some of the nearby coffee plantations. I go off to explore the other side of the island on my own and with a new found positive energy become grateful for what I've still got.

Having had a clean diet from eating off the hostel's farmland here has helped me think more clearly and move on from being annoyed about Ometepe, despite it not being the fun-filled adventure that I'd dreamt of during my desk life. Perhaps the organic lifestyle that the island depends on and this hippy or sustainable living has rubbed off on me after all to put me in a better mindset? Or perhaps that's what a one hundred and fifty dollars hole in your pocket and a whining Dutch girl does to a man.

Elements of Nicaragua – Best served missing something. 14.3.16.

The diversity of Nicaragua helps me recognise the differences in a little place. With a disjointed character from its politics which still scar the people, there is still a charm that makes it a likeable destination, when in my month here I've tasted the highs and lows of travelling.

After the tourist attractions of Sunday Funday and the museums and more, the real Nicaraguan life is focused on the family. My time in a home stay and in the jungle offered me an obvious insight, but even whilst on the tourist trail in San Juan I met, by chance, the owner of a sugarcane farm who provides the sugar for the Flor de Caña rum. The spirit was a great accomplice of mine on the beach during surf sessions. A millionaire in his own right, he is part of the family business and, despite all his riches,

65

still works with the elders chopping the cane in the field so they can spend time together. The process of selling food and drink in Nicaragua is one of the leading sources of revenue, be it the desperation of selling anything on a bus, to the touristy restaurants that provide jobs. For a growing influx of tourism in the country, food and drink are a big focus.

I had offered Juan Ardillo a book that I had finished as a gift to help him improve his family's English. The simple joy on his face was priceless and a highlight of the jungle experience. Understanding the simplicity of his life and seeing how the rich and poor live side by side despite animosity between the classes, is humbling. Nicaraguans' home environments are their comforts as they stick together, almost to spite the split the country is in where the rich and the poor live side by side. Naught point five per cent of the country is incredibly rich, yet their mansions share the same view as a village slum next door. A common trait across the country, I saw a drug addict openly mainlining next to the glamour of Leon's main attraction. Those who have nothing and are more sustainably aware (in a country whose government chooses not to be) live off the land, be it jungle or farm, which is admirable in an era where processed food has never been easier to access or worse for your health.

But even after the kindness of the home stay, I had low points in struggling to keep up in Spanish lessons. Paying to learn something and not enjoying yourself is glum as that first moment of being homesick but without wanting to be home; I just felt lonely. Despite Ometepe's beauty, the scooter incident annoyed me with its outcome, just as the owners trying their luck a bit too much with the gringo money. A common trait across the country which is understandable – from being frisked on the streets to buying snacks on a bus. Being asked several times at the home stay to babysit I could deal with, but it was a final incident in Nicaragua that annoyed me.

My boat's return journey to the mainland was straight forward, allowing me to catch a bus over the border to Costa Rica. With a two-hour queue at customs, the bus driver was keen to take off leaving bus passengers at passport control as he'd be late arriving at the destination that his slow departure had created. Arriving at the front of the queue at long last, the driver lurked behind me to hurry up proceedings. He communicates with the customs official in the corner of my eye with a hand gesture. The customs official claims my ticket to cross the border that I've bought from the driver is not valid and I must buy a new ticket at an inflated price of three times the normal value for a journey. I leave the queue to find an alternative ticket to take me one hundred metres when the driver threatens that unless I pay him off, he's driving off with my bags which are on the bus. The only thing on me is my passport, which isn't a bad thing to have, but with the urgency arising that this driver was going to con me or leave me at a no-mans-land checkpoint, the extortionate fee to cross the border is what I had to pay. I paid him, and a wave from the customs official was an adequate visa check, just to cross the red line of the border.

I understand that Nicaraguans have to try their luck, but it's an annoying way to leave a country and another reminder of how unimaginable a stunt like this would be in the first world and the sour taste it brings. The disdain for the wealthy and the need to capitalise on that for the poor is understandable, but the greed regarding the canal and the damage it'll do is equally frustrating. It is a country whose waste policy allows it to ruin itself without the help of further bad decisions on destroying their land. Nicaraguans understandably feel they're always one step away from being forgotten and left behind by their own government and the world all over again.

Costa Rica

Costa Rica – Best served eating a Breakfast Burrito.
- 1 big flour tortilla
- 20g of cheddar cheese
- 1 sliced avocado
- 1 tbsp. of sour cream
- 1 Scrambled egg
- 1 slice of bacon
- 100g of Gallo pinto

Grill the bacon for 5 minutes either side, scramble the egg at the same time, pile all of the ingredients into the flour tortilla, wrap it up and it's ready to serve! Eaten hungover in the rain in Puerto Viejo.

Costa Rica is one of the standout tourist destinations in Latin America. I sometimes find that you know the least about places which you hear about most, and whilst I knew the gist of its tourism, I was never that clued up on its pull. A retirement haven for wealthy Americans, I was hoping that this would be an easy place to travel around and see wildlife, as opposed to being an old people's Disney Land. It was never on my bucket list for this trip, but as my recently retired mother has started to travel herself, I couldn't not make our paths cross for a few days. I had no desire throughout my trip to be connecting with family as much as I had been, yet I also hadn't had a family holiday in over ten years, so if nothing else, this should be interesting…

Monteverde, Santa Elena – best served with your Mum 16.3.16.

Santa Elena is renowned for its 'Cloud Forest'. Sitting at altitude, the thick cloud that covers the area makes it cooler than I'm used to. For my mum coming from winter, she's feeling as I was in El

Salvador – close to melting. I need to adjust to people who have just arrived and perhaps aren't used to travelling – another reason why I chose to travel alone. Insistent that we keep well hydrated in the heat, with cocktails, I am able to have a look around the small hillside town of Santa Elena. Tight for time, it's beneficial to have an abundance of travel agents who can manage you from one place to another, though it does take away my incessant need for independence.

A guided tour into the Cloud Forest, however, doesn't seem to offer anything we can't do for ourselves. Sure, they guarantee a glimpse of wildlife, but come on – we're in the middle of a jungle... I think I'm capable of spotting a few things here and there. After my experience with Juan Ardillo in the jungle which this country shares with Nicaragua, the idea of not being able to navigate this national park – with its paved walkways and signs – is hard to believe. I can find us some animals. So with my new sense of wildlife confidence (mainly based on having just spotted a sloth climb up a telegraph pole outside our room), we set off without a guide.

We arrive at the Cloud Forest confused. It's a beautiful warm day, but without a cloud in the sky. The colourful flora in the park lives up to expectation, with each variety intertwined with the next in full colour. Despite the fact that we're here out of season, it still feels amazing. The soundtrack of the rain forest is all encompassing as it echoes around, identical to the rhythmic sounds on a gimmicky stress release CD. I know this as I once downloaded one to try to help with stress in a pathetic attempt to relax. In fact, it did quite the opposite, but here, in the cloudless Cloud Forest, it's truly enchanting.

Now, I never promised to be a good tour guide, and I soon realised neither Mum nor I had a clue as to what we were looking for. On a day where there are no clouds, no animals and no tour guide, we haven't seen much so far. Plus, the humidity is increasing by the minute and I wish I'd managed to down a few more of those cocktails.

We decide to head back with a sense of disappointment, having seen neither clouds nor animals. I walk on, and then suddenly realise that I'm walking alone. Even at my mum's age, she's still got that explorer in her, and in testimony to this she appears to have wandered off. I've lost my mother on a one-way cemented path. I had been feeling less and less confident about my tour-guiding skills as the cloud-less, animal-less day had progressed, but now – alone in a national park, sweating out my margaritas – I was sure that this was the last nail in the coffin of my short-lived career change.

I wait around for five minutes in case I've walked ahead and not noticed. She definitely hasn't gone ahead of me. Perhaps, after four hours of searching for animals, she's found something and stopped to look? As I slowly start to walk back I become more and more apprehensive. I begin to panic that I've lost a sixty-year-old woman, or even worse, killed her off. The hills are pretty steep… can she have fallen off the edge amidst the heat? I pick up the pace and, after nearly an hour, decide to head to the bus stop to see if she's gone there to return to Santa Elena. Only my mum (or, perhaps, I) could get lost on a one-way path. This is why I travel alone.

Soon enough, my hot and bothered mother walks up to the bus stop, asking – as if we'd only seen each other moments before – where the bus is. The bus has long left and it's a two hour wait for the next one, which allows plenty of time for me to quiz her about her off-the-beaten-path adventure. It appears we both fancy ourselves as a poor man's David Attenborough and she went off in search of animals, lost the way back to the path and forged her own back to the bus stop. With both of us now calm, it's a great moment to sit and laugh, and for a fleeting moment I remember what fun it can be to travel with a companion. It's also nice to be around someone who is at the start of their journey, and still gets excited by the smallest of things. My mum is fulfilling a dream of her own, much like I am, and I realise how much I've been taking for granted lately, the things I've seen so far.

So the day was notable, but it made me swallow my pride and rethink the 'guided tourist' experience we initially turned up our noses at. Later in the week we took another swing at the Cloud Forest, but this time at night.

The guide had a good sense of humour, although perhaps the majority of the humour came from his broken 'Spanglish'. Straight away, just as with Juan Ardillo, glass frogs, spiders, scorpions and snakes were all pointed out to us from the most impossible angles. We saw the kinds of animals that you never imagine seeing because they're hidden in a world that you only look at through a television screen. The guide even picked up prey for the tarantulas and nonchalantly tossed them for their feed, a blink-and-you-miss-it moment.

Whilst being educated about each animal's presence in the Cloud Forest, the eponymous cloud finally appeared. We had finally started to experience what we came here for and it delivered. The disappointment of our first tour here had now been well and truly forgotten.

Staying in a more upmarket hostel than I was used to, it was nice to have a bit of luxury for a change. Crisp clean sheets, no selfish dorm mates who point the fan on their beds to add to the discomfort and awkwardness that dorms provide, this was the kind of accommodation that I hadn't longed for by any means as I didn't consider it an option but still loved it. I hadn't had something like this for years, even trumping my overpriced, stuffy, tiny box room I rented in London to save for this trip which I called my home; this was plush in comparison. When booking a dorm room, it can feel like an ill-informed gamble of what you'll get but this is a welcome change in the type of travel, from the dorm, the companion and the tour – and I was more than fine with that.

Manuel Antonio – best served in a tourist trap 19.3.16.

First impression? One of the most cringe-worthy touristy places I've been to… but what a beach!

Major global cities like New York cater for tourism as a reaction to the visitors, but Costa Rica's tourism trade is the second largest industry behind their tech world, and they cater accordingly. Never enthused by tasteless overdevelopment, I can accept that Costa Ricans are well aware that building a McDonald's in their rainforests would destroy their prized commodities of the wildlife and kill their tourism. An apathetic effort to recreate an American steakhouse by the beach is more endearing than offensive.

The excitement that the surrounding rainforests offers comes from the infectious joy that Costa Ricans have with one another. Always laughing with each other, our shuttle driver from Monteverde even offered to take us on a scenic detour where he helped us spot animals and explained volcanic formations. We finally drove onto the iconic Pan-American Highway and the driver catered to our hunger, stopping by one of his favourite one-man-band sandwich cafes that lived up to the hype. He said that he was used to feeding American passengers' stomachs. I loved that he was always on hand to give a constant lesson about the country and its products. He told us all about the process of cashew nuts, from growing on a tree to the product you eat – it's a huge process; no wonder they're so expensive!

Along with learning of Costa Rica's dependence on their global fruit trade, from just passing by fruit plantations, we were getting a free agricultural lesson too. All of this was just an effort from a bus driver; it wasn't in his job description at all – he was just being friendly to the tourists as part of an industry which he clearly loves.

Off the back of a more successful night tour of the Cloud Forest, I retire from my guide experiences and treat my mum for her birthday to a tour of the Manuel Antonio National Park. Not so convinced that the night tour could be improved on from the previous one, I felt a little bit sceptical, especially as Manuel Antonio is more known for its beach than jungle. My cynicism instantly came to fruition as the small group I had signed up for turned out to be a group of two hundred amongst ten guides, it was Spring Break and the place was packed. Just like that, my chances of seeing animals was taken away by moaning Americans on holiday, in what felt like entering a Jurassic Park tourist attraction.

Twenty metres in and some clumsy American smashes his camera lens into the scabbing wounds on my arm, making me hate the cattle procedure of this tour. Surely crowds of this size would scare off all the wildlife anyway? This tour seemed like a bad idea, too crowded, too touristy. The guide was charming enough, again explaining more about how the animals make the most out of their surroundings, as opposed to how humans do. But, man, this group was annoying.

Having been to a couple of rainforests I was beginning to compare and contrast them. I get the impression from my mum that I sound annoying and brattish. I start to become that guy who says 'this one time at...'

Santa Elena was certainly more impressive but the guide here is better. The tour began to grow on me and as the path widened, more animals started to creep out into the quieter spots with clear views close up to iguanas, monkeys and sloths, all acting normally in their habitats.

The cringe-worthy chaos of congested tourist crowds really was a pain, but seeing animals up close was a never-ending source of entertainment. Watching them fight amongst themselves, groom and stalk humans and steal their food put us back in our place for intruding on their lives. Unlike us they're able to do it in a humorous way, which was worth the chaos.

The entire area is involved in that tourist process: hospitality-transport-wildlife – everyone! More civilised than the monkeys was our final meal when, again to Americans' over-indulged standards, devouring enormous platters of fresh mahi-mahi fish from the ocean that we looked on to, albeit a change of scenery, the touristy element of Manuel Antonio was actually pretty great.

Puerto Viejo – best served in a tent in the rain 22.3.16.

I make a brief stop to San Jose to drop my mum at the airport. It's been a short visit but a poignant one, as neither of us were sure when or where we'd meet again. Leaving without closure, more of a lingering goodbye that must have been hard for her – she's as clueless as I am as to what I want to do next, although I know I still have more to see and explore.

Now comfortably in the routine of a life of leisure, it's taken this long to unwind from my brain-sapping, mundane work life and relax. On the bus journey down to Puerto Viejo, I had my first experience of tropical rain which continued through the day and into the night. The sulky London life engraved into me makes me feel sorry for myself. It's typical that the rain would arrive when I'm about to go somewhere where there's little to do but enjoy the beaches.

To pass the time, there's no option but to drink and be sociable. As much as I love my mum, it would be good to spend some time with people my own age. I check myself into one of the more popular and recommended hostels in the area with the hope of meeting people. I arrived with a pack of beer but the reggae-infused postcard town that I'd heard of wasn't what I'd expected. Quiet, gloomy and grey, the white sands were now flooded and the waters too strong to swim in. Having avoided extortionately increased hostel prices for the Easter holidays, I went for a cheaper option than a dorm, which was to sleep in a tent. From a nice hostel to this – I was back to reality. I make the best of the situation by polishing off all of the beers alone. Surprisingly, nobody seemed keen to join a guy drinking on a bench by himself in the rain. It was obvious that I was going to retire to a hot, sweaty tent floor – oh the glamour of travelling solo. I didn't need travel companions anyway…

I wake up feeling ropey and tragically pathetic in my efforts to be sociable in an awkward environment, reminded of the smell of rain that I haven't had since leaving England. It's time to go and face the elements and make the most of being here without getting tragically drunk on my own. It was either that or become further sucked into everything I hate about a 'party hostel' which doesn't have a party: the food. Although I'm told otherwise, I remain unconvinced that a 'Costa Rican Breakfast Burrito with American Cheese' is a Costa Rican dish of any authenticity, perhaps mere justification of how American tourism has influenced Costa Rica. Fucking hell this is lame; it's a real shame I've been sucked into the gringo trail here.

I rented a bike to pedal around, which wasn't as easy as I had imagined. I realised there was an issue of contention for the leasers, considering I had evident grazes from my previous accident, but I didn't think I'd have to practically beg to rent a bicycle, proving my ability to ride a bike.

Within a ten-kilometre ride of Puerto Viejo there are a number of beaches, broken up by natural rock formations, which can be cycled to. All of the beaches are immaculately maintained and information on the area's conservation efforts to maintain their good work and the life of the area is well-informed.

Cycling to the beach with an American girl I met on the bus down here, I continue to adapt to companionship as I remember that some people are just so bland. I find it uncomfortable to force myself to be social when there are some people I'd rather not spend time with. When travelling I feel that I have to be sociable, when really that shouldn't need to be the case, it's OK to be anti-social. The thing that irks me is when people experience their travels through the lens of their iPhones. Surely the beautiful view in front of their eyes is so much more authentic than a Snapchat filter can convey? What is the point? Telling the world constantly on social media that you've been somewhere by enjoying it only by showing off – the arrogance and boredom of that alone make me despise the way certain people travel. I am no model traveller; it's your choice on how you travel, but having intentionally kept my phone at the bottom of my bag for a lot of my trip, perhaps suggests how I prefer to travel whilst also dealing with sporadic contact with the GBH.

The sun tries to break through all day, but it seems like a forced effort. The weather is a real shame, but it's one of those things that can't be helped. At least I have learned that I will never force myself to spend the day with people when I'd rather go it alone.

Costa Rica – best served 'Pura Vida Baby'.

This was always going to be a touristy country to visit, being more built up and developed than other areas I had visited in Latin America. Costa Rica is far less troubled than its more dogged neighbours, and their image of being friendly (the happiest country in the world) is mirrored in their politics. They have no need for an army, but rather push their energy to being hospitable and making the most of their tourist economy. They're not 'over the top' or sleazy in a persistent way but seem humble and helpful without being pretentious.

The influence of America here means that food portions are huge, even in the most basic of eateries. In the spirit of the country, food here is plated to be over the top as opposed to suffice – there are no airs and graces. Whilst using the basic recipes of their past – with farmlands of rice, maize and potatoes – they're more expansive on their meat and seafood offerings. Each dish is made in a simple way, with some dishes only containing one or two ingredients yet still tasting delicious. As a more developed nation with a stronger economy, the people of Costa Rica have more options because they have access to a wider variety of ingredients.

Westerners who visit third world countries become disappointed by the limited cuisine options and Costa Rica is a country more beautiful than elegant for its cuisine. However, as tourism is stronger here, they can charge almost the same as someone would pay in America for a meal, so it's harder to live on the cheap during this part of my trip.

Budget living here isn't how it is north of Costa Rica, but the good thing is that rice (which is always in abundance) *should* be the same price as in the other places on my travels – if you're being overcharged for a bowl of rice, then you know that you're being conned. Eating a basic diet of fruit and rice dishes is wallet friendly for travellers and a more realistic insight into how Costa Ricans live. This was a much better experience than I expected; perhaps tourism and the Pura Vida – 'good life' – isn't as bad as I'd anticipated.

Panama

Panama – best served eating ceviche.
- Half pint of peeled prawns
- 2 tbsp. of Bocas hot sauce
- Quarter of a green onion
- Handful of coriander
- 2 tbsp. of white wine vinegar
- Pinch of salt
- One tbsp. of mayonnaise

Thinly slice the onion and soak in cold water for ten minutes, afterwards – throw all the ingredients into a cocktail glass and mix together. Eaten in the main market of Panama City with football fans.

Bocas del Toro – best served in Caribbean waters with too much rum 31.3.16.

Attaining a Costa Rican exit stamp in my passport, I start to cross the border to Panama. The two countries are divided by a narrow river bridge, and there is a big feeling of change. The imposing bridge crossing structure towers above me as if to boast that this is a country of engineering significance for the entire world.

I went to Bocas del Toro, a cluster of islands in the Panamanian-Caribbean waters that are only accessible by boat. With the rain continuing, perhaps my dreamt-up love of the Caribbean isn't meant to be. Bocas town itself doesn't initially strike me as the best place to be, but it serves as a hub for water taxis, taking visitors to other islands for day-trips or longer. I arrive too late to go anywhere else, and with the beach being a washout, my only option was to eat copious amounts of food in consolation. Nearby Jamaica inspires the cuisine here, and I can't complain as I drink my rum and eat slow-cooked jerk chicken served in a polystyrene tray as locals laugh away the rain under umbrellas.

Bocas is a known gringo party destination, so it seemed appropriate that I should at least try to make some friends in my hostel and, if possible, avoid getting drunk on my own. It had been a while since I'd had to endure the new-hostel-small-talk procedure, but I seemed to be getting better at it. I felt more comfortable and relaxed than before, not feeling the need to force myself to make an effort for the sake of the autonomy of the gringo trail, allowing myself to accept that the trail and its elements need to be embraced slightly.

Some of the bars in Bocas town are suspended over the water on wooden stilts. Totally idyllic and unique for a drink, but certainly have the Tiesto effect which I despise, accepting that I'm no longer drawn to what eighteen-year-old partiers go out of their way for. The excitement of the gringo trail nightlife that appealed to previous generations has become mundane, unoriginal and unappealing to me – like going into a sleezy bar when you're sixteen and thinking it's amazing as opposed to going in it now, it's nothing that hasn't been seen or done before. The crowd of travellers in Central America tends to be somewhat older and more interested in a cultural experience, so it's not somewhere that has blown me away with its nightlife scene.

Having spent days waiting for the rain to pass, I add some productivity to my life and book myself on a tour with surfing and snorkelling – this is more to my home life's visualisation than procrastinating with a bottle of rum in a bar with eighteen-year-old Australians. Having someone drive me around on an island boat tour whilst I snorkel, watch dolphins and sit on the beach without any extortionate financial commitment (or requiring any level of skill) was the right degree of productivity for me.

With the bad weather I'd had on the Caribbean coast, I was yet to see the postcard images of deserted islands. Despite another day of bad weather, I want to persevere with the trip to see if photographic dreams were really true. I met some Dutch people in the hostel, who bring a football on the boat to kick a ball around with a crate of beer: the postcard image was close. The day seemed too good to pass on, whatever the weather. Islands with no bars, no buildings, nothing but sand and palm trees were absolute paradise. The sun eventually crept out, making a bleached white, photoshopped style beach against the turquoise waters. I couldn't quite comprehend how good this beach was. It was our paradise for the day, with no distractions other than to start playing football. And when it got too hot, we snorkelled in the waters at the nearby reef before cruising in the boat through mangroves and watching dolphins playfully showing off next to us. This was the postcard shot that I'd envied back at home. The moment of something you've been waiting to experience, being tangible, is a special feeling.

Easter weekend in a Catholic country means one thing which isn't to a lot of backpackers liking: a booze ban. On Bocas, soaking up the sun, drinking Caribbean rum with a portion of yucca chips – the paradisiac Caribbean version of fries – was the normal thing. Streets were now filled by passionate religious parades as psalms were read out on megaphones, which made a change from which bar was announcing its happy hour. Wrapped up in the bubble of the tourist trail, this was a chance to remember that people live here. Easter is the highlight of their year, and it makes me realise that there is more to Bocas than a visitor's first impression.

Whilst being surrounded by a greater number of tourists in comparison to other places, just like Costa Rica, a lot of Americans migrate here for a better life. Warm Caribbean waters where you can rest and surf are certainly more relaxing if coming from the hustle and bustle of a first world city. Spending Easter Sunday on a beach with a BBQ grilling behind me, I meet a sixty-year-old American named Bryan. Tall and skinny, with bags under his eyes, there's a sense of rejuvenated happiness on his face despite his warped leathery tan. Bryan had moved to the island of Bastimentos near Bocas to live a simple life of selling hot dogs, burgers and beers during the peak seasons whilst maintaining a millionaire's yacht as a place to live. Cooking is a hobby that he makes money off, an easy earner with a sea view – a nicer, simpler life that reminds me why I did this is in the first place – to discard a complicated and hectic life that I couldn't deal with and to do something that I enjoy; otherwise, what is the point?

The way people emigrate to countries, it seems, is often based around lifestyle and opportunities – the opportunity for a slower pace, having been too engrossed in their own bullshit. In the areas of Bocas, which have obvious poverty, people are welcoming, smiling and laughing (probably high...). Even the kids, who have nothing but their baseball stars to look up to, are engrossed in a culture of having the time of their lives. Communal activities include playing baseball with a two by four plank of wood and a crumpled-up piece of paper. Grouped around eating Caribbean food, watching chaotic baseball and listening to reggae music whilst friends laugh and joke – that's what this place really is all about.

I sit with families on the beach and by their food stalls who live in complete poverty, but are full of happiness in acceptance of what their lives are. They tell me how the development of Bocas has boomed over the last ten years. The options for accommodation, tours and dining are endless, but the local housing, security and basic plumbing are very third-world. Drains run open in the street, amongst litter and broken glass. You see mounds of waste that will never get cleared outside a house that has no front door, sitting incongruously next to a fifty dollar-a-head restaurant. There is an awkward imbalance with no sign of it ever becoming equal for those who live here, as opposed to those who come and go at leisure. Providing hospitality for tourists is their joy, be it sat around together on the stools they provide in the street or the overpriced tourist restaurants that locals work in, albeit extremely unbalanced to an outsider like me.

Taking on Paradise one wave at a time 1.4.16.

Waking up in paradise and choosing between which beach you should go to is a wonderful ordeal. This beach you can swim, that one surf, this one you can hike – tough daily decisions that a traveller sometimes encounters are involved. The water taxis in between each island are a fun way to explore when you're on your own and able to take in the scenery, although it's not quite like sharing the moment with someone. Amidst small talk in the hostel, I meet two guys travelling together, who met by chance on the gringo trail. Ben and Chris (nicknamed Panda) both made their wealth by their own means, but got sucked into the nasty end of working too hard and not enjoying themselves, so they packed their bags and headed to Central America. We instantly get along as we exchange stories of our routes down to Panama. An average bar can become a great night out when you're with the right people.

Ben is a keen surfer, and as Bocas is one of the best places to surf on the Caribbean coast we decide that going surfing together hungover would be a great idea. Surf-culture food shacks plotted along the beach and the idea of washing up on the shore (quite literally, for me) for a bite to eat is ideal in principle. I am still very much a rookie when it comes to surfing, and being dropped at a reef a long way from the coast on only two hours' sleep was something I started to regret almost instantly. The chance to gently float back to shore as I had in Nicaragua wasn't something I had the chance to do here – it was ride a wave or get battered by it. After what felt like twelve hours of being bruised and battered (though Ben and Panda insist it's no more than an hour), we called it a day and floated back inland. The hardest part of this surfing day was knowing how and when to catch a wave. Understanding the ocean is the hardest part, and it's easier said than done with a raging hangover. I laid in the water, blankly staring to the palm trees and desert to what I hoped would become my surfing lifestyle…

Of all of the bars in all of the world, the most fitting place for what feels like paradise was named the Blue Coconut. With a backdrop of mangroves and a fifteen-minute boat ride from anything else, only fish swim around the bar, which sits on stilts in crystal clear waters, a common theme for bars in the area it seems. There's no traffic or chaos from the Tiesto effect, it's certainly not expensive and the owner has a Labrador that dives into the ocean with you. He doesn't allow the bar to get overcrowded amidst the day drinking culture like Bocas Town – I have found a new favourite bar in the whole entire world.

After a few hours it's still only the middle of the afternoon, and I've lost count of how much rum I've had. Sat in a hammock, swinging into the waters and I couldn't care less and neither do the locals who act like the tourists here. The atmosphere is only about having a good time. The sun is out, the water is warm and it's all about the good life in paradise. Who you are with makes such a difference, and Ben and Panda are great company. Yet as the sun goes down, sat at the edge of the dock in Blue Coconut, there's something missing. I am grateful for the company I am with and I start to think about who else would love this, and who I'm not with. The glass tilts half empty. I try not to think pessimistically, but even whilst I'm sat in paradise – that still after three months – I missed the GBH.

I feel guilty that she's not here, and that I told her not to come until further down the line. There have been times of not knowing what we should be doing. We didn't want to break up, and we don't want to talk all the time. Brutally long silences have been peppered with cancelled Skype calls whilst I run around having fun, but despite time and physical distances, she's coming to visit in a few months. Sharing memories with new friends is fun, but it doesn't quite have the same connection, especially when the GBH is that specific type of character that you can travel with, be engrossed with, go through anything with. Of all the attractions, places and people in the world, I think about and miss her the most. Other people are just nice pieces that make up the bigger picture. The chance to have amazing days like today and dare to hope that they can get ever better is another motivation to keep enjoying myself and to not get distracted about what's at home.

Panama City – best served in between the old and new in a fish market 2.4.16.

Arriving at the crack of dawn in a capital city is, more often than not, a nuisance. It's busy, confusing, difficult and foreign, yet arriving in Panama City was so easy. It feels like a miracle after a cold night bus journey.

In a taxi to the hostel, driving through Panama City, I start to think about the definition of 'developed'. Language, education, technology? It's apparent from the off that there are two very different sides to the city: old and new. The new looks like Dubai, with towering skyscrapers and slick office blocks in a modern superpower image that light up the left-hand side of the freeway on the city. To the right are belittled three-storey-high narrow, colonial buildings off cobbled paths, with grey, beaten-up, post-war image housing estates in-between them in what is affectionately known as 'the old town'. Even the bursting colours of the sun rising doesn't mask how extraordinary it is to have two such different sides of the city stand off against one another.

Settling in, it's time for some life admin – the part of travel that is like household chores, the stuff you need to get done to make sure the next thing you do will be decent. Boring, time-consuming but laborious routines of home can at times be hard to shake off, and going from store to store in the centre of the city, filled with coffee chains and numerous shopping malls. The quality of cars on the road everywhere has improved the further south I've travelled, (it's part of the changing landscape) and with that I need technology to find a replacement camera charger. This seems an achievable task given the modern nature of the new city. The travel often provides the most interesting of anecdotes and conversations as the taxi driver's story proves to be the most interesting part of the day. Taxi driving is not a lucrative career in Panama. The enormous high-rise flats we drive around in the city are extortionately priced between one thousand and five hundred dollars and three thousand dollars a month to rent, compared to the government supported buildings that are one hundred dollars a month. Unattainable rent pricing literally towers over the poor.

Walking the old city in the evening, I realise just how diverse and far apart the wealthy and poor are. You can be walking on a cobbled street with quaint colonial buildings, and behind you there is a beautiful and clean, European-styled plaza with restaurants around it, benches to sit on, freshly cut grass as you walk with a view of a slick, clean, big skyscraper. However, the street which you then turn down, the dynamics change in a footstep as you stand in murky waters of piss and shit running down the road. Kids playfully run around you in the freedom of their homes, with broken windows lining the street behind elegant restaurants and cafes, but their clothes are tattered, or they don't have any clothes at all. The hostel had warned that if you feel like you're walking down a dodgy road, go down a different one, and quickly. Unfortunately for me this meant I ended up going down an even sketchier path. Five minutes before, the Old Town was beautiful… now it's a mess as I walk with my sandals acting as ploughs through rubbish and waste on an unattended street. Ahead of me is a group of elderly people sat within a cloud of smoke from their chicken cooking on the grill that's fired up on the street corner. Potentially an image of hopeless homeless people gathered around an oil drum at night somehow changes into a positive idea that perhaps this is a good spot to try to figure out where I am in this ghetto which I've ended up walking in and to get a bite – food over safety, always. After their initial concern as to why I was there, and that I mustn't walk home in this area, eating and yakking with them was some of the best company I'd had yet on my trip – and entirely in Spanish. Exploring off the 'well-lit path', in this instance, has some obvious risks, but some high rewards, be it speaking in Spanish, the company or just great food. Probably a combination of all three made me feel really good about myself. For now, some Panamanian Jerk Chicken can solve any immediate issues. It is obvious the locals love cooking for themselves, but welcoming a lost traveller and making me welcome in their conversation, it seems that they open up to the 'gringos' more than I'd expected from my first impression.

Panama's western ideas create a travel bonus in the shape of home comforts that I forgot existed: hot showers, cleaner bars and a fifty cents happy hour. When these opportunities come around it's necessary to take them and stock up. Needless to say, taking advantage of a cheap bar allowed me to lighten up from being engulfed by travellers, due to the international airport, making it so easy to get access to Central America from here. I guess a fifty-cent bar can make me less pessimistic.

For a city with two sides, there is a food epicentre of the city where both sides from the Old and New Town congregate: the Fish Market. Tourists and locals are sardined on stools or squished onto anything with a ledge, locals having more assurance and confidence in how and where to sit, as waiters, covered in fish guts nervously serve different ceviche and seafood combinations from their counters. There's chaos and amusement for everyone under the warehouse roof as the main focus, apart from food and giving aggressive stares at anyone who slightly knocks a cold beer in someone's hand, is Real Madrid v Barcelona. The market is the place to be. Like the pub in England, this is where they come for their beer, food and gossip. Amidst all the chaos of a football game going on, it is very safe, happy and customary to their routine – as if people have been doing this with their friends and families for years – all with a modern twist of the New City in the background.

Dwarfing the city is the iconic engineering feat of the country: The Panama Canal. Allowing cargo to pass through from the Pacific to the Atlantic in eight hours as opposed to weeks in a journey around the continent makes it one of the most significant industrialised constructions of all time. I knew of the canal, but didn't know a lot about it, so to understand how important it was helped me to gain perspective of how the city is as brutal as it is now. Run by Americans in Panama, keeping slaves from all over the world busy in 1800s. Basic machinery dug the equivalent of eight storeys deep – a skyscraper's depth. No coincidence that the New City's infrastructure has gone for 'big'! However, for a generation that's now so dependent on technology, it's sobering to see that labour as brutal as pulling tugboats through the mud is still significant in the modern era and how something created by people from all over the world in a small country like Panama can have such influence. It's a shame that it took America until 31st December 1999 to allow Panama to run it themselves. For better or worse, it has certainly helped the country to cement their status as a powerhouse, holding all the cards, to continue their development as a growing influence in the world.

The San Blass Adventure – Best served in doubt 3.4.16.

Panama to Colombia has two options – fly or go on a boat through the Caribbean's deserted islands of the San Blass. I looked into it and it was a no-brainer – a boat trip offered desert islands, no communication: just powder sand, blue waters and coconuts – it was an easy sell.

I had kept in touch with a friend who I met in Xela, Fiona, who planned to be in Colombia around the same time as me. Both of us being on a budget, a mini-cruise around the Caribbean is far from a budget-friendly excursion, so signing up for the same boat meant that should our financial worries mean that it turned out to all be a bad idea, at least we would have each other.

Neither of us are keen on big gringo trail-escorted tours and are more interested in finding more authentic experiences. The financial commitment that tourist operated tours involve always feels like a big deal. The operation of a boat tour for several days and at a supposedly dangerous border crossing requires a regimented briefing. The ten or so people that we had imagined to be on the boat with us in this romantic rum-drinking paradise crusade turned out to be a group of thirty!

Sat in a cramped room with a group of people I'd never met (and, frankly, couldn't be bothered to meet for what was going to be a short space of time). It was all a bit disheartening that I didn't in fact have a Caribbean cruise all to myself. Forking out for what would be paradise for me was in fact the most budget boat tour possible. It usually costs thousands; hence why so many others were also signed up. My dream trip was still alive; it was just changing.

I wasn't sure what it was turning into, but excitement grew as we were told of our narrow boats, to be driven by Kuna tribesmen through the islands with all the rum and seafood you could imagine. I'll believe it when I see it. Bocas islands were pretty special after all.

The San Blass Islands – best served on a boat. 10.4.16.

Twenty-eight gringos line up on a boat dock, fresh-faced and excited. Amidst unloading supplies of rum, rice and a bunch of oversized backpacks with tacky gadgets on, onto the boat we go. There is a sense of togetherness that is shared in the group and everyone is keen to get along even though no one knows each other. Boat trips are usually fun, but extra effort to get along seems necessary as if I'm stuck on a boat, or even desert islands, with people I don't like or I am being antisocial, it's going to be a long couple of days.

The boat motors steadily away from the mainland until we suddenly go full throttle further into the depths of the ocean. The water goes from turquoise to dark navy as the coastline disappears into the distance. The deafening drone of the second-hand motor that encourages people to sit in silence ends up prompting small talk and pleasantries. This helps me adjust to admitting that I have become part of the gringo trail, although yet to become something I hate, my lack of resistance in avoiding being a gringo is slightly endearing but to me, it's pathetic.

Within an hour, we are coasting towards one remote, desert island demonstratively named 'Band of Coconuts', we pull up to the island to stop for lunch; our own island with just us. On the opposite side of this island, further at sea, were hundreds of these remote scattered islands, some with solitary palm trees, some with huts, but all of them exquisitely beautiful in their own way, and we'd only just arrived at the first one. It was a twenty-metre-long island with a few trees growing out of white sand and a single Kuna tribesman selling cold beers from a polystyrene cooler. He paddles out to more expensive yachts offering to sell beers to them and his homemade rice and fish head dishes. The desert island life that I had dreamt about, the beauty, the life people live here is real and not just what I'd imagined, but for all of those with me in the group too. The sense of relief and joy in knowing that this part of my dreams weren't lies is amazing.

A group of backpackers from each corner of the world celebrated a communal happiness by completely letting down their guards in their new surroundings straight away. When I was at home I'd have a drink as a way of celebrating an occasion. Today, as a group, we celebrate as if a goal of all goals has been achieved, in realising that this paradise the world has created does exist.

I think about the GBH again, but I don't feel guilty any more, I'm glad I'm being selfish and doing this now. This is all real. Caught up in my dream world, I grab a snorkel and mask and even try to swim to another island, like in the movies. I make it but nearly drown in what was a surprisingly strong current that you definitely don't see in paradise movies – at least I'd have drowned in glory!

Desert island dreaming gets my brain thinking of other fantasies – the lottery, for one, so that I'd be able to buy one of these islands! So beautiful, so remote, so perfect, they look as if they're newly discovered. In fact, the islands that stretch between Panama and Colombia are all owned by the Kuna people. Familiar with the dollar currency, their happiness and purity of the lives they live is their highest commodity. After that, it's their coconuts. Tourists taking a fallen coconut without their permission is theft. To buy a beer from them or any material goods, you need to exchange cash for coconuts to deal in.

What seems like blissful ignorance is actually acknowledgement and commitment to not being like the 'real world'. They will never sell their islands; this way they aren't involved in corruption, inflation rates or any other difficulties which could change how they are, whilst still accepting that they're part of Panama. The Kunas have no envy of the bright lights of Panama. They can have their own fun with beers in the sea, having bonfires and drinking rum as they play their version of 'hide and seek' with the group of travellers, hiding in boats and climbing up trees.

The novelty of sleeping in hammocks strung up between palm trees on desert islands is something that I won't stop smiling about for a long time. The novelty of waking up in a hammock with the worst hangover I've had in a lifetime, being swung side to side as I'm told the boat's leaving any minute is something I want to quickly forget about. Dehydrated, confused and still drunk, fast motion is the last thing a castaway wants. I was ready to stay there forever, for it being a paradise and also because of my inebriation. The double-edged sword of a tour means that you move on – a tough life, but as we head for another paradise island I get over it.

Busting my foot, all I wanted to do was play football, while injured. Doing something, or being somewhere that you can't, is agonising, so playing football on a paradise island before swimming in the sea with a beer is a hangover cure for months of wanting what I couldn't have. It was almost worth the wait. Running around laughing with new friends from all over the world like a child, I felt like I was an advert for some overpriced cringe STA Travel tour for ten days in Thailand, but instead it was our own happiness.

Interacting with the Kuna people briefly whilst they steer their boats, I was looking forward to the evening on one of the larger islands with a bigger population of locals. With their lifestyle of carefree and non-materialism, this was an occasion where having been introduced to something culturally, the chance to then go further into it and know more was there.

The Kuna weren't an influencing factor for me coming on this trip, although it has certainly added a fun mix and an interesting cultural dynamic to a glorified border into Colombia. From arrival onto the small island (albeit bigger than the others we'd visited so far), paths are laid out in-between thatched handmade houses. It seems that my first impressions were accurate with the Kunas' positivity, or perhaps that was my change of mind set from being here. The Kunas' happiness and jovial antics hit me straight away, as a child jumps onto me and slaps my white skin and curly ginger beard. The street filled with children who erupt with laughter at my appearance. The laughter becomes the continuous soundtrack which provides the whole place with a spring in its step like some over-the-top Disney musical. The kind of happiness here is the sort that must be instilled from the very start to the end of their lives; it doesn't seem diminished to anyone on the islands regardless of their age. The central point of the housing cluster is a dry, dirt square where kids chase each other around playing football with a plastic bottle, as the older kids play basketball above them on the same pitch. Running around each other in happy chaos.

The island has a population of one thousand which holds a democratic vote every few years for who should become the leader and, effectively, the voice of reason for the island. The leader makes decisions such as where and when their thatched houses should be built in the format of a planning permission process, the newly acquired solar panels that the mainland government provided them with. If you have a lot of coconuts, you can build your house...

The new infrastructure being built is a big deal for the community, which is why one person is elected to take decisions on behalf of everyone and make an executive call. Although proud of their independence, the influence of the mainland donating the solar panels is seen by both parties as allowing each other to carry on with their lives and not interfering with each other. Allowing the Kunas to remain happy with themselves and use the mainland's help for their resources is something that can't be manufactured on the mainland. They can build their own basic infrastructure, and trade with coconuts, but other than fishing for food, lifestyles are basic but as equally wonderful.

The green in the Kuna flag represents a portion of how they are aware of their background and being a part of mainland Panama. Their difference, despite their dependence on the mainland, is summed up in their community where children are thrown to the forefront of society, being free to ask the leader anything they want. Should a kid have a query, they don't go to their parents, they go to their leader for an answer. When sitting in a hammock with someone, be aware that, should you swing seven times, then that's your wedding ceremony and you're married! Not quite like the mainland – that wouldn't happen in the skyscrapers of Panama!

Heading to South America was exciting, but I was gutted to be leaving these islands which had all been so perfect. I was ready to leave the boats– I love the novelty, but riding waves that, when further out to sea, are capable of drowning you and soak you from head to toe for three hours a day... The novelty wears off within twenty minutes, especially when the boats keep breaking down. Having said that, it's not a bad place to break down in comparison to being at home on the hard shoulder of a motorway.

When approaching Colombia, it only seemed fitting that we would break down again, for one of the group to then notice a wooden crater box floating nearby in the water whilst we were stationary. Pulling the box into the boat it weighed about eighty kilograms, the lid slides off to reveal packs and packs of cocaine. The Kuna driver quickly slams the lid shut and gets his Kuna friends and assistants who have been on the boat with us, to help him store the 'rice'. Code?

Having spent four days with the Kunas, this was the happiest I'd seen them yet and I'm not surprised – they've just come across around eighty kilograms of cocaine washed up against the boat! But aren't these people who have no motivation by money? What good is a million dollars worth of cocaine to them? What are they going to do with it and why are they so happy? The concept of selling the cocaine for convenience in their location near Colombia to visiting tourists in such a safe environment had come to mind.

The Kunas are certainly aware of the benefits selling can bring but are aware of the trouble involved. Without wanting to be involved, they claim to work with the authorities by handing over the coke whenever they find it. Why are they so happy then? Why did they charge one of the group twenty-five dollars dollar for a plastic stool which broke by accident when it couldn't have cost more than five dollars? Why are the boats so expensive to hire? It creates a doubt in my mind about what I've learned about them, and their values maybe aren't as genuine as I thought. Either way, catching a crate of cocaine amidst the obsession with coke on the South America gringo trail, informs us that Colombia is definitely the next stop.

Passing through Panama 8.4.16.

I was sad to leave Panama, both for the enjoyment of the country and the memories I'd made, and were it not for the draw of arriving in South America I probably would have stayed longer.

Panama leads the way with abrasive and developed infrastructure as well as its business acumen. Costa Rica is developed, but their focus is on tourism, as opposed to what feels like a more corporate world here, gives it an economic nudge. The financial loopholes on offer here offer that taste of the first-world corruption, as whilst I was here 'The Panama Papers' were leaked identifying politicians and millionaires hiding their wealth here, something that other Central American countries could only wish for. Panama has an edge to it; the business acumen and growth element is evident but so is the history of the Spanish and Colombians here and their basic living. Much more than other places in Central America, you feel convinced that Panama is a country that is progressing at a rate of knots.

It perhaps also explains how things are aesthetically sharper, as they've been inherited from American ownership of the canal and a savvier business acumen – knowing that they can get away with American pricing on their commodities and food. Also, a reflection on how they charged the Americans the same as they're used to back home as they hated their prize asset being owned by Americans. The development and accessibility of destinations in Bocas and how the ease of travel through the San Blass islands perhaps cover the cracks of those being left behind on unattainable house prices. Genuine poverty exists next to fancy hotels and indigenous tribes who do their own thing, yet hold a connection with mainland government that isn't quite so clear.

Whilst there's a western feel, the massive influences of their own Caribbean vibe, the dependable and reliable cuisine of chicken and rice, which are so easy and cheap to make, are made fancier and altered along the way with the famous variations of hot sauce. Panama seems to have taken ideas from the business moguls of America, and the lifestyle of the Caribbean, and made it their own – seems logical. What matters most though, their number one joy, is everyone enjoying themselves, enjoying their company and the beauty of their surroundings – what bliss.

Crossing borders and continents 8.4.16.

Chopping along the sea in a boat, we curve close around the coast to our guide screaming out 'Welcome to Colombia'. Looking up at the aggressively rugged landscape of cliffs which are covered by grey cloud, it's as intense as you'd expect the densest jungle in the world to be. This area, known as the Darien Gap, which Panama and Colombia share, seems intimidating from so low down, sat in a boat, as it towers over us. It's inadvisable to go over land from Panama to Colombia due to cartel traffickers, another reason to choose the happy-go-lucky San Blass tour.

Currently floating in no-man's-land, having just had our exit stamps from Panama done in relatively hassle-free circumstances, we are no longer in Panama, but don't have the entrance stamp to Colombia yet either. Only a geographical map identifies our position. We pull into the dock and all pile out, stumbling onto the dock as the tide's undercurrent pulls our standing position on the boat back and forth. Flailing around over one another, whilst the boatmen wade through with ease.

As people wait in single file for entrance stamps, I walk around the small village which seems lined with armed forces. The village has a lot of fierce-looking people staring with intent; I instantly feel uncomfortable. The area feels abandoned and soulless, yet overpopulated and cramped. People are sleeping on the streets, on their patios outside battered shops and tents are everywhere. It's an eerie vibe, not only because it doesn't feel friendly or safe, but because it's something I haven't seen before and don't know how to describe it to myself. I have been in unsafe areas, but this is different.

I head back to our boat which is tied to the dock, and our group begin filtering back, refreshed and with a passport stamp. We get back in the boat to go to a more viable place in Colombia to set off from. Just as we sit in the boat and patiently wait, the dock over from us has a queue for customs which stretches at length, its huge fishing boat and its passengers are all carrying everything imaginable in buckets and bin liners, from blankets and clothes to a kitchen sink and a pitch fork – everything. As our boat slowly turns around someone pointed out that the boat had come from Somalia and those in the queue had recognisably African features. The traveller translation of a 'border town' usually means 'shit hole', and everything suddenly clicked. This was a refugee town.

In their plastic bags were tents, their clothes and their lives that they'd boarded the boats with to run away from Somalia which is painted on the side of the fishing boat they'd arrived in… and this shit hole was their freedom. They probably paid an arm and a leg to get in that boat, and I can't imagine that the Atlantic is the easiest ocean to cross in comparison with the bumpy few days we had in the San Blass paradise. If this place is a better life for them, how shit can Somalia be? Europe has an immigration problem and this is another one I'm seeing in front of my own eyes.

When seeing things like this for the first time it can feel uncomfortable and agitating. I feel helpless and ignorant not knowing more, and angry that the world is like this. I arrive to my hostel in the evening, still feeling numb. The beautiful yet terrifyingly rugged untraceable mountains and jungle that our boat had gone through in the water is home for these four million illegal refugees who are joining guerrilla wars because it's a better life for them. How has the world got to a point where that's a better life, to be an unidentifiable refugee, fighting a war in a foreign country with no legal proof of existence? How is this a better life? It's a serious reality across the world on all levels of poor to rich countries.

Amidst having had the time of my life – all the postcard-photographs, the laughs, games, friendships made and cultural exposure I'd had – I was grateful to be entering Colombia with a group of people who, without saying, I knew held sympathy for what was in front of us. Now a group of happy travellers sit in a deathly silent boat, on their tourist trail, soberly entering South America. Deep down we all held a feeling that the adventure ahead of us, for all the great things Central America provided, would be going up a notch.

Colombia

Colombia – best served eating Bandeja Paisa.

- beans
- white rice
- chicharrón
- carne en polvo [powdered meat]
- chorizo
- fried egg
- ripe plantain
- avocado

A portion size of the above all to choice, mixed together in one hearty platter from the locals of the Paisa region, eaten in Medellin.

Viva Colombia – best served cold, wet and tired 10.4.16.

The town of Capurgana is small and frankly, underwhelming with there being nothing other than wet travellers from the SBA that can't seem to warm from a cold and wet boat ride. The group starts to split up as some people plan to go to Medellin and others to Cartagena within the next few days, the two choices for the gringo trail. Being so close to the Panama border, transport police can hold those needing to use the pathway to ransom, so their choice to strike, banning all transport in and out of the town for the next few days, meant that it was either leave tomorrow (the next available time being at the extortionate inflated fee of a seventy-dollar boat-then-bus ride) or leave whenever the police allow. Most of the group were keen to leave ASAP, and as Capurgana didn't offer so much straight away to me, I was easily swayed. I am well and truly becoming influenced by other gringos now, I may as well embrace it for a short while at least.

The two-hour boat ride leaving at the crack of dawn was always going to be arduous. Looking at the size of the boat, the thick dark clouds ahead, and that it was necessary to put all of our possessions in a waterproof liner protection, set the mood of what was coming up; I was apprehensive. Spending my days cold and wet wasn't what I'd anticipated arriving into South America to be like.

We set off and it was a breeze in comparison to our boats with SBA, despite being crammed in like a chicken bus. The boat was quick and dry; it was easy and almost relaxing without the occasional wave bump. The further up the coast we go, the further away from the land we go, the more treacherous the waters become, deeper waves, higher falls from the waves, bringing the inevitable soaking. Still going as fast as seemingly possible, the length of this journey is two hours, but appreciating the speed that we're going – it feels like a water ride at a theme park that could be over pretty soon. Pulling away even further from the coast, the height of the coastline reminds me how intense that jungle by the border is where the refugees are, and that a trip up the coast to Cartagena is actually more of a mission being almost the length of Central America, if not a big chunk of it!

As time passes we now begin to laugh about the audacity our driver has in driving directly through waves that dwarf our overloaded boat as people hang off the sides, having stopped to pick up the driver's friends. Being on the front row, I had the best seat to a death by drowning, as wave after wave leads the driver to take a pause. He must be exhausted from getting battered by the waves himself. After some time, we noticed that we've actually been stationary for a while, and the captain has unsuccessfully been trying to flag down other boats. Thirty minutes pass being stationary as he remains silent. We were lost. In the middle of the ocean, with only dots and specs of coastline to see. The driver being dismissive and ignoring any questions was creating a nervous atmosphere, as a passenger eventually hints that the boat also needs more fuel.

Patience is the key to a lot of travelling. People on the boat were tired, cold, wet – all the criteria that patience tests. Fortunately, within some of the group, another trait was good humour as hopes of a five-star cruise picking us up and taking us all the way to Cartagena began to be suggested. Gringos however, are not a patient breed. Coming from fortunate backgrounds with lots of money and built-up stress, they have rage which creates the opposite effect to patience and threatens to create a toxic environment. Whilst people begin to vent their anger at the situation, I was embarrassed and irritated to hear a loud English-speaking voice shout slowly, loudly and in a condescending tone to a Colombian boat driver who can't speak a word of English. To the famous HR question: 'If you're stranded on a boat, who do you kick off first?' there's a few I would have thrown off to lighten the load as we hit the hour mark of floating abandonment.

Then out of nowhere, like an oasis in the desert, a sixty-foot cruise boat arrives pointing in multiple directions. It eventually flings us a gasoline barrel for us to fill up on. The dream of salvation is certainly a reality as we notice other travellers on this boat who have seemingly had no issue with a transport strike. Raised high up like royalty on their boat in jeans and warm clothes, they're even drinking lattes in mugs in a café. Meanwhile I have a bag of onions pressed into my back!

As we go from stand still to full throttle, the coastline appears and we rev up again to go through a massive wave. BANG! We've hit something and the boat spins and skids across the water. The thud of the collision rattles through to the back of the boat as those behind us scream and the boat tilts onto its side. In slow motion, I look to my right and the only thing in between my head and the water is my friend Duncan's head vertically below me; we look at each other with a sense of disappointment that this is how it's going to end. Our friend in front, Chris, turns behind to look at us, begrudgingly agreeing, without saying a word, in a silent movie, all about how a group of gringos die in an over-priced boat ride. Accepting that it was our destiny and wouldn't be the worst way to go out, after all.

Just like in a movie, there's a snap back to the real world when the boat lands with a bang on its side, thrashes back to balance and spins as the engine blows out and throws everyone over each other in their compact rows. We stop and a few loose bags are flung overboard from the jolting. Screams and profanities amongst the boat erupt, followed by a couple of laughs as the two-hour ride up the coast was now at four and a half. The novelty of boats has well and truly worn off. For some, the boat ride is about letting the Colombian captain know exactly what they think. I find it all hilarious, but there isn't much room for humour in what I thought was going to be certain death.

We pull into the dock, packed with police and locals who find it hilarious that an overcrammed boat of gringos has made it to the dock with a massive hole in front. The crowd shows little sympathy in between their hysterical laughter at the boat as if they'd known what happened to us. Stepping onto the dock was nearly impossible with no moving point for those who want to 'help' carry your bag ten metres to the station or to sell you bus tickets. I am tired and can't be bothered to be harassed right now as that patience I've been clutching at was being tested to the full. Unfortunately for me, I'm starving and there's nowhere to buy food ahead of the ten-hour bus ride that's now required to get to Cartagena which strangely helps me accept that this was a bad situation and there's nothing I can do at all about it. Nonetheless, ten hours of people not talking to one another is exactly what is needed to calm down.

Only when we reached the road sign at the six-hour mark for Cartagena do people begin to lighten up and jokes start to be made again. Sure, there would be the battle of going through the admin of finding a hostel with a wet, heavy bag when I'm starving and tired. I think the Scottish guy on the boat who hated the Colombian driver the most has burst a blood vessel now, but Cartagena is a food haven and I'm guaranteed good food – what more could I want?

The Cartagena Carry-on – best served at a street party 11.4.16.

The first two days in Colombia were not quite the endearing entrance to the country or continent that I hoped for, but then again it's not like I was owed the red carpet treatment. So far it has been hard work but after the San Blass Islands, I was due a reality check. Arriving late at night the acceptance of becoming more and more gringo is taking over me, a few of us explore the cobbled streets of Cartagena.

Tall buildings give the ambiance of a classic, classy, well-polished colonial city, intermingled with the history of a city of crumbling walls and erosion all around. It's a beautiful city, especially at night as it lights up, and I now feel that after two days I'm somewhere in Colombia where I feel comfortable, excited and relaxed. The city feels enormous, having been on desert islands, small towns and cramped buses. The crumbling city wall circles the old town area of the city which looks out to the busy city of skyscrapers, similar to how Panama City was laid out.

The first day of exploring in Colombia with friends from the boat – again the favourite hobby in a new place – we walk aimlessly, soaking up the atmosphere and street sounds of what instantly feels like a happy and beautiful people and we stop to break for the best coffee that I have had in my life. It is light in density but strong and with a refreshing kick; people-watching has never tasted so good. With most of our group from SBA in Cartagena, meeting up for an evening of drinks was inevitable; in between sitting on the city walls drinking cocktails, this was a classier and definitely more expensive way of enjoying a city.

The gringo obsession with Colombia's biggest export – cocaine – it was inevitable that it would be going around amongst the SBA group. I am not too phased about it myself, nor do I know much about the history of it here in Colombia and the damage it has previously caused. However, the way it seems that it transcends and is accepted by normal society here in comparison to the first world is almost comical in comparison.

Close to the old town, the backpacker region Getsemani was where most of my new fellow gringo friends are staying whilst six of us had opted to stay in the nicer part of town and take advantage of prettier surroundings. Our path to meeting others in Getsemani was shady, breaking open into a large square where food vendors grilled kebabs, blast out music on each corner, selling big bottles of beer cheaply as the food stalls set the tone for a street party, on a Sunday. The street food is so delicious and cheap, it's an easy party starter, a convenient way for people to socialise together, a foundation of how Colombians spend their money and time with one another.

From SBA, two of the people I had got on with best were Fiona and a Londoner called Chris and it was one of those trips and groups of people that you just laugh with the whole time. We continue in fine spirit, reminiscing with everyone over recent fond memories, partying away and falling in love with the city that is the foodie capital of the country – new anecdotes were being made.

I was having a great time, well and truly accepting that despite my best efforts to be authentic and less of a gringo that this moment and the last week or so, being with travellers who had come to Colombia almost principally for cocaine, I am now also part of the gringo trail, for the time being at least. Each to their own, after all. Travelling to learn a language, to learn about how the food infuses into the culture, for many that would be the last thing that they would want to do. As the night escalated with drinks somehow getting cheaper and cheaper the later it got, 'white gold' was around just as someone stated – 'when in Rome'.

Allegedly 'the best' in the world, I have never cared to rank drugs in such a way. With a sense of low risk and a convenience of price and accessibility, it seemed too easy, especially considering the reputation of dangerous drug barons and wars here. Coke is undoubtedly a huge part of the country's history so a taste seems the best way to find out more about it and if it is worth the fuss.

Amidst the fun and games and the inevitable effect of cocaine kicking in, there is not a care in the world. New and old friends, the atmosphere feels like we've known each other for years but without having to know each other and share the baggage. Partying and cheaply, the relaxed nature of the evening with the intensity of a big party vibe is right up my street, not having to worry about what shoes I'm wearing in a bar, not having to pretend to be sophisticated, totally relaxed and having, if anything, too much fun as I ride the SBA wave through Colombia. Still not entirely sure that coke in Colombia is worth the fuss, but that doesn't matter right now.

Having been discreet with the coke for the evening, Chris, Fiona and I take the relaxed atmosphere literally for a walk down a quiet road which we consider safe enough, enjoying the warm air and finishing the small bit we have left. Content already with the evening, I am not bothered about having much more and just enjoy the good company of laughs and absorbing the moment of again feeling completely content, with or without cocaine. A tiny amount is left to finish and requires my driving licence to be used before we walk back. A luminous green moped screeched to a halt, suddenly pulling up around the corner, is now stationary in front of us as we sat on a street curb.

Clenching my palms closed with ID in one hand and cocaine in the other, the police step off the moped and I am a sitting duck. I have no idea of the possession laws and I'm drunk beyond speaking good enough Spanish to wiggle out of this one. This isn't like asking for directions to a hostel or a bus terminal; this could be an issue. The moment of being relaxed, liberal and carefree has crashed and burnt into a wall as the cocaine kicks in and my adrenaline doubles with anxiety as the officer asks me to open my hands. Almost sensing my fate, I do it slowly – ID first then the cocaine – hoping to delay an unknown inevitability that I cannot predict.

The officer speaking Spanish orders me to stand as he confiscates the cocaine and I am aggressively and thoroughly searched as Chris and Fiona remain seated. I figure I'm best to stay quiet as I look at Fiona who seems close to tears and I feel guilty; the fun has ended. I have nothing of worth on me to be taken or confiscated other than about twenty US dollars in Colombian currency, but the damage is already done.

Turning to Chris and Fiona the officer says, 'This is very illegal in our country. He must go to prison for this. We take you to the station. You can meet your friend there.' He steps towards me and pulls out his handcuffs with a disappointed and authoritative look on his face. I shouldn't feel surprised but I was. His stuttered English slows everything down as the fun of the last few weeks, the evening and the rest of my trip come into my head – is it worth the fuss? Right now, absolutely fucking not.

I came off the boat three days ago to emails from the GBH, counting down the days till she came out to visit, of how hard she'd been saving and I could hear her excitement in the emails. I was excited too, but what am I going to do now? How long will I have to be there and what about the GBH? She will be heartbroken all over again and wouldn't forgive this one. A silly and relatively innocent mistake but one that seems unforgivably stupid out of context. I think about what may or may not happen between us as the officer talks to me in Spanish. I can't even be bothered to understand what he's saying, I'm too annoyed with myself and all I think about is the GBH. This is a real fuck-up. I always tell my friends not to mess around with drugs when travelling. Be smart and just don't get caught out – you don't know what will happen and I haven't taken my own advice. Hypocrite. Idiot. I am sick with guilt as my pending new experience tonight will be very real and unknown.

I have to do something, stop being quiet. I need to take a chance to somehow get out of this. I wasn't in a position to run, too drunk, too slow, and they have bikes. I am certainly not in a position to have thrown the drugs away or denied anything that happened as it all unravelled so quickly. I clear my throat to say something as Fiona begins to frantically beg in an exaggerated, Welsh-Latino accent. This is a great idea – beg! I start to say something again but she's off, doing her upmost to defend me. I start to listen to the translation again as the officer asks where the drugs were from, where we are going next, why we are here and so on. We are all on the same page and all on the gringo trail as we answer unanimously and promptly. The officer begins to ease up and starts taking a liking to Fiona's gringo blonde hair, blue eyes and impressive Spanish – thank God she is here and that we went to the Xela language school. The police have now made it quite clear they are only interested in talking to her, so I'm keeping quiet. Fiona is talking at a thousand miles an hour, probably from the cocaine, and the officer is now at the point of wanting her to either calm down or shut up as he proposes a fine.

Standing still waiting to be handcuffed, I am ready to pay whatever it is not to be arrested, happily accepting the gringo money can get me out of this horrible situation. The officer wants one hundred US dollars, this is a bribe. Knowing I only have twenty US dollars, he rejects my offer and tells me to get on the bike – perhaps this is a fixed price fine after all. I really am an idiot. Why do I not know the laws, but then why would I know the laws? Why have I let myself get into this situation? More begging and pleading begin as Chris empties out his wallet to make up one hundred US dollars. We have been paying one US dollar for a beer all night. How or why he has that much cash on him I don't know or care but I love him. I count the money out as the officer lifts his hand to suggest that forty US dollars was enough and I sign a dubiously photocopied fines form of my crime. I hand him the cash which he then refuses to accept. He lifts the seat of his bike and tilts his head for me to put the cash in. Bribe. What a dick. We had bought his bullshit, desperate to get out of the situation. He tells us to go and leave Cartagena first thing tomorrow. Heartily, he tells us doing cocaine is fine at home and lets us leave, as we quickly pace in the opposite direction.

After a long pause, whilst getting our heads around what had just happened, we crack a nervous laugh of relief as I pay Fiona and Chris gratitude for their part. We agree to not let this ruin the evening but I need a drink.

I want to leave, I want to get out of the city and the country. I can't be bothered being in situations like that, and as with any pathetic knee-jerk response, I want to leave. That was nerve-racking and I want to be alone; I don't want to talk. We head to the bar where everyone else is, to a number of curious-looking faces as to where we have been and why we look a little preoccupied. The idea of heading to a three US dollar, all-you-can-drink bar is not high on my list as I feel awkward to be out anywhere. The reality that our first night out in Colombia has involved an intense altercation with police which could have been a lot worse, our faces paint a picture where news of what happened filtered through our group. The loveliest Irish couple from SBA asked for some of the cocaine we had. I tell them it's gone, to which the girl asked innocently naive questions of the rush and what it was like, unaware of what has just unfolded. She's sweet and curious enough to ask, 'is it worth it?'

Hypocritical to say you should or shouldn't do it, for me it was being caught in a moment which the surroundings dictate, as opposed to curiosity. The rush is there for sure, and I was having a great evening, but more than I would have had, if I had not been an idiot? No. I wish I could listen to my own martyrdom advice sometimes, but perhaps the problem is that I don't like the advice or what I say or do. The anxiety about the unknown was probably at the back of my mind but it was walking away and then explaining the story to my friends when I realised I was now more annoyed about adding fuel to the fire of this issue. Buying coke as a traveller is certainly nothing new, but I have encouraged and allowed the locals to keep selling it to 'gringos', and travellers like me maintain the demand for sales. Yet I have also allowed the police to feel that they have done themselves and Colombia a favour by taking a bribe, a source of income for themselves, but who knows what they will do with that money? Frankly I don't even care now. Perhaps with hindsight I should have let them lock me up for a night by refusing to pay a bribe and fuel their corruption; amidst the blur of it all, paying a fine seemed like a great idea!

At the bar it wasn't long before a friend, with the benefit of hindsight and the internet, tells me the amount I had on me was not a criminal offence. I absorb the confirmation of this having been a bribe and threat with a pinch of salt, accepting that this is a country known for its lovely friendly people, but those ones just did a number on me. Good job this place is an all-you-can-drink bar, and that from traveling I definitely have some good friends.

Carrying on and Chilling Out – best served by the beach eating from fishermen's boats 16.4.16.

The day after was a day of nothing. Everyone was hungover; the last thing I wanted to do was to be mentally or physically active. Instead I did some life admin, planning a few things that I could do on my last day before Fiona and I would have a few days chilling out away from the temptation of spending money and partying up the coast around the Santa Marta area.

Cartagena is not a cheap city in relative terms. Colombia so far has been up and down. People aren't as friendly as expectations promised they would be; it's not that cheap and the pricing isn't kind. A good thing about exploring is there's no cost to walking around aimlessly taking photos, being able to practise my Spanish skills while turning down the offer to buy tacky souvenirs or cocaine.

Eating cheaply is certainly possible though. A picnic pieced together by the local bakery of pastries and fruit costs about one US dollar each – there's always a bargain somewhere even in this expensive foodie-city. For all the partying, the good eating, the paradise boat ride, had I booked these from home and not winged it how we did, we could have spent thousands, when in fact we probably didn't spend anything close to that amount of money. We have had a blast and a splurge. For a while I felt like some kind of Hollywood baller which is so far from the usual for me back in London where it can feel impossible to dream of doing anything close to this kind of luxury.

Goodbyes are in order as the SBA crew begins to split up. Exchanges are made of routes and suggested dates and locations around Colombia are thrown around based on people's itineraries and there seems a good chance of seeing each other again at some point on the continent or around the world – a final evening last-supper style, taking advantage of the city's cuisine. We compared this to the street corners where with their own party atmosphere that they create, the oily foods they fry add to the heat in the streets. Positioned on the coast, the seafood is amazing as Colombia takes on its own style of ceviche. Being so close to the jungles nearby, the array of different ingredients and spices gives the quality of food an edge, less vinegars and oils, more plant-based supplements to complement its dishes. A freshness and originality, along with the beauty of the city, the food makes Cartagena a destination in itself.

Up the coast towards the north east is the city of Santa Marta, a base for anything that you could want to do from jungles, mountains, rivers, beaches, wildlife, coffee – it's a great place to base yourself in as it's also somewhere that as soon as you arrived you'd want to leave. The city itself is a dump filled with travel operators and little else. Fiona and I chose not to get the adrenaline going with a hike just yet but to do nothing but sit on a beach and see my friend from Caye Caulker, Nick, who was working in a hostel in Taganga to save some money. Working in a hostel is often a good way to experience more of the area, free board in exchange for around six hours work a day.

Taganga is a small fishing village with a handful of restaurants, bars and hotels which are populated by weekend visitors and fishermen after they have sold all their catch on the beach that same day, fresh from the nets that they were caught in as cheap as one US dollar. Fishing and diving are the main pastimes here, so for me it's perfect to do nothing but relax and have a change by cooking for myself with the freshest fish possible. Fiona went diving, and was able to figure out from the divers' community where there were any parties should we want to participate, but I had no interest in being sociable. As soon as I saw a hammock by the hostel pool, I soaked up the sun all day. Walking along the beach littered with fishing boats was as energetic as I got.

The beach is so peaceful in the morning, come the afternoon, as fishermen start to end their day on the water, they line up on the beach in their boats and sell fish to the locals of Taganga. A fish BBQ seems the thing to set the tone for those partying here in what's a buzzing nightlife spot. Fishermen out at sea have no shame in heckling to get punters to come to the table they set up by their boat for trade. For Fiona, being a blonde-haired girl however, walking around in a town with fishermen who had been at sea, the word 'bait' was thrown around casually by locals who love trying their luck in charging an extra forty per cent gringo tax on anything they sell.

I love being by the sea. It's therapeutic and the old element of fishing adds so much charm as seashells glisten on the waves as they ripple on the sand. Perfectly shaped upon first look, they seem like they could be fish gills that had been shaved from the knives of the fishmongers. In fact, they are ringlets from eroded plastic bags in the ocean that have swept up onto this beautiful beach. This isn't even that big of a bay so it seems unfathomable how much more waste is in the ocean, treated like a rubbish tip, a sewage for hundreds of years as the ocean erodes away, killing nature and supplies that we require to eat and survive. Colombia does not have the tools to deal with waste, rectifiable with investment support. The culture change required through education is the hardest challenge. Impossible to trace where this waste has come from, the ocean is now a global trash can.

There is waste in all oceans and beaches I've been to, locals and tourists being culprits too. Japan and Norway are two countries I've been to with fantastic philosophies of not leaving litter around and aesthetically they're much nicer; they set an example that we should all look up to. The first world must begin to take more responsibility; finances help but education seems the paramount method for improving. We must all play a part not to ruin the environment further both aesthetically and climatically.

The Lost City – best served sweating, eating nothing but rice 19.4.16.

Santa Marta is the base for departing treks in the Colombian jungle which spreads into the Amazon. The Lost City is an indigenous and spiritual ruined city, built hundreds of years ago within the jungle which requires trekking to so Fiona and I sign up with SBA friends, Duncan and Marius, for four days.

Living out of a bigger bag and needing to condense that bag to a smaller one for a four-day trek requires more time to pack intelligently and lighter than moving everything at once when changing location. Choosing to detox in Taganga had been with this trek in my mind; I needed to give my body all of the help it could get, having done little exercise since breaking my foot six months ago.

Before we set off we are briefed by our guide that each day will be a different length and terrain. There was little leeway in which was the best day for hiking in terms of a challenge. The real challenge was going to be the humidity of the jungle; just standing at the start of the trek, we're all sweating profusely. Feeling excited but still in the mood to be lazy and relaxed, my last serious hike had been in Nicaragua. Our group had an American girl who has brought her dog along for the 'walk'. However hard it may be for me, it'll be a lot harder for him, underestimating that this is the jungle, not the park.

Several hours of hiking can be so good for the mind and uplifting. Surrounded by nothing but rugged, imperfect jungle scenery for miles and miles it's hard not to love the Colombian spirit of beauty in between its rougher parts of dirty paths and broken fallen trees. The awe of walking past mud huts where kids dressed in potato sacks run inside as the 'white man' is a new specimen and not a friendly one on the eye. Donkeys trudge up the hill past us carrying hundreds of kilos of weight on their back. The crime, coke and dangerous cities which I had been taught about Colombia growing up is apparent, but the isolation of those in poverty here is new for me.

I always love the idea of hiking, but when actually doing it the reality is that it's on muddy and awkwardly footed terrain, it's sweaty, and conversations are mostly non-existent with long awkward silences of struggle which hiking entails. This is no different with the added bonus of a crippling, never-ending humidity. Surely it's impossible to sweat this much. Every item of clothing is soaked all the way through to the liner of my rucksack within five minutes. We take rest stops in lagoons and natural pools along the way. Ironic that we look like we've already been swimming with the sweat and our stiff bodies, although the cold water is a godsend to help the muscles. Drying off isn't an issue; I'm sweating as soon as I step out of the water.

With the conversation being limited from the challenge of the hike, following a dusty path often in pairs or on your own, I try and start a conversation with our tour guide and his translator. There's only so much effort one person can make in asking questions about the jungle with one word answers or no answers at all from the grumpy guide, and a translator who doesn't seem keen to talk despite her profession being to talk. The area is beautiful and it's nice talking with our small group from the SBA but mostly, this is a difficult couple of days.

I love the remote sense of abandonment, being dropped in the jungle with nothing but a need to explore and survive. Cutting down bush en route through this vast Sierra Nevada de Santa Marta jungle and mountain range as we follow the river, the sense of exploring and adventure is high even if we are all like the donkeys themselves in following a path. The convenience of a tour this time is welcome, as opposed to the remoteness of Nicaragua's Rio San Juan which is more unique yet a bigger and more challenging commitment.

This is why you pay what you pay for a tour. The chance to buy a water or energy drink from a donkey owner who walks the paths that we do, or have your food prepared ready for you by a villager upon arrival, is welcome. The food is basic; boiled rice with a chicken stock broth is a fair representation of how this area is, basically with nothing here but jungle. We pass small clusters of a dozen or so mud huts perhaps once a day so far; the abandonment their lives have, how basic they are being eye-opening. Children don't have clothes. They're wearing sugar bags to cover them; it's not poverty, it's nothingness. Yet somehow there's an element of earning money and existence here that would seem impossible upon looking at it. After all, these donkeys carrying drinks for hikers are earning money for their owners in these tiny pockets of civilisation. The benefit of having a drink at breaks was a blessing in this heat, a lifesaver even, but it makes the sense of adventure become much smaller than hoped. Having felt so excited by what the surroundings represent, it feels awkward to be able to buy a Gatorade which has been carried up by the tour venders. Maybe this isn't as abandoned as I thought it was, or hoped for it to be, as we arrive at a pre-designated 'base camp'.

I still wonder how it is possible to become fully engrossed in the communities that are here, to drop yourself into a remote place but the reality of falling onto the tourist trail makes it hard to do. I love this adventure; this trek is hard but it's beautiful and doing it with friends is more fun than with some of the random people that can be on treks. I am craving some time off the gringo trail though and need to go and engross myself in something less convenient than this without alienating myself completely.

Entering the Lost City – best served uncomfortable, still eating rice 21.4.16.

After two days of walking on a dry, dusty path that changes from clay to chalk on each and every other ascent and descent, humidity and rain are still making me sweat an amount that doesn't seem possible any more. The sunburn makes us all crave shade so badly that whenever a cloud comes to cover us, our spirits go up a notch. Even after three days walking, mules are still carrying sacks of sugar and rice for the villagers and, for our comfort, even a kitchen sink on one.

The guides so far have done little in the way of offering information on the history to the Lost City. Being in the middle of nowhere, it was only information that the group had read beforehand about the site that we shared amongst ourselves that educated us at all. A city built for immense sacred value, it was abandoned later after an attack by the Kogi people. The Kogi's were a tribe of descendants of Colombian history based close to the site. They came across it by chance in the 1970s. That is the kind of adventure and discovery I would love to do, a one in a billion chance of finding something like that, climbing mountains to find a city in a forest! Everything in existence has to be discovered at some point, there's no reason why more can't be discovered, especially in the areas where it's thought best 'not to go'.

The walk through mountains to discover the lost city is under a thick and claustrophobic canopy of humid jungle. Arriving at the base of the Lost City, we begin climbing twelve hundred steps of rock, which is covered by a low arch of trees and plants resembling a secret garden passageway, our route up to the Lost City. The climb of twelve hundred steps is the last thing anyone can be bothered to do, with everyone's kit soaked through from sweat. It's so humid there's no chance of it drying over-night either. The climb is tedious and ongoing as we slug up the unbalanced rocky steps. Amidst the heat and trying to squeeze enthusiasm and information out of our guides, who have not improved, their lack of ability to guide has added some camaraderie to the group, on top of pulling together on a tough hike, albeit a forced effort when the novelty of the hike and discomfort had started to wear thin.

Scaling the steep climb, the tree canopy arch we've followed up begins to open and the trees become taller above us. The mountain plateau's flat as we reach what must be the top with the site of large, perfectly circular rock formations which are laid out on the floor. They had moss on them as if they've been there for centuries. Our guide finally does something decent and brings us together at the summit to explain what this hike we've slugged away at is about – better late than never! The city was made by the indigenous people as a place to live, like any area of habitation today, whilst the rock formations were to celebrate those who lived in that spot and who have been buried, hundreds of years ago. With the remoteness of the location, the city took one hundred and fifty years to build. Thinking about how tough the hills are to climb, it could have taken longer; I'm not convinced this guy is giving us the whole picture.

Until there is another climb! I've done the hike, now I'd like the view, this is dragging on a bit now. The top of the mountain was designed by the indigenous like a wedding cake with enormous grass circles on each tier. The final climb is cruel and hard work but it feels like we have discovered it all over again, with no one else there, with nothing else but jungle-covered mountains in sight. The guide keeps saying every climb is the last one; I really hope this is the last one now. Should this still have been inhabited, the site itself would house thousands. Now popular with tours, it's not crowded as other indigenous sites can be. This is one of the blessings of a treacherous trek being the only method of getting here; fewer people come here as it's so difficult to walk the route.

The dog, which after three days of endless energy and sniffing every tree and rock in its enthusiasm as any pup would have, is now exhausted and struggling. Every twenty metres or so the dog collapses in the heat and crawls under shrubs for a chance of shade. The dog got a big laugh when he decided to piss on the sacred trees which are directly next to one of the largest memorial sites with a 'do not pass' sign. The intensity of the climb up the repetitive and arduous steps has been broken by our four-legged friend as we reach the summit. I know we've now reached the top as we're able from the highest point, to look over the thick jungle we've walked through, and down over the layers of circular formation. It's quite the view, but the sobering thought of how remote we are is most humbling and satisfying both for the difficulty of the walk, and how this place came about in the first place.

Our guide finally does something decent. He calls over a tribe leader from the bottom of the mountain for a 'Q+A' with us. He's done nothing but walk in front of us without saying a thing the last few days but seems to have saved a final trick! The leader, however, seems annoyed that we are there. He respectfully admits he knows nothing about our culture or lifestyle and doesn't mind us being there for a short while, but informs us that for certain parts of the year, he hopes we do not visit as there will be spiritual events taking place amongst his tribe. He painfully requests that the tours become more controlled, with a firmness as he looks at the tour guide implying that he is in fact bothered that we are here. Unable to quite see into their lifestyle or have it explained, perhaps this is something that the guides and tribes need to take up with each other in what is without doubt a sacred and important place for the tribes. The Kogi are content here and don't have to deal with any of the 'outside world's' nonsense whilst we have walked straight into theirs.

I felt none the wiser as to how this city became what it did from our guide, and I felt out of place being here, not just as a tourist but as an intruder. The line between being intrusive and inquisitive of this nature of living is fine. This trek was not possible to do solo so trust was given to the tour operator, and that's where I feel it has to lie. The last day of walking back was tough and just as gruelling, as new toes grow on feet in the shape of blisters. With water running low and refill opportunities apparently limited, rationing water meant that the final day is a welcome one. I've had enough of mosquito repellent, sun lotion and sweat constantly dripping in my eyes and feeling slightly dejected. The experience of culture and cuisine here is the basic cooking of rice, rice and more rice, fruit as snacks, and sugary water drinks – a fair representation of how they live, off very traditional and simple basics. But when the guide is rubbish, and the locals don't want you there, it's hard to find out more without further intrusion. We arrive back to normality, treating ourselves to a gin and tonic in the hostel pool. A tough but beautiful hike, our tribe leader who we had met couldn't be further away if he tried.

The Travel Companion II – best served trying to understand companionship.

Constantly doing things and being in situations where you meet

114

people, sharing a room with someone you talk to, or someone you meet in a bar, or with a guide, you're easily surrounded by people, looking like a tourist with the shade of skin and accent, it can be easy to pick up a conversation and introduce yourself a lot of the time. Choosing to spend time with them or become friends with them is another dynamic entirely, just like meeting people in the real world is.

I know when I can click and get on with people straight away and without much fuss. When starting to get on with people, you inevitably socialise more with them and do excursions together. Then when separating from each other to go different routes, it's polite to say 'let's keep in touch' when really, unless you are heading for the same route, the chances of that happening are quite slim.

Nick is someone I met in Belize through our hostel and we got on really well. He is planning to go to the Rio Olympics which was a base for us to keep in touch, and to try and meet up, along the way. I want to learn a language whilst Nick wants to do some teaching so our interests overlap. As it was my plan to travel solo, to be hassle free, the last thing I am going to do is spend time with people I don't like or change any plans for them. I meet some people who hold huge regrets and fall out with their friends by being stuck after falling into that trap as they like the comfort of being in a group. Solo travelling suits me to a tee even though I am still with people from SBA, because I know that when I want to go solo, it's just a matter of time.

The difficulty with a travel companion is when either mental guilt creeps in or you physically want to but can't get rid of the companion, as happened with Wesley in Rio San Juan. I knew within five minutes of being with him I wouldn't like him and that I wouldn't be able to lose him. Clingy, irritating and awkward to socialise or communicate with, he had a gift of appearing from nowhere when I tried to lose him. Patience is fundamentally travelling and accepting that not everything can be perfect, while trying to see the positive side in the grimmest of situations. So being with people who complain of not being able to get any Wi-Fi, the good thing to remember is that the world existed before Wi-Fi and everyone was just fine then. It's a useful device to communicate with and research destinations on, but also a social killer if everyone is on their phone, as in Puerto Viejo where people were more obsessed about looking at their screen than around them, drives me insane.

Travelling solo has prompted me to consider my pessimism for trusting people. I am isolated and at times need assistance or can't be bothered to do everything for myself. Having better Spanish than me I became reliant on Fiona at times when I was lazy, but there is always a chance events could go wrong and the people I meet for a very short time screw me over. What is it to them that they drop you as quickly as they find you? It is easy for people that you make friendships with to turn on you, just as the Dutch girl I met in Ometepe did after insisting on sharing the cost of the damaged bike and then changing her mind to pay me. When you've just met someone it can be difficult compared to people you have known for a long time.

There are often travellers you meet on a different kind of budget. They can be much more willing to be generous with their cash to help when they know you're on a budget, like Ben and Panda. I met two guys travelling independently, who met having had a very similar journey of working for the man, earning good money and becoming unhappy, so travelling was their escapism to become happier, not dissimilar to myself. Generous and fun to be around, it can be a challenge when the travel companion is willing to pay a lot more for something unnecessary, such as a quicker transfer and in comfort whilst I'd be happy to rough it for the sake of being able to stretch my money further.

It all comes down to, just like the real world, which drove me mad, not allowing yourself to be surrounded by people who don't make you happy. Even if you can't emotionally or physically leave them, you have to try to make the best of it and control your emotions to make it bearable and enjoyable for yourself wherever you are in the world. I felt that time on my own, being quiet or meditating helped me with this. Luck and determination to put yourself in situations where you're more likely to be around like-minded people helps; your opinions of others reflect your own state of mind. Whilst being here, I've formulated a mindset for the kind of people I want and don't want in my life, I don't miss those I don't want, that's for sure. I guess you do learn things about yourself when travelling after all.

Medellin Madness – best served partying hard in a changed city 30.4.16.

Amidst the winding roads through all of the mountains of the west of Colombia sits the city of Medellin in its basin. During the nineties it was the most dangerous city in the world, the home town of one of the world's most infamous criminals and drug lords. The hills spread for miles and miles and there are still untraceable hidden drug farms, here; the drug problems aren't anywhere near as bad as they used to be, but the stigma that Medellin is the cocaine capital of the world still stands. The images of Medellin during the troubled era of the late eighties and nineties are of a war zone but the district of Palermo that I am in is now an expensive, European-styled area. Within five minutes I'm offered cocaine at least twice although the surroundings feel strangely safe and peaceful for such stereotypical behaviour. Each shop vender or person I come across are openly friendly, helpful and welcoming, much more so than other places in Colombia.

Once a war zone, it's now a popular place for students to come and study and then stay to live after their education. Welcoming new faces is part of the city's culture of moving on and the Colombian tradition of forgetting things – literally for better or worse. Drugs are still producing two to three per cent of the country's GNP, and the country has rebuilt and rejuvenated itself because of the consequences of the drug's war. Even buildings for governmental and authoritative use were inherited from the Infamous Criminal which were built after his death in 1993. The stigma is hurtful and embarrassing for the locals and the nation; they can't try to hide their history. The attitude of the locals, Paisas as they're known, is to celebrate the good times, fitting as this is the party city of Colombia, and one of the best nights out on the continent.

Soon after arriving, it seemed quite a good idea to meet with some of my SBA friends along with Ben and Panda. It was a night that didn't disappoint – the lively nightlife scene of consecutive bars and liquor stores selling onto the streets was an energetic and heavy evening of partying.

On first impressions, downtown Medellin doesn't have the atmosphere of fear you would have expected from its reputation. A mixture of European and Latino architecture is silhouetted with friendly street food vendors and bakeries on almost every street. The flow of road into road with the chance to eat on every corner makes the city more absorbing and addictive to see what's coming up next on a variety of Colombian street food snacks.

The culture of trouble in the eighties and nineties actually started in the 1940s after a popular presidential candidate, who was trying to change the country for the better, was assassinated. As left and right-wing politicians clashed over his death, their supporters fought each other as a revolution began – apparently this was the first time that Fidel Castro held a gun as he waded in on the issues as a protester. Revolutionary personnel who formed themselves into armies as part of a war, were mostly from the lower classes, particularly farmers, as well as different left and right illegal paramilitary groups. Most of the battles happened away from the city, out of sight of civilians in the hills which sprawled for miles and miles out of Medellin. I had driven through them on my way here.

A generation being born into this turmoil and discomfort of a war created violence as they grew up in ferocious surroundings. A new income opportunity was then created for their escapism, called cocaine. As violence mirrored the demand for cocaine outside Colombia, the need to protect the product grew so the younger generations of these right and left-wing guerrilla groups would be played off against each other to protect the farms, and also kill anyone who tried to disrupt the cocaine production. Playing each side of these groups off against one another, their anarchy-craved mindsets were taken advantage of as they were set up to compete with one another on who could do a better job for them in protecting their cocaine plantations i.e. who killed more policemen who tried to disrupt their production. Of course, from the money from selling coke, they would be handsomely rewarded for murdering. Making the demographic from which these 'soldiers' would act on, meant it made them rich beyond their wildest dreams.

The global demand for cocaine is the country's biggest problem. As demand grew, the richer the drug barons got and the chance of having a glamorous city lifestyle grew. Barons would bring their crime with them into the city, adding fuel to the fire on what complications drugs caused people as it became so accessible. Cartels began fighting with not just guns, but bombs, which killed thousands of innocent people, all from the demand for the drug.

There is still a shadiness of rough and ready here. A cable-car travelling over the city highlights the poor derelict housing on offer for many on the outskirts of the city. Football matches for the two teams in the city have a never ending enthusiastic energy and ferocious love, the more successful team previously being owned by the Infamous Criminal who gained fanship from both his workers and locals. At the same time the demand for prostitution never being far away, the oldest church of the city is a popular spot for hookers to congregate at and allow 'buyers' to confess their sins after their dirty deeds.

Knowing their history, Medellin residents are the friendliest people who make a conscious effort to change their reputation. I have never been asked to be sat next to by so many people in my life as I was at the football game I went to. The national dish of Colombia is even named after Paisas; after all it is one of the most influential cities in the country. A bandeja paisa is a combination of everything you'd imagine in a football game, a meal in a country whose cuisine and culture have no frills – unhealthy meats with rice served from a pig. So fatty and heavy but delicious, washed down with beer, it's a magnet for locals to come to you, wanting to crack jokes with you all game even through torrential downpour. With strong pride for their football club and city, after the Infamous Criminal's death in '93, they were the first city in Colombia to build a metro in '95 which brings the city together logistically and metaphorically. Squares have now been built as event venues to celebrate and to forget the troubled past.

In 1995, when Medellin appeared to have turned a corner, a huge bomb was activated at one of the event squares killing many children with no activist group taking responsibility. A statue, which was completely destroyed by the bomb, remains in situ next to a bigger identical version which was made to show that their past cannot be ignored. However, now the city's people are stronger and better than they were before.

The Paisas welcome visitors to their city like no other, and they party hard with you like no other! There is no 'gringos only' area; they seem happy to mix with you and educate you about their lives and city. For all of the options for expats moving to Latin America so far, I understand why here appears so popular. The partying and cocaine dominates their reputation, but that's just a scratch to the surface of this great city.

Bogota Bound – best served eating something new at altitude, inspired by creativity 1.5.16.

Leaving via the mountains and hills through the night from Medellin to Bogota, going higher and higher, reaching two thousand three hundred metres above sea level, this is the highest altitude I've been at since Guatemala, and it's cold.

Arriving early to get the most of a full day and meet two friends from SBA, we take a cable car up to the view point over Bogota from Cerro de Monseratte, surpassing three thousand metres. The main attraction up Cerro de Monseratte is a church; the novelty (now in my fifth month of travel) of colonial churches has evaporated. I was more impressed by the line of food stalls and markets of which there is a mixture of authentic colonial weaving and 'gringo tack'. Boasting an enormous view over the city of eight million inhabitants spread across a crater tucked into the mountains, the vendors are selling a food I haven't yet seen on this trip before: pig intestine with chorizo and baby potatoes fried in butter and oil. It sounds awful, but the imagination in the dish is intriguing so I have to give it a go! The altitude had me feeling quite nauseous and the first mouthful made me gag. The awkward chewiness, the fatty, heavy butter, and being reminded that it was a pig organ, this is an ordeal. I swallowed it and go for another piece only to spit it out with a mouthful of bile – the worst thing that I have ever eaten anywhere, ever. I gave the food away to a beggar. To my disappointment, and wishing to explore Bogota more, my first bout of illness comes on. I guess it hasn't been a bad return on the months travelled so far, but exploring the capital would now be more limited. Recommended to ply myself with coca tea as much as possible, usually a plant drink from the highlands, it's apparently the miracle cure for any bad health, including stomach issues of altitude.

Capital cities on this continent hold a preconception of being dirty, dangerous and chaotic and arriving here, the assumption is legitimate. There is a lot of unattractive graffiti tagging on dirty battered walls which had been my first impression on entering a wet and cold Bogota early morning. The government, however, has created several enormous walls and given permission for a number of buildings (some which are three hundred years old) to be listed and painted for street art decorations by local artistic groups.

Still desperate to explore Bogota which has an artistic scene that connects the community together, albeit whilst clenching all stomach movement and nausea from the previous day's experience of pig intestine and altitude. Artists of all ages are involved in riding the wave of the country's progression in the capital which is the fastest developing city in South America, making it an artistic haven as well as a commercial superpower. Artists are commissioned to paint about the history of Colombia, whilst photographers are offered prizes to have their work enlarged in popular areas such as the Bolivar Plaza, the main square of the city. To celebrate the creative imagery of the country's artists, the government also set themselves up for a battering with Colombians taking advantage of having this freedom for creative expression on their route to the escapism they need from the country's troubles. Many nationals feel their home is in one of the most corrupt countries in the world. More aggressive and less subtle street art paintings don't have permission for art as they're on an unlisted wall, an act which historically used to result in punishment by death. These are strongly motivated paintings which are creatively inspiring, intelligent and imposing with a positive effect on both Colombians and visitors; however, this art is what makes the city look ugly.

A population of eight million, the community is tight-knit and not as conflicted as I expected from opinions. The rich to poor gap is obvious but the will to pull together for the better overrides indifference. An enthusiasm for defending the arts culture provides their chance to stand up to the political troubles, welcoming travellers to the city and building infrastructure which will soon include some of the tallest buildings on the continent. Bogota has made impressive progress.

With their approach to global warming, it's illegal to have a car of a certain age due to Bogota's emissions laws, and roads are pedestrianised on Sundays so people can explore economically on public transport or on foot as they play their part in environmental development. Colombians adoration for cycling is obvious as the number of bikes used here perhaps could rival Amsterdam. It's a city which beyond its stigmas and first impressions, can be enjoyed and praised for their work to enhance the lives and interests of both the past and the present.

Zona Cafetera, Salento – best served drinking a hot mug of political coffee 3.5.16.

Colombia is the third largest coffee provider in the world, and coffee is the country's most popular export. My idea is to have a couple of days in the wilderness of a coffee plantation – covered mountains, a welcome change to city living, and to remember that, as 'tranquilo' as travelling can be, it's nice to travel into remote areas, where clocks, rushing to places, and security issues are things that aren't thought about for a second.

Another bumpy road as I travelled from Bogota, I then take a van ride for the tail end of the trip to Salento, distancing myself from city chaos, despite the van giving a bone-shaking ride! With a number of plantations to visit for a 'Colombian coffee experience', it's an hour's walk away from the pretty, cobbled town square of Salento which is decorated with cheap-eats, bars and trinket shops.

I set off walking from Salento for the day, up and over hills, following small handmade routing signs which lead the way to the several plantations which are available to visit. Tired billboards with the most persuasive, broken, written English possible, try to tease walkers into their site for a coffee experience. The Ocaso plantation is a stunning background of rolling, lush, plantations for miles, in deathly silence and a smell of morning dew accompanies the school-like class on the process of coffee making and the history of coffee in the country.

The history includes the coffee crisis in the 1980s and '90s, adding to the dysfunctional time of the Infamous Criminal during that period. However, it wasn't cocaine and drug cartels causing trouble but fungi and insect issues. During that period, coffee plantations were still figuring out the best techniques to get the most out of their plants and now they understand on how to reuse the plants three to four times, helping them to avoid contamination from insects which caused the original problem. Old and used coffee beans, which have been burnt or not grown well enough, are also used for compost in the soil.

Invited to try my hand at coffee picking whilst I walk around the plantation, my own coffee picking basket in hand, the guide is offering a constant education about their own picking techniques in this enormous and global industry.

Colombian coffee is naturally the sweetest in the world; even the berries are sweet from the plants in the fields which I pick, tasting like sugar cane. The difficulty of the plantation's remoteness for transport to keep up with the demand for their uniquely sweet beans is a huge challenge for them. There are only so many trucks that can take so many beans on these tiny roads. Logistics come after the dependence on climate and ability to turn the coffee around through all its stages. From picking to roasting to packaging – it's a long, patient and precise process that's admirable in the face of their challenges.

The demand for exportation is not directly rewarded to the plantations but to the groups of owners who have several plantations, the franchises, and then above them, the government. The Colombian coffee, that's sold by larger foreign corporations who have bought it from the government usually has one coffee bean out of one hundred from here, allowing it to have that name 'Colombian', when it's probably as Colombian as I am. As far away and beautiful as this area is, it still holds the admirable Colombian charm and resilience, but also the politics that at times hold them back too, no matter how far you go – 'you can't take the Colombian out of its coffee' – which for the people of Salento is bitter-sweet.

Salsa Capital, Cali – best served trying to dance with eating Arepas 5.5.16.

Another city with its own drug cartel nightmares, having been bullied and terrified by the Infamous Criminal, Cali is without a doubt the salsa dancing capital of the world, something they boast about more than their cartels.

It doesn't matter who you are, rich, poor, fat or small – everyone loves to salsa. If you're a local here (known as a Calelos) and don't dance, you're a black sheep. If you're a gringo who doesn't salsa, you're not worth their time and are quickly dismissed, even by those who want to be your friend more than anything. Like all Colombians, they want to talk you to death; every conversation starts with, 'you like salsa, like chicas?' There's no waiting to find out anything else!

A short walk of the city with some bad navigation on my part, I quickly find myself in the rougher side of Cali, conveniently marked on the map to reassure me of my location and my mistake as 'dangerous, do not go'. Unattractive, hectic, dirty, it feels fierce. The part of Cali they don't want you to see is easily reachable and a reason many tourists don't visit as it's not a pretty place. If you don't like salsa it really is a legitimate question by locals: 'why are you here then and what's wrong with you?' As put so eloquently by a taxi driver I flagged down to help me get my bearings, helping me out of my situation but still making an honest and comical way of putting it across to sort out my lack of map-reading skills. After a three-hour detour, I asked myself the same question every minute, 'Where the hell am I?'.

There are newly designed boulevards and churches in the city centre intertwined with charismatic, boisterous second-hand counterfeit retailers. They don't look much different from other road sellers anywhere and the novelty is almost wearing off but the hilarious jokes the friendly locals make with you as you walk past makes it entertaining in itself!

My friend, Zoe is one of many expats in Colombia. The advantage of having a resident show you around opens the city up for me and prevents me getting horribly lost again. Zoe introduces me to the salsa nightlife and it's so different from other night spots in the country. For all the fiery antics and charisma that Colombians have, when it comes to working they're professional and focused; they go out dancing every night till two a.m. but won't drink alcohol. I go to attempt some salsa dancing and after a few beers quickly realise that it's wiser not to drink. Salsa, for an uncoordinated man like myself, is hard enough sober, let alone after a couple of trips to the liquor store over the road for a cheaper beer!

The common practice of dancers is to go outside for a drink;

it's also the only place feasible to have a conversation. When inside, the intense, sweaty atmosphere from the salsa music is deafening. Even whilst ordering a drink, the bar staff shake maracas in front of you almost intentionally so they can't hear you and can carry on dancing to the catchy music in the background. After all, they work there to dance too!

My dance lessons in Guatemala at a snail's pace are no match here, despite my best efforts of going at full pelt which results in more crossed feet stumbles than anything. It's more fun to watch the athleticism and aesthetics of the dancing and to hear about how being an expat, moving abroad can open up so many wonderful options for your life. The chance to live in a complicated, but wonderful country, especially for Zoe in a city where her passion to dance can be easily accessed. Leaving the comfort zone of home in England and throwing herself in this new environment has been a life changing experience.

Cali of course has similarities to other cities. Areas of poverty are next to the posh and well-maintained boulevards, and there are areas where both the rich and poor mix in the markets of La Galeria Alameda, where you can eat and drink anything you could think of. The same with downtown, there isn't a class divide as obvious here as it feels so welcoming, even when I don't have a local guide like Zoe with me. The divide of rich and poor is huge but the effort to allow everyone to mix and be as one is unique here compared to anywhere else. Of course, for a country which loves its street food, no food symbolises this social characteristic more than an arepa – a circular corn cake stuffed with cheese, the go-to Colombian dish any time of the day, eaten by everyone. Going for a dance or grabbing an arepa is done by all Colombians. Everyone comes together to celebrate the city and country. Even when they do drink, they have their own special cali-cocktail drink, Jugo Borojo, fruit and wine in a jug to ease back into the groove of the night!

Cali has its own dance and its favourite lyric to the city's anthem is the line: 'Cali is Cali' – a sense of pride in the differentiation to the rest of the country.

The Infamous Criminal – best served with cocaine.

The man who most Colombians don't want to talk about, don't give the time of day for, who some feel caused an incomprehensible amount of trouble and problems in their beautiful country, who Colombians refer to as 'the Infamous Criminal', is the drug lord, Pablo Escobar.

Even years after his death in 1993, the country vividly remembers the havoc created across the country. Crimes included murders, bombs, bribes, kidnapping and corruption which still linger today in the country. Deaths of thousands of innocent people for no reason as he targeted rival cartels and politicians who were against him in his surge to control the exportation of cocaine that his Medellin cartel used to carry out. Along with his own aspirations to be involved in Colombian politics, he went about seizing control so violently that thousands suffered as a result.

Cocaine has global issues that are no secret to the world, yet being the drug's biggest global exporter, Escobar took responsibility for the role he played in creating a drug that caused these issues. Of course, the demand globally wasn't his own, with America being a huge factor from a demand-supply chain. Once cocaine is in America, it's cut with addictive chemicals to keep the drug's demand high, an issue Escobar may have had little to do with, yet he was the one supplying and the problem is still very real around the world today.

The tragedy is closer to home for Colombians as, when the demand escalated, drug addicts in Colombia could no longer afford the cocaine, even at three dollars a gram. Addicts were (and still are) then sold the excess waste and scum off the production of coke which is highly addictive and has the same effects on the body as heroin. This is their modern-day drug issue and the grievances Colombians have with Escobar's legacy of coke. Having met some of these addicts who loiter outside salsa clubs in Cali, they look like they have been in a concentration camp; it's harrowing and obvious to see. Zoe told me stories of their demise and lies to get money to fuel their addiction, tragic stories of drug problems which are all over the world but the reputation of Colombia's drug problem doesn't always go as far as the victims of it closer to home.

Despite the animosity towards American visitors resulting from their country's political interference, on the whole Colombians wholeheartedly welcome tourism, grateful for travellers coming more to visit, especially over the last ten to fifteen years. It's part of their recovery process of moving on from their label that they're so embarrassed about from Escobar's era, feeling guilty that they're still recognised as this dangerous country where 'everyone is a coke addict' when most of them despise the drug. Their attitude to change and being positive is taken seriously with immense pride for their country, pride is fuelled at times by hatred of Escobar for controlling this 'evil' and the awful crimes he committed. These are the reasons why instead of referring to him by his name, he's referred to commonly as 'the Infamous Criminal'.

My intimate experience of understanding the local opinion was getting to know an Escobar, meeting a girl with the same name in a bar in Medellin. In Colombian character, she was friendly, willing to talk openly about her country, more so than in other Latino countries I've visited, sharing some honest opinions.

While with my friends in a bar, this Escobar asked me where they had gone and assumed, that they'd gone to buy cocaine. Cue rage, disappointment, aggression at 'irresponsible tourists', adding fuel to what has ruined their country and the exhausting stereotypes they have from visitors, but also for when Colombians travel and the awkwardness that her surname brings her. Such an outrage of emotion was terrifying. This wasn't a tour, a museum or book, but a local's opinion from a girl in a bar. I hadn't brought the topic of conversation up; it was on an assumption, and even the thought of it made her furious.

The murders of innocent people were a daily occurrence as Colombia became the most dangerous place on earth in the nineties. Upon reflection, this was soon after I was born, and locals I have been meeting are of similar ages and would have grown up in the equivalent of warzone Syria today. Brutal public bombings developed into assassination attempts. A presidential candidate who was a rival of Escobar, went to board a plane from Bogota to Cali, Escobar sent one of his lieutenants aboard with a bomb to blow the plane up and kill the contender, and in doing so killed all passengers on board. By accident, the candidate hadn't even got on the plane in the end – a brutal act of terrorism that's been replicated since, all for the sake of killing a political rival. Nothing would get in the way of Escobar and it didn't matter who was killed. He killed who he wanted.

Achieving these goals to get what he wanted was what Escobar did, so what did he achieve? Control certainly, and ludicrous wealth. Earning sixty million dollars a day, that converts in the modern day by a multiple of six, being in a third-world country, this made him one of the richest men in the world, recognised in Forbes's 'Richest Men Alive' list. Impossible to spend that amount of money, there are hundreds of anecdotes worth reading about what his wealth was spent on. Escobar owned eight hundred houses where cash would be buried for safe keeping, much of which is still being found today in the walls and floors of homes across Colombia. So, if you own a house in Colombia, try your luck and knock down a wall, rip up a floor or dig up the garden to see if there's a loot of cash!

From Medellin, there are accessible trips including to the small town of Guatape, a town with a lake purposely creating remote lake-islands, and a new source of energy for Guatape. Escobar owned one of the eighty hectare islands and built a house which he visited three to four times a year. Guatape has a viewpoint at the top of a volcanic rock overlooking the lake which was used by Escobar's security men as a vantage point for intruders attempting to take on the Infamous Criminal.

Fitting into Escobar's mental behavioural approach, this is no normal house. Pulling into the dock of his island, the scenery is beautiful as you walk up to a lavish building with stone white pillars. This is no house but was Escobar's restaurant and nightclub which is at the entrance of his mansion. Lavish lifestyles hit a new level when you have your own nightclub in your garden! The house actually got bombed by the activist group called Los Pepes after his death. They had the sole aim of aggressive tactics to destabilise Escobar; the bombing was a final 'fuck you' to him.

The building's interior is gutted, dusty, stained with smoke and eroding, but enormous, a mansion like no other: swimming pools, jacuzzis, a BBQ the size of a bungalow, three eating areas (outside!), a tennis court, football pitch, guest houses, stables, farms of imported exotic animals and a helicopter pad. The debauchery and lunacy that would have taken place here are the stuff of Hollywood dreams. I find it hard to even comprehend how much money can be created by one man. The tour of the grounds is a 'who's who' of imported goods glorifying the obscene. Maple trees from Canada on one side, bonsai trees from Japan on another, cork trees from Australia, all brought to a remote lake island in Colombia in the 1980s. Today these importations are almost impossible. The customs official bribes and expense to have pulled it off, along with the ridiculous notion of it all, helps convey his attitude of nothing being allowed to get in his way, it borders on the admirable.

The guide who showed us around Escobar's estate, however, gave a different side to him. Explaining his life as a child and how Escobar improved his family's lives, they lived in one of the houses which Escobar built for many of the poor along with sports facilities. Was Escobar sharing his wealth, or was it a tactic to get them on his side for his political aspirations? When someone living in poverty has their life improved like that, naturally they will defend the man and support the idea that Escobar was wrongfully criminalised and driven to his death.

Away from his island, getting what he wanted went all the way to the government. When Escobar faced jail time for his crimes, authorities gave permission, after heavy influence from Escobar, to build his own jail and serve time there. The jail sounded like a Vegas resort where he continued to run his empire exploiting the government's ignorant belief that he wouldn't while in prison. Once they got wind that it was still business as usual for Escobar, they stormed the prison, only for him to escape via one of the underground tunnels which he had built; the fugitive fled into the mountains.

Escobar went on the run to avoid full imprisonment. After Colombia struggled to find him, American advanced technology intervention came in to help. Months later the search ended in a classic rooftop shooting. The responsibility for his death was unclear with three different parties celebrating 'who killed Escobar', such was the demand and attraction for doing so.

The Americans claim their SWAT team shot him, which upsets Colombians as their police force also claim responsibility. For Colombians, it was impossible to understand the extent of such a manhunt, although it may not have been an American gun which killed him, the American intervention and help in the search was unquestionable. However, the Medellin cartel claim that Escobar was never caught, and that he would have killed himself rather than allowed himself to be caught and extradited. The cartel lost their leader and people mourned his death in their thousands; he never lost his dignity in their eyes. His death was celebrated as a win for Colombia, a landmark for the country to turn a new corner.

Despite the Colombians doing their best to move on, they're well aware of the past and their stigmas. The police museum in Bogota even claim not to have a shrine of their 'biggest catch', yet proudly display Escobar's custom-made silver and gold Harley bike which he rode, and the solid silver revolver which he used. While rebuilding their infrastructure, lives and reputation around the world, the demand for cocaine has reached the point there is now a Netflix show 'Hollywoodising' the nightmare that the country lived through and still suffers from. Cocaine is Colombia's double-edged sword. Despite so many amazing things in Colombia, the Hollywood story that a script writer couldn't write, and the country's cocaine, are what bring a lot of tourists here without any understanding of the damage it's caused. Ignorance around the world referring to Escobar as a legend, hero and man of the people, are uninformed assumptions as to how he built that reputation with the poor people in Colombia. I cringe when the Western world jumps on this bandwagon to fuel the ego of this evil and stain that is on Colombia. Supporting his trade, adding to his empire and ego, and while doing so they leave most of the country to pick up the pieces.

Cheerio Colombia – best served with two sides 5.5.16.

Colombia feels like a dramatic, intense Shakespeare play; beauty, love, drama, history, tragedy and a scenery to match. From cobbled Cartagena, clay in the jungle, to busy cities and tranquil mountains, I recommend Colombia to anyone. The beauty of the place has a twist and the beautiful women sum it up. Wanting to talk you to death, they are a lot of fun, but their beauty is often a result of the saying in Colombia: 'Honey, there is no such thing as an ugly girl, just a girl without money'. Referring to the high amount of plastic surgery that takes place here, a beautiful face has a sad story behind it, just as the rest of the country does.

As expected, an underprivileged lifestyle is common here, as they crawl away from the tragic history and corrupt politics which dominate Colombia's story, increasing the lack of equality with wealth, not just from the Infamous Criminal's antics. One of their most popular and successful presidents known as the 'Iron Fist' (elected in 2002) still turned out to be as corrupt as anyone else. The Iron Fist was so named after his strong take on security and the money he put into making Colombia safe. Making an agreement with G.W. Bush to tackle the cocaine problem by increasing the price of cocaine so it became less affordable, meant unhealthier cocaine was created and consumed. By borrowing American money to spend on armed forces to wipe out the guerrilla armies in Colombia, rewards were offered for the authorities to kill guerrillas, the opposite of what Escobar did when rewarding the murders of police officers. The crooked ways of the law led to innocent peasant farmers and the homeless being taken from their villages, dressed in guerrilla uniforms and killed for cash rewards. The president knew this was going on and played it up in order to show that they were winning the war against the guerrillas from the high death counts his forces were achieving – innocent killings again for the sake of money.

However, the Iron Fist did set up some positive legacies. In 2002, fifty thousand tourists visited the country a year, it's now four million. The enthusiasm to welcome you, and wanting to let the world know the positivity of Colombia is relentless, but they don't need you here. Why accept the help of external nations like the USA who took advantage of them and caused their demand for coke to keep the drug a major issue for the country? Does Colombia really need the rest of the world to help?

Even with growing infrastructure for tourism, Colombia doesn't need tourists to flourish. There are the hydro-ecosystems they have, coffee trade, fruit plantations and an increasing number of well-educated expats improving their teaching system. Infrastructure is already in place from the drug money which is now being used for the authorities' headquarters which makes Colombia the fastest growing economy in South America, with Bogota being the fastest growing city. All before any tourism influx, their economy is booming.

Colombia's desperation to move on is handicapped by the knowledge of corruption within the authorities, which I experienced first-hand myself. The government even hinder their ability to move forward, recently selling off one of their largest hydro-energy plants in a dubious auction where the undervalued and third highest bidder won, a Canadian firm whose owner is coincidently friends with the president. Being controlled externally and reselling the energy back to Colombia at a higher value, it kills the longevity of fair-priced energy. Friends do business all the time, but by the locals' admission, this stinks of corruption. Even the coffee that's exported isn't sold by the plantations but by the government and they of course keep an unfair proportion of the sale. The finger can be pointed at who voted them in, but voting is hard to do here and can take some people thirty-six hours of travel to get to a polling station such is the geography of the country. Adding apathy and mistrust for candidates only seven million out of forty million voted, the size of Bogota, an unfair reflection of who wants whom in power.

Colombians are mocked in South America as having a short memory; they try to move on and celebrate. The celebrations of James Rodriguez's World Cup 2014 goal are documented as one of the biggest parties that Colombia has ever seen. Replica shirts are on sale at every street corner for scoring a famous goal; it wasn't even the winner but the moment is cherished! The Escobar era is put behind them with their pride of Medellin being the first South American city to install a metro transport system. They allow their street art and graffiti to celebrate their cultures and history, while also giving people a voice on their political views – they openly share their emotions.

Colombia is unquestionably on the up, and for all their torment, they deserve it. The once dangerous Pacific coastline has an opportunity to be used for new hydro-energy and exportation routes around the world. The government are holding peace talks with FARC for them to hand over their weapons and with the plan of not punishing them, but integrating them back into society.

The government and police need straightening out though, it's not OK to take bribes or rob tourists which happened while I was chosen for a random search in Medellin. It's not OK to do dodgy deals with your friends which hinder the country. They don't need intervention from the USA. Rebuild the country themselves, and they can be left to do this themselves too. Let them show their strength and be resourceful. They use every part of their stock, recycling all their coffee procedures and using every part of the animal's body for their soups; cows' hooves are used for stocks, and cows' lungs are found in the Galeria Alamede – every part! The creative, weird and wonderful food bags a lot of surprises, from the amazing Cartegena food to the awful pig intestine is how Colombia is. Trying everything, I appreciate the awful with the brilliant, Colombia is just that.

Ecuador

Ecuador – Best served drinking a Batido.

- 4 oreo cookies
- 1 tbsp. of instant coffee granules
- ½ cup of water
- 1 tbsp. of sugar

Throw all ingredients into a blender and fill with ice, blend and drink. Ingredients are to taste, predominantly for the sweet toothed! Drank in the middle of the road surrounded by cracked roads in an earthquake zone.

Quito – best served at 0° latitude eating in a market 6.5.16.

The journey from Cali is the first bus ride which comes close to a night and day journey, hitting nineteen hours door to door. The final and first impressions of Colombia and then Ecuador are of my wallet being emptied of cash. While I was asleep a thief went through my bag that was next to me. I was helped out at the border by a lady on the bus to pay for entry fees, with no cash machine in the area. She was so helpful, only for her phone to then get stolen as she slept on the second leg of the journey. Oblivious and completely unaware, driving through the enormous and impressive Andes on a bus full of people choosing to play dumb, tired and frustrated I was helpless, irritated and annoyed at being robbed but perhaps thankful it was just cash. This isn't a fair reflection on Colombia, but my first impressions of Ecuador are mixed.

The bus crawls into Quito, the city spreads for an eternity and it appears that Quito's an ugly city to drive through, getting to the Old Town where I am staying was an effort in itself. Meeting friends from SBA for a night it'll be nice to have some company after a tiresome and frustrating day, to have a beer and go on a walking tour of the Old Town in the evening. I can't mope around;

I need to get back doing what I usually do, besides, I've just spent a day bored on a bus.

While exhaustedly absorbing an abundance of heavy information about Ecuador's economy, there's a lot to take in. Ecuador carries a huge reliance on their exportation of oil. The practicality of trading with America is beneficial as Ecuador uses the US dollar, after a governmental screw-up resulting in bankruptcy in 1999.

Using the dollar isn't a bad thing for gringos travelling, it's easier to calculate what you're spending. Ecuador's repayment system following their financial crisis is that using the dollar means they pay three per cent interest to America for every dollar spent. A cruel repayment scheme, especially as the use of notes means the USA benefit the most. The Ecuadorians have their own dollar coins, which are only used in Ecuador, so the USA benefits directly and they aren't inflated. The good news for Ecuador though is their two per cent inflation rate is actually the lowest in South America.

Learning all of this with sleepy eyes amidst the hustle and bustle of a capital city is intense, but the Old Town and its beautiful architecture lit up at night are gorgeous. The city, which continues to expand further and further, is a colder, gothic style. Even the banks are grand and as impressive as the cathedrals. Relaxed and hospitable locals make it easy to fall into an evening of beers and cocktails around the Old Town to knock the intense and exhausting day on the head. Raising a glass with friends to exploring a new country.

On the edge of the Old Town is Central Market, the food hub of the area and a great place to aimlessly wonder and start to taste the weird and wonderful styles of Ecuador with two new friends I'd met the night before, Scottish couple, Fergus and Lou. An entrance with parked pick-up trucks with horse hooves leaking blood onto the parking bays, to fruits and soups galore from the almuerzo menus, it's a cheap and cheerful place to soak in the city's atmosphere. Without being harassed by the traders to check out each stall; it's more of a welcoming to sit together and feel comfortable.

Quito was a city I knew would be fun to explore but I didn't quite appreciate that it would be a city to connect the whole country by excursions on such a varied level, close and far away. The convenient and cheap bus system logically charges a dollar an hour which helps to get around. Famous for being the only city in the world where the equator line goes through flat land, sitting at exactly 0° latitude, I went to visit the equatorial line.

After a touristy hour of photos, messing around jumping between the northern and southern hemispheres, the walk around the museum, which the line goes through, suddenly becomes a science experiment. With the correct latitude of the equatorial line only being realigned and discovered correctly when GPS came in, the original thought of the location of the equator was unluckily only a few hundred metres away – not a bad effort with no measurements!

The physical force of the equator line, lined out in thick red, makes it difficult to walk in a straight line. Watching water drain both sides of the line in different directions was a layman's science tutorial! Having a balance of twelve hours night and day, the weather remains steady with no drastic seasonal changes or cyclones.

Ecuador has extremely volatile plate tectonics, recently causing a destructive earthquake in April which has put off a lot of travellers from coming to the country. Something I always think is a bit of a pathetic thing to do, when people find an excuse not to go somewhere because of an event or stigma.

A city of constant education, you mingle amidst the friendly locals in the main market where everyone sits together for cheap tasty food. I think I'll like Ecuador!

The Quilotoa loop – best served thinking about cheese toasties 12.5.16.

Whenever there's a mountain, there's always a hike and with the

Andes it's almost guaranteed to be spectacular. My plan was to use Quito as a base to do hiking from and I wanted to hike up the Quilotoa crater. Once a volcano, there is now a lake inside the crater. There are a variety of routes and paths around the region, starting or finishing up in the town of Quilotoa with a view into the crater.

Still being in a slight routine of laziness with planning, I've started to become scattier after a couple of tours, relying on someone else to do everything as part of a group. Fergus and Lou were coincidently planning the same trek at the same time as me, so we chose to plan together. I now had to do something which was great to have my independence and adventurous energy back. As much as I love the sound of my own thoughts for hours on end hiking on your own can be dull.

Our bus journey starts two hours south of Quito in Catachunga where our old, tired-looking coach slowly bends round impossible angles on hairpin road. Gazing terrified, but entertained by the sheer drops our bus tyres cling to. While at the top of the Andes along roads of loose rock and dust, it's a nervy ride as we haven't seen any other vehicles for miles, probably because it feels impossible that buses survive this route at all. Suddenly we turn a sharp corner onto a perfectly smooth road from no-where; our vehicle continues to struggle and grunt uphill in first gear. I begin to trust the driver and his ability as on the hundredth potential death-drop over the edge we survive once more. I start to enjoy the balance of feeling that we are away from the chaos and bustle of an exhausting city life, yet close enough that we won't be so abandoned in the Andes to risk death. A fine margin that I've decided is in my line when doing independent travel like this. Go off path with someone who knows what they're doing, where you're likely to learn more and appreciate it is great as opposed to not having a clue and not enjoying it at all, although sometimes people who claim they know what they're doing seem like they don't at all!

The bus journey is breath taking, never-ending Andean mountains and I realise I'm in one of the smaller countries of South

America. The Andes start in Colombia and go all the way to the south of the continent. I feel insignificant and miniscule in comparison but invigorated and excited to be here for those reasons. Just like in Central America on the buses, drivers and locals know where to jump off in the most random and deserted of places, walking down the mountain with nothing in sight, but heading to something; it's fun to imagine where they'll end up.

The air is thin at this altitude. Becoming lightheaded it sounds as if our voices can't travel far. The serenity of our height and where we are, is spooky in the cold mist with there being little visibility but also exciting as we plan our route, of which several are available to us. I wanted to climb volcano Cotopaxi before I came to Ecuador but my foot still isn't quite strong enough for a more advanced hike; the chance to hike through the Andes is a great compromise.

The region here is known for cheese making, so setting off excited on a cold, damp morning with cheese at the end of a long walking day is exciting in itself! Hiking with two people who have a similar mindset, food is a topic of conversation which dominates the day. Hearing about the different foods we like, what we crave and what motivates us up each climb is a great way of getting to know each other having only known them both for three days. A Cotopaxi cheese toastie in sight is a nice reminder of home food, a far cry from the norm of rice and beans in the market!

The foreground of the beautiful Andes is rolling green fields of nothingness; it would be a fair distance of walking till we come across bony living creatures or people. Occasional farm animals such as a pig, donkey or cow tied to a farmer's fence would be on our route, usually next to a stand-alone house with no one at home along a stream which is our path to follow through the beautiful Toachi Canyon.

The walk is pleasant and flat, just how I like it, to be able to have a conversation while walking through the stunning canyon. Climbing a volcano, however, means you must go up, and up we go, almost vertically as we climb out of the canyon to new terrain using our hands for support along the path. The change of dynamic had its perks as I was able to look down on where I'd walked and enjoy the view. The privacy of seeing only the Scots and me for miles was so peaceful and relaxing. With no need for introductions it was great to enjoy good company intensely (as hiking with no one but ourselves is) but in a relaxed environment, I was unconvinced the Scots felt the same. Reaching the summit, we looked down the rigid, steep layers of canyon – they could only eff and blind at how hard the climb was. We laughed together about it which is a reality of climbing. A lot of the time it's really hard and exhausting, although it was certainly beautiful.

I rarely need an excuse to eat and having had copious amounts of rice lately from the two-dollar almuerzo set ups in Quito's Central Market, I craved something a bit dirty! The town for the night on our trek of Chugchilan is what the travel guide Lonely Planet would describe as 'remote', translated as, 'about four hundred people live here and there's nothing there but a school for the kids'. Fortunately for us, three ladies were huddled around their food grill, dressed head to toe in beautifully coloured handmade shawls and jumpers with the biggest smile on their faces to serve us chips – perfect!! Named Pito Mixto, the bowl of deep-fried chips with a fried egg on top was wolfed down, to be then offered a portion of chicken on top. The chicken was the giblet from the bird, fried and spooned on top of the chips with all the oil and juices, so dirty, and so good after a long hike in the cold talking about food all day!

Hard to get a lot of meat off the bone it was underwhelming, but for the novelty and that for fifty cents a warm meal wasn't too bad! Lou hadn't gone for food with us, later joining us with a smirk on her face as she saw us chewing the bone was concerning. What happened? Amidst our excitement to devour our meal, we hadn't noticed that we were actually chewing a fried chicken neck, head still on and fried to a crisp beyond recognition. Fergus had already sucked the head dry as we had ravenously devoured our meal. Tasting some of the head and guts, it was disgusting with a hint of chicken stock – for the effort it was to eat it wasn't as good as egg and chips! My meal could have been one of the three chickens I'd seen while walking earlier; the happy farm animals wouldn't be so happy now.

Without being repetitive, our next day is much of the same. The canyons which we walk through, however, aren't hundreds of metres wide any more or lush fields of beauty, they're half a metre wide. Our only way of passing through is to scale the narrow wall of clay-mud, legs stretched like a spider across the width as it is too tight to walk through. When larger streams appear, the river crossings are no longer hopping stones but logs are used as makeshift bridges. Balancing isn't a forte of mine, so I'm walking a tightrope with a real possibility of falling to my death. After yesterday my legs are feeling OK, but tight, like I haven't done any exercise in a while. The canyon keeps going up, it's staggered formation through beautiful, lush green hillsides give a beautiful view from the top. The intense climbing is due to the altitude, but even walking through quite similar green landscape in the mountains has a nice variety. Cornfields, pine trees, fields, are everywhere as we pass through, with enormous Aloe Vera plants and eucalyptus trees, scattered as natural route markers to guide us to the start of the ascent for the Quilotoa crater.

The accumulative population of villages and towns we pass through mustn't be any more than three thousand people. Local school children (randomly dressed in all grey matching track-suits like a prison) continue to charge up to me, to then realise how shy of western travellers they are, to then run away! The locals seem shy and distant. When they want to be hospitable and friendly they certainly will be; once that barrier is down the conversations can be great. Friends have said similar things about the English to me which is perhaps why I feel a sense of warmth and familiarity towards them.

Hiking so far has not been brutally hard, but with the altitude I'm maybe thinking this could become much harder than anticipated as our final climbing point is very much up to the crater rim and Quilotoa. Should this climb now start to be hard it's not the end of the world. When envisioning something beforehand, it very rarely is how you imagine it to then be.

The final day is more eerie than usual as the clouds so far have covered everything in sight. Up to today I've woken up and gone to bed in the midst of the cloud, although, as we scale up to the crater of Quilotoa, mist is still here and it comes and goes, yet the cloud is now below us as we've reached such a height. With nothing but clear sky in sight, we are above the clouds, reaching one of Ecuador's highest and most scenic points, and an adrenalin rush kicks in.

The walk carries on; the repetitive one foot in front of the other carries on. My mind skips the monotony and starts to get excited that the end is in sight. As we walk zig-zag up the side of the crater to the summit, I forget altitude and I start to walk quicker. Wanting the ascent to be over, my legs are tight in the cold, my ears keep popping but this is so great and I'm feeling like I'm about to look over the world from the Andes. Yes, I know it's a small part of the Andes and my body is now falling apart, but I'm excited – knowing the size of what I'm looking at feels enormous but actually covers a continent, and I've not come close to the surface!

The three of us have now spread out quite a bit at our own comfortable pace. I was enjoying my own thoughts and taking photos, racing ahead, ignoring my own advice to pace myself, made the last ten minutes of the ascent incredibly hard. Mind over matter as I kept my legs moving as I struggled to breathe, I should listen to myself more often. The Scots gradually catch up as we roll to the top of the summit of Quilotoa together, peeking over the crater rim and looking down at the crystal blue lake at the top of this mountain.

The circumference of the crater doesn't do the climb justice as only specks of people can be seen on the other side; the crater takes five hours to walk around. Soaking in the gorgeous view as well as the satisfaction of our hike, the truth of standing still at the top of the mountain is that it's freezing, my legs are sore and of course it's started to rain. Tired, the hike isn't finished as on the other side of the crater is the town of Quilotoa and one last, cold, wet slog is required for an hour and a half on foot. The rim undulates a lot through mud to sand and at this altitude, which is now three thousand, nine hundred metres, it's hard and I want to be somewhere warm. I've run out of water, I'm tired and cold am getting hungry.

I walk as fast as I can as the photos of the same crater from different angles don't really do it justice. This amazing volcanic lake is now a beneficial attraction from the evolution of an earthquake. As opposed to how earthquakes in Ecuador have recently caused problems for them, a hard bit of walking is a blessing by comparison.

Galapagos Dreaming – best served with pelicans 14.5.16.

As far as extravagant destinations go, the Galapagos are something I'd love to do if the chance presented itself, but it probably never would – a long way from home, and even further when trying to afford it. David Attenborough's glamorous TV documentaries, create a feeling that his work is unreachable, that only a select few have been chosen to go there. A visit to the Galapagos I thought would surely be on another trip, but I had a contingency fund for an emergency. Being paranoid I thought it would be used for a family funeral, or a friend stupidly getting married that I'd have to go back for. The chance to go to the Galapagos was an emergency; it would be a travesty if I didn't make my best attempt to get there on my tight budget. The chances are, I'll never be so close again.

I spend my travelling weekly budget straight away on flights there and back from Quito. Daunted by the expenditure, but so excited on the plane from the mainland in Quito as I extend my time with Fergus and Lou and go to the Galapagos. Flying over nothing but blue waters, islands begin appearing in the distance. Travelling is a holiday, but this is another holiday of a lifetime within that, a honeymoon but on a whim. The wildlife that I've seen so far has been amazing. Reading on the flight over I sense it's going to get better as forty per cent of the wildlife on the islands are nowhere else in the world. I am guaranteed to see something I haven't before.

I land at Baltra airport; the tropic heat hits me as I step off the plane onto a barren cacti field which is the runway, with strange-looking shrubs either side of the tarmac. Walking through customs, the welcome of how expensive the islands are, I'm met by a one-hundred-dollar entrance fee. Wincing, I feel that it's the first of many big expenses. Our bus driver from the airport drives slowly, manoeuvring around an enormous yellow and multicoloured iguana that's sunbathing in the middle of the road. Steering around the creature I get a closer look at the iguana, his chin proudly up, looking at the bus passengers' stares, he's giving us a warm greeting.

A short boat ride to the main hub of Santa Cruz island, Puerto Ayora, which I plan to use as a base, is a ten-minute show of pelicans and herons fighting for fish as they dive into water for food. Imagery I've seen on wildlife documentaries is unravelling either side of our boat journey. Stunned and in awe, being able to share the excitement with Fergus and Lou makes me feel that it's OK to get carried away by how a typically routine journey from an airport to a hostel can be so amazing.

The dream to keep us motivated when hiking the Quilotoa Loop, was the idea that we'd be able to talk our way to a discounted cruise here. Tour agencies lining the streets here have last minute departure deals but even with their discounts they're far beyond our budget. The dream quickly came and went as we began lining up tours and day trips to the various islands that make up the Galapagos, to see as many different species of wildlife as possible (each island has its own special wildlife), without breaking the bank. On top of that, the great thing about the Galapagos is that even though it's expensive, there's a lot to do that is free, and avoid spending money which is easily done here, the obvious one being to spot wild animals!

After two separate trips to a cash point in an hour, a week of excursions is paid for at four hundred and sixty dollars. I am broke but excited and I'm relieved to have a plan, knowing our expensive trip here wouldn't be spent twiddling our thumbs and thinking about what could have been.

We drop our bags and I decide to make the most of being here, wandering into the town with Fergus, excited to see everything I can! We strolled down to the water front to see fishing boats, water taxis and cruise liners in the water, and at our back, tacky restaurants and souvenir shops which sell all the same stuff with slight differentiation – as if all variations of the gringo trail so far, have bumped up a gear but in a peaceful environment. The promenade has a small fish market, made up of two tired-looking work benches piled with fish. The local fishermen catch, gut, slice and sell the fish up to lengths of 1.5m to order, the size of a child. As crowds of people watch the artistry of these beast-sized fish being handled, herds of pelicans join the party. The pelicans wiggle their feathers with excitement as the fishermen toss scraps of fish to them, acknowledging the locals with a long nod of their beaks as they fly and perch themselves on the work bench for a better chance of being fed ahead of the competition, and that includes paying customers! Having never been this close to wild birds before and intensely observing their mannerisms and beauty, I'm close enough to make eye contact. They aren't phased by humans in the slightest; these pelicans are behaving like they're going about their weekly groceries and we're the weirdos who don't know how to do it.

Absorbed by the pelicans, I'm startled as, lying next to my bare foot, is a dark, dinosaur-looking, vicious-clawed marine iguana. With mean-looking eyes and its battered peeling skin, it looks fearsome, despite its smaller size. Sat just like the land iguana on the bus ride over, bulging its chest, it's unphased by me like a host proudly welcoming me.

I am loving taking photos of the animals. Iguanas are great to snap as they move slowly and generally stay still long enough to get a snap but move enough to be attention-grabbing. Whilst taking photos of my iguana friend, a smack on the floor behind me grabs my attention. An enormous sea lion is slapping the floor. Eyeing me he barks and tilts his head; he bats his eye lids for a photograph, a true poser.

These animals are all within touching distance, posing for selfies and entertaining the tourists while they get their dinner. It is like a hallucinogenic drug as animals keep popping up all around me, as crabs then climb vertically up the pier dock. Sea lions then queue in orderly fashion for food between people. I feel like a kid in a sweet shop; I don't know where to look; all I can do is laugh and smile, instantly wanting to see and explore more. Suddenly I don't care about the money any more.

Conservation and Evolution – best served with Charles Darwin 16.5.16.

The Galapagos are an enormous cluster of ocean-volcanos that make up the islands which Ecuadorians boast are their country's crown jewel. Puerto Ayora on Santa Cruz is the HQ for the Galapagos National Park. Santa Cruz is clean, tidy and without 'over the top' touristy tack in the shape of the Tiesto effect or McDonald's.

Darwin, the scientist and genius behind the theory of evolution, was only twenty-two when in 1831 he joined a voyage to the Galapagos where he collected information for five years. Known as a great traveller, this was the main voyage that he did while the rest of his life was spent doing experiments and writing from home. A reason why locals love him so much, they feel like he's theirs. Appointed with the title on the voyage as an 'Environmental Gentleman and Companion', for a twenty-two-year-old who was about to change science, that's a pretty cool title!

Darwin, is a demi-god here; roads are named after him as is the conservation centre. A centre built in his honour to conserve and protect the animals here, helping them with health issues or abandonment, allows the animals to build their own lives naturally in the area of Santa Cruz.

The centre creates the benchmark across the world for conservation, while being very honest in explaining the problems that the animals face on the island. With the demand and need for items to be imported to these islands when things can't be created here, rodents and feral animals get on the boats accidently and are then unnaturally introduced to the wildlife on the islands. At customs, bags are searched thoroughly, not for weapons but for possible intrusions of ants, flies or the like that could infest birds' nests. The centre now nurtures intruders for research to study how they can merge into the surroundings in the most positive way, allowing them to become part of the islands' evolution as opposed to exterminating them.

The iconic animal of the Galapagos is the giant tortoise and the Darwin Centre has a large enclosure where you can see them up close. Even knowing that I would see them it was still a surprise and shock to see them first hand, another creature that always felt so exclusive to those working in TV, never for the ordinary. Enormous and genuinely prehistoric, they look old too with their sad, wrinkly faces and slow movement – correlations to old people make sense! Since Darwin emphasised evolution so much, it was timely to see two tortoises have very slow and grunty sex. Darwin would be proud that visitors got a first-hand viewing of the creation process, especially as at the time Darwin arrived they were being eaten by pirates and close to becoming extinct.

Ever filled with knowledge and enthusiasm for learning about the Galapagos, there's still room for doing nothing but relaxing as we walk to Tortuga Bay, one of the most beautiful long, wide and white sandy beaches I've seen anywhere and the best part of all, no shops, cafes or any buildings at all. Just a beach left for the animals and iguanas to live on in their natural habitat, they leave them to evolve on their own accord. Not only do the islands have remarkable animals but now amazing beaches, as well as volcanic rock pools to visit, this place is one of a kind.

Island Hopping – best served broke and living off rice, but being worth every penny 19.5.16.

Our first day away from Santa Cruz is on the island Santa Fe for snorkelling in what is a swim in a tropical fish tank. The boat drops us in front of a cliff face with the water full of tropical fish, it can't be real; it feels like they've been planted there on purpose for tourists. Swimming with shoals of fish the size of my head, they carry on around me.

Under the water it's so tranquil and therapeutic. So silent, just the noise of bubbles from the fish motioning past, having time to yourself to enjoy the nature. Sunbathing sea lions watch us snorkel, they join us for a swim and play around us underwater, circling us, diving around us and under or in-between our legs, like Labrador puppies! Up close and watching their mannerisms feels creepy, as if watching a human when they yawn, stretch, roll over in their sleep, just as we do, but in a slapstick manner. A marine iguana swimming past in-between our view snaps us to the real world. Although this is the real world, I'm perplexed to be in one where a form of dinosaur, that looks so fierce, can just swim past so casually, completely unphased by my human presence. This isn't an information overload but a visual, incredible intake of existence

When it's not wildlife blowing my mind, the landscape is equally impressive. With hundreds of different plant species, the terrain alters at each height; there's no metre with the same shrub or plant; even the grass alters every moment under foot. Looking up, the trees and cacti change as an ever-evolving science project laboratory is around me. The volcanic islands create an urge to visit the largest island itself – Isabella. The boat ride again puts the magnitude of the islands and water into perspective, as we see two enormous whales within one hundred metres of our boat. They could easily flip the boat as every new experience here is of the grandest measure.

Arriving at the next island: Isabella, however, was a shock. Compared to Santa Cruz, it's a dive. The island's volcano, Cierro Negro, erupts every few years, it's impossible to maintain developed infrastructure as it keeps getting destroyed. So they leave it how it is, basic and dirty, the bonus being that the volcano itself is an attraction. In comparison with other volcanoes I'd visited, this wasn't as good, even if the rolling clouds through the crater were impressive. It was an expensive short walk, the fortune of being fortunate.

The lava tunnels and bridges that have formed from the eruptions have created perfect habitats for wildlife and marine life. Weaving in and out of lava boulders and arches amongst sharks, turtles and even a seahorse, crushes the myth I'd created in my head that seahorses didn't exist! Turtles eating and swimming casually around me are enormous. Even as a grown adult, it was impossible to get out of their way and swim in the salty water. They move around you and feel comfortable staying around; they don't swim off scared. I thought that the novelty of snorkelling would wear off but I'm convinced it won't if it carries on with the chance of similar encounters. When on the land, the iconic blue-footed booby of the Galapagos waddled and posed in a recreation of Basil Faulty. I don't have enough superlatives for this place.

While the sun is setting, it's a short walk back along a lake where flamingos elegantly stretch their legs as they wind their day down, sucking water up like a vacuum as they feed off the algae. I know already that I want to come back here; the GBH would love it here as would anyone. I usually feel guilty when something is so good while she's at home in the cold, broke and saving, but this is too good to feel bad.

For all the weird and wonderful animals, the visitors here are even more obscure, from the wealthy, ungrateful, spoilt tourists and families who stand out, the 'this place I've been to is better than the Galapagos' tourist. There are some idiots in the world but I'm now more able to zone out negativity. To a lot of people it's someone's first, and something astonishing. For my firsts here I'm happier than I have been in a long time even though it's blown my budget out of the water. It's unquestionably the most expensive place I've ever been, even after eating nothing but the traditional cheap-eat menu meal – menu del dia for six dollars each day – rice and soup after rice and soup – this is an amazing place. Eating rice every day is fine if you're sat next to a sea lion in a bar.

Goodbyes to the Galapagos – best served looking ahead to sustainability 19.5.16.

New friendships formed and almost by accident over two weeks with Fergus and Lou, it was now the last day before we went our separate ways. Another impulsive bond made in the most spectacular of places is cemented while snorkelling on the last day around the island of San Cristobal before we return to Santa Cruz for our flight.

As ever, we're spoilt as we swim with turtles in shallow waters, and even a water snake which made me shit myself. Not knowing that snakes swam here, to see it inches from my foot as it chased a fish, a hunting experience in front of me – underwater – another surreal moment.

A landmark of the Galapagos is the snorkelling spot, 'kicker rock'. Our excellent guide explains so much about the islands and what we are seeing. Setting out to see hammer sharks the area was intimidating being so far from the coast and waves crashed against the rocks that surrounded us. Unlike other ventures there was no sandy ocean floor under foot for reassurance, just the dark ocean abyss below us. The snorkelling became unglamorous hard work as the cold waves took its toll; other tourists from our boat needed to return on board. Close to freezing myself I am determined to get every penny worth from the last tour of the most expensive week of my life. Silently screaming through my mask with cold, we are well rewarded as sharks appeared! So calm around us, it was only to resurface for air and go back under water again for a platoon formation of stingrays to also appear from the dark of the sea floor. In a blink they appeared and stayed nearby for an hour. The bewilderment helps thaw me out and I contemplate on what an amazing time it's been here and to enjoy it with friends. I didn't want to go and was sad to leave; the phrase 'once in a lifetime' isn't only for how expensive and far away it is, but because you really do remember it forever.

The price is a deterrent for many and doing it on a budget is hard work. Rice every day is boring, the unspectacular truth of budget travel. The islands have their own challenge, being geographically distanced from the mainland, the logical way of travelling is instantly expensive – flying or a cruise ship. So detached from the medical and educational support they require, doctors and teachers leave the Galapagos for more money, while those with money on their boats and yachts, who generate fifty per cent of the islands' income, rarely stay for long enough to make a sustainable impact.

As people come to the islands, there's a balancing act of growth and maintaining sustainability. The islands can't get any bigger to balance out visitor number growth which threatens to destroy the islands, but growth for business and economic survival will never change. To limit the need for importation which results in feral animals arriving, organic farming is increasing locally and locals and tourists are encouraged to eat and shop for organic produce. They must balance the commitment of paying more for the 'value' of food with the islands' long-term sustainability in mind despite the cost being higher.

Wind turbines and solar panels have been hugely invested in as the Islands are an ideal place for them and they plan to be fossil fuel free by 2017 (spoiler alert – it wasn't). They are four times the price of the mainland for energy. The cost is high for the life, I guess, and not just for tourists, but it's nice to see a positive local input into it, as opposed to a wallowing self-pity that's often the response to isolation. The right attitude echoes around this amazing place, it really is unique.

Canoa, Ecuador Earthquake Response – best served with a Batidos rebuilding 28.5.16.

While I was in Colombia, Ecuador was hit by an earthquake that measured 7.8 on the Richter scale. I have visited areas that have recovered from natural disasters, but never passed through a country so soon after the event. Neither have I had the chance to help in a way that doesn't feel disconnected the way sending money does via the Red Cross or the like. Being here I feel involved with a chance to make a positive impact in the flesh to those who have had their lives ruined.

I didn't want to head out to the coast, where most of the damage was to be a nuisance. I signed up on waiting lists to volunteer with a number of crisis-support organisations, to be accepted and given a period of dates to go to the damaged surf-town Canoa with the 'All Hands' volunteer group. I was pleased to be able to help, to almost re-establish that not all 'tourists' or 'gringos' are happy to turn a blind eye to the difficulties countries face away from the glamorous attractions. Out of sight, out of mind, can be blissful but when it's on the tourist trail, more often than not, out of sight is from convenience.

I knew this would be an experience that would be difficult to envisage and therefore really prepare for. There was a recommended list of donations to bring, not tangibles like bedding which first come to mind, but stuff that can help rebuild the town – ropes, electric tools, building equipment. I was told I would be sleeping next to the refugee camp with other volunteers, people whose houses had been destroyed in the earthquake. This meant I needed a tent which required two days of vigilant shopping in Quito and a trip to the markets of Otavalo where they sell 'everything'. It's quite an experience albeit incomplete, as they sell 'everything' apart from tents. After much fuss and effort, I was able to find a tent and felt relieved. Relieved – what a bitch I am, people are too scared to go home or can't as their homes are ruined so sleep in tents and I'm relieved to find and buy a tent. There goes my first-world problem's alarm.

Arriving in the dark at five a.m. from Quito, I was still half asleep as I navigated my way through an army secured refugee camp. Surprisingly organised and laid out like a newly laid village. The reality is that this large rocky field is in fact now home to Canoa's inhabitants, and that these three by three metre tents are their homes for the foreseeable future. I was prewarned that the demand for tents is high with people being unable to, or wanting to, live indoors in case the buildings collapse in another tremor. I don't feel tired, just exhausted with nausea, and the silence of the camp hit me, like they're in mourning.

To live in a country where earthquakes are a minor occurrence of little damage, it's hard to understand what is in front of me in Canoa. Scenarios like this can be traumatic, but I can't help but think that the first-world traveller needs to be helping less developed countries. When the reasons to avoid an entire country become to do with someone's short-term gratification, I think it's cowardly and pathetic. My journey through Ecuador has been amazing and it's a place needing the economic support of visitors more than ever right now. Locals are even more friendly and welcoming, making the experience unique in itself.

Twenty-three thousand, five hundred people lost their homes to the disaster. My first day, after not having worked in months, felt like the first day at a new job. Learning names and where things were, more so than in a hostel, I set out to find saws and rope to build housing. Temporary shelter to rehouse the victims means housing for around the next two years in a house that's three by four metres and made of bamboo and held together with string made by volunteers. The walls are second-hand billboard vinyl posters. The battered and used vinyl is waterproof but acts as a greenhouse in the humidity. With little ventilation, the heat just builds up as the families squeeze into these tents. With mattresses, portable stoves, clothes, lives in a tent are held together with string. It's tough to see, but it's more important than ever to be the face to help these people and try to make them feel better, than to drown out any emotions on show. Making the guilt and tragedy of the situation even more tragic, as putting on a brave face isn't always an honest expression.

Carrying tortuously heavy bamboo canes to be sawed, measured and sawed over and over again in humidity is tough. When disasters happen, people flood to the areas to volunteer at times which can cause more problems – too many chefs in the kitchen, so to speak. Money is donated to help, but little is put towards the equipment for volunteers to use; sawing one bamboo cane to its various measurements with a handsaw can take up to twenty minutes, to split it with a machete sometimes up to an hour. With an electric saw, the process takes around ninety seconds. Time restraints on top of the logistical work for disaster relief are enormous; from organising volunteers, where people go, how, equipment, on top of an emotional and physical toll.

The crisis has prompted a positive impact from the Ecuadorian government who have invested wisely and intelligently to the cause. With most people in tents and rubble from destruction everywhere in sight, the clean-up effort at only three weeks in is impressive and things aren't as bad as I thought they'd be. Canoa is a tourist destination that has been badly damaged. With its importance for tourism, for any country, let alone Ecuador, the strategy to rebuild the touristic areas first made sense in showing the world that they can recover quickly.

Investment and effort are dear, but the presence of the army is reassuring for an anxious community. Direct from government orders, the major of the army comes over to us volunteers, deploying twenty-five troops to help assemble more temporary housing and gazebo-style tents sent from China Aid; investment aid has stretched to a global scale. Sharing anecdotes of their time in the forces and travel advice on the continent all day while we constructed the housing together, lightens the mood given the reason for our work in hand. The army, along with the locals, seem emotionally and eternally grateful as every member of the forces goes out of their way to shake our hands and thank us at the end of each hot, laborious day working outside with no shade.

This is the first time I've done 'work' since my old job over five months ago and I am reminded that working hard can pay off but there are always things that go wrong. Power shortages for electrical equipment or tools not working makes the labour hard. Bamboo shrinks in the heat as soon as it's cut, making the frames unstable. In this case it's not some office job going wrong which has little importance, but people's homes; it's significant.

While the focus is predominantly on tourist areas, the small 'remote and nowhere' villages haven't been ignored either with teams being sent out to drive almost aimlessly down dead roads to find destroyed houses. One day we ventured to do a 'demolition' job, demolishing a house that was unsafe for those living in it to remain, so their new home could be built. Using a sledgehammer all day and being destructive for a beneficial purpose is inappropriately quite fun. Arriving at the site, my ignorance embarrasses me when I ask where the house is. Standing in a small field surrounded by jungle, my supervisor laughs and points. From what I thought was a scrap pile in front of us, an elderly man crawls out from underneath a tin roof leant against the once-built foundation beams. Debris of photographs, possessions and wardrobes are scattered around the slanted building that has been his home for the last three weeks. So isolated and with no help he has been there since the tremors three weeks ago, obviously devastated by his situation which he seems to think is his fault. Emotionally it's heart-breaking to see and within an hour, six volunteers have ripped apart his home and made an orderly scrap heap for a bonfire while he stares aimlessly at where his house once stood in a dusty dry dirt patch.

In pragmatic fashion, our work is done, and when asking what more can be done for a man clearly fragile and now with nothing he responds, 'You have helped me clear up my mess; what more could you do – thank you.' Tragic, it's awkward to take personal satisfaction in my work from only being able to make this guy feel a bit better with his current life being a mess. His gratitude is a motivation when carrying heavy bamboo for the rest of the day; this man will soon have a new home again. Perhaps this is a new lease of working life that motivates me which I'd never really had doing a crap job in the past. It's certainly something I can take as perspective of the struggles people have compared with cushy first-world living as these tragic situations happen all over the world every day.

Canoa itself is a small seaside town which reminded me of Taganga and El Tunco with its simple layout and laid-back attitude inspired by the Pacific Ocean beaches. Again, I was becoming that traveller who compared, place to place, the gringo chat everyone hates to hear, both in hostels and back home. The beach has a dozen or so huts with three or four stools at each one where you can buy a drink or a plate of ceviche. There are two nightclubs where locals and tourists used to go to in the evening. It's the perfect beach town that's small enough to walk across, simple and not spoilt by too many options or chains. Everything is run by locals and offers the opportunity to mix with the locals too. The plummeting tourism and fear of another earthquake means every bar, restaurant and hotel is closed due to damage or not being able to justify being open in what is an indefinite 'quiet season' from now on. During the week though, in tandem with the full circle of a house being demolished, rebuilt, and a family moving in, another restaurant opens up on the beach. I can smile and feel good to see a place physically appear and economically slowly start to rebuild.

One local man and his food truck sells batidos drinks to passers-by out the back of it. It was closed for three days in the aftermath of the earthquake but has since remained open as his personal stance against Mother Nature and the fear of another quake. Batidos are an Ecuadorian drink typically of tropical fruit and ice, but with their sweet tooth, often with a sugary cookie or the like as a treat. Business was of course slow after the quake, but with so many places shut, his van became a popular haunt for volunteers after a day of hard graft. Sharing his appreciation for our business and the help from volunteers all over the world, he was overly generous with portion sizes as his way of paying us back for helping rebuild his home. Before the volunteers arrived, his only method of getting business was by setting up his plastic picnic table and chairs in the middle of the road; that way passers-by would notice him by stopping to move his furniture out of the road and end up buying a drink from him – determined and whimsical in his methods to get back on his feet, it worked for him!

I was sad not to be able to stay longer and do more work but, understanding the needs and the responses required, I hope others will help too, so that this awesome town, with the locals' magnetism and determination can become a destination to visit again in Ecuador very soon.

Ecuador Essentials – best served as a rare experience 29.5.16.

Similar to a lot of Latin America, the history of Ecuador has been turbulent both recently with earthquake devastation and the dodgy politics. After the currency change which was taken so bitterly at the time, with world economics wobbling regularly, travellers can now freely spend the dollar, which is convenient for any traveller. Ecuador now has the lowest rate of inflation across the continent, so today they're in a good position.

The president in power now symbolises good, evidenced recently by the speed of response to the earthquake, but also protecting the country's leading asset – oil. He signed the agreement to not interfere with untouched oil land in the Amazon, a leading destination of Ecuador but also of immense cultural value to the indigenous tribes, somewhere I wasn't able to even get close to. While oil is their number one export, the protection of the Amazon is protection for cacao fruit which is used for chocolate and cocoa butter (both for food but also for therapeutic purposes). The importance of safeguarding their biggest food export in order to support their oil-reliant economy is huge, offering an insight into how the food culture creeps into how Ecuadorians are.

The everyday menu del dia is the low cost and filling way to get two courses, it's quick, practical, and always in a friendly market environment of people being together and being grateful for their company and what they have. The novelty of eating it every day wears thin. While enjoying the variety of the dishes which are prepared to each chef's liking, it also sums up most of what I ate here, whether penny-pinching in the Galapagos, or eating in the refugee camps in Canoa, it didn't matter. The novelty of rice everyday topped with chilli to make it tastier, wears off quickly. The love of stews reminds me of the British tradition of having everyone together, all eating from the same cauldron of stew for warmth, the warmth I desperately needed hiking up altitude, dreaming of my own home comforts of a cheese toastie and Pito Mixto – even if a chicken neck with head still attached was a revelation!

At first I found it hard to get to know Ecuadorians despite their polite enthusiasm (which is mostly haggling passers-by with their best menu del dia offers) and in the abyss of the Andes. It's so remote it's hard to gain understanding of their local lives other than their emphasis on agriculture as you hike through the beautiful farmland. They are kind and hospitable, derived from their love of a sweet tooth with all ice creams and sweets being available on almost every street corner. Even when they have nothing sweet to eat in Canoa other than batidos, in comparison to the rest of the sugar-crazed country, locals would always offer their fresh juices as a refreshment in the heat when they didn't have access to commercial goods, making us feel welcome and showing their thanks.

I leave, regretful, because I couldn't stay longer, but pleased to know it's a country that has so much more good than bad about it.

Peru

Peru – best served eating Churros.

- 1.5 tbsp. sugar
- 1.5 tsp. cinnamon
- splash of water and salt
- 2 tbsp. of oil
- 2 tbsp. of flour

In a small saucepan over medium heat, combine water, 1.5 tbsp sugar, salt and 2 tablespoons vegetable oil. Bring to the boil and remove from heat. Stir in flour until mixture forms a ball. Heat oil for frying in deep-fryer or deep-frying pan to 190 C. Pipe strips of dough into hot oil using a pastry bag. Fry until golden; drain on kitchen paper. Combine 100g sugar and cinnamon. Roll warm churros in cinnamon and sugar mixture. Best eaten with the GBH in Cuzco.

Travelling to Peru – best served hungry travelling south 31.5.16.

Finishing volunteering in Canoa, I went from town to town to cross the border into Peru via buses, hitch-hiking and walking. By now I think I have the hang of that, but having never been to each new place, I still had no idea on where I was ever going. I just carried on, hot, hungry and lost but certain that I was gradually getting to Peru, if I could find the right transportation. Driving from the northern border of Peru south, carrying on and on, the Peruvian desert goes on and on, forever. Dry, barren, scorching land, I gazed in confusion as to how this journey was unravelling, not that I had a preconception of the Peruvian landscape.

Sat next to a Peruvian on the bus who now lived in Ecuador, speaking in Spanish, he shared stories of the hardships growing up in the Third World, with little but his affection for his family, home country and newly adopted one. Kindly offering to buy me lunch for my efforts in Canoa which I passed up, I took up his offer of Peruvian destinations, of which his first, and the one closest to our route, was Huachaco. I was able to jump off at the next stop. Having been in transit for over twenty-four hours, Huachaco was a welcome surprise.

Another surf spot, the beach stretched for miles, albeit not an aesthetic town. This was a good spot for a night in a bed and not on a bus. I've lost track of days and haven't walked further than the bus aisle in a while, although I'm not sure how long – it's one of those journeys. Finding my hostel and turning my phone on, I get a message from Fergus and Lou who coincidently were in the same town. While I was in Canoa the Scots took a different route, but a quick reunion with friends when far away from home, even after a week, feels like an anniversary with old friends. The cliché of a travel companion!

Easily falling into the pattern of drinking by the beach, I hadn't drunk much lately as I was saving cash for the GBH's imminent arrival, but also starting to think how far my budget will go on this trip. Along with waking up early for volunteering, hiking or seeing things in the Galapagos, having beers again felt like another bonus on top of seeing them, a materialistic pleasure in a basic but rewarding time living out of a bag. Unpacking and repacking the bag to move on again the next day wasn't an option; I couldn't be bothered – I am too tired and just don't care. I looked at the bag and ignored its existence. I was happy to talk about how we'd get to Huaraz together over some beers; this would be a lay-over and catch-up to make my way slowly to the GBH, who was shortly to arrive in Peru.

Huaraz – best served hiking 2.6.16.

I had the image of Peru as a small, cute, little country, almost patronisingly small in my mind, when really it's enormous!

Huaraz is a base city for hikes nearby, from week long ice pick challenges, to half day strolls. Content with the hikes I have done so far and keen for a shorter hike, we chose the highly recommended Laguna 69 – a hike through the Andes ending at a lake, fittingly named because it's the sixty-ninth lake out of two hundred in the National Park. After all the stupid and difficult names to pronounce that have no correlation to the area, this one makes sense.

The hike starts at around the same height as the Quilotoa loop, so well and truly in the mountain tops. Going up to 4,600m the scenery is now snow-capped mountains forever in sight in the distance, as opposed to previous Andean farmland in Ecuador. I constantly have a headache that rivals the kind of hangover where your head could split in half. It was essential to keep the legs moving as we ascend higher into suffocation with the lack of oxygen in the air. Paralysed by a delirious surrounding of bright white snow it's cold while the sun burns my face, an uncomfortable combination of being hot and cold at the same time. The beauty of Andean snowy mountains is of course greeted with some dick-head playing Tiesto from his phone as we walk. The need for crap music as you walk through incredible beauty is beyond me. My headache worsens, the altitude is only increasing and this hike is becoming more difficult than enjoyable. I stop to catch my breath; the scenery is breath taking and worth a pause in itself – the fortune of travel where pain is worth the struggle. We arrived at the lake which is shining, ice cold from the melting ice caps and crystal blue that allows a refreshing dabble for the sweaty feet and a drink of cold water. Sat next to the lake, was it worth it? This is nice but the altitude is a bitch. I'm tired and hungry, all the feelings that your postcard photograph don't ever tell.

The next day I'm sore all over, like my legs have been through a war. Keen to keep exploring light heartedly, the convenience of a lighter walk with a tour guide to Ishinca Glacier suits me. Stocked with a carrier bag of beans from the market for my fuel, I board the bus full of retired holiday-going Peruvians, uncertain of the clientele I've joined on this day tour. Stopping on the bus at sights on the way, the ease of a tour and when tired not having to think for myself is great. The bus continues to stop to take a photograph with a llama dressed in sunglasses and a hat, a cringe-worthy addition to the gringo-tourist trail, and I remember again why I try to avoid tours. Nonetheless, I can't escape the tour in case I get abandoned by the bus in the Andes. This continuous stopping for gimmicky attractions is like sitting through something you can't tolerate, but can do nothing about.

Finally, I have freedom to leave the tour at last for a walk, with a condor hovering above my head. He's like a guide eerily swooping metres above me, circling the path up the glacier I am heading to, as if he's wanting to catch me in his talons. The walk is more altitude climbing; I drag myself up the mountain. Feeling weak, I consider the risk of the condor taking me just to feel a different kind of pain from being at this altitude.

The view from the glacier and the air being so fresh and clean is uplifting. I'm deliriously convinced that Mother Nature is rewarding me with a new chance of life and no more pain with clean air inhalation. The view, as everywhere has been the last few days, is amazing; beauty is easy to see here, yet my expectations of a glacier are dampened.

Melting glacier markings show that over forty years, like a tidal line on a beach from the ocean, ninety per cent of the snow has now gone. The lagoon looks like a warm cocktail that has melted particles of ice slowly moving around on top; the ice is no longer the chunks or boulders that I'd imagined but damp cold slices. I listen to the crackling of ice breaking, like pouring lukewarm water over ice cubes in a glass; everything is melting around me. Noticing the streams of water on the walk to Laguna 69 which ran over the roads and paths, global warming is melting the glaciers here too. I didn't even think of it. Although this is a problem with the inevitable disappearance of the glacier for tourism or natural purposes, there must be greater and more significant underlying issues with global warming all over the world. This is a large glacier, but nowhere near as big as the ones I've seen elsewhere or those further south on the continent. To see in front of me glaciers melting was alarming, and not how it is on TV where it looks sped up; it's happening.

The end of the day it was time for another farewell to Fergus and Lou. My time spent in Canoa meant I couldn't do the Santa Cruz trek that they were off to do; I was becoming a bit tired of hiking, my foot hurt and I was constantly exhausted from the altitude. I wanted to move on to Lima to meet the GBH, a new travel companion now, one I'd never travelled with before; things are going to change.

Lima Layover – best served over thinking 3.6.16.

Lima – 'The City of The Kings' – a destination on the 'gringo trail' which people describe as a shithole. I arrive a day before the GBH so I have the chance to see for myself just how right the chat on the gringo trail is.

The Plaza de Armas, where the presidential palace and cathedral are, resonates a European megaton. Steeped in history and modernisation along its clean pavements, if this is a shithole, then good luck to travellers going to other parts of the continent.

Arriving on election weekend there's a more vocal atmosphere than I imagine normal. A booze ban on the city today forces people's voting decision to be distorted, with voters seemingly scrambling for a drink on the sly, making things seem nervy and anxious, let alone an important election taking place.

Peru has struck me as a gentle and friendly country. Watching the changing of the guard at the palace with a performance that could be likened to a North Korean war march was comical in comparison to their kind nature. Seeing the army soon afterwards pile onto a bus laughing and messing around with each other in a troop eradicated any thoughts of underlying aggression they had.

The brightly-coloured buildings are a feature of Lima. Recovering from a city fire one hundred and fifty years ago, when reconstruction took place, infrastructure was painted brightly. With the city being on the coast and having a constant smog lingering, the colours brighten the mood and give people some effervescence. It's a small but captivating method to improve the livelihood of residents in Lima.

The longer I spend in Latin America and begin to understand more of the language, the more I understand of the news and its politics and with Peru – it's a soap opera. As elsewhere, voters in Peru vote for someone they can relate to – usually a working-class hero. However, this year, that candidate is a woman and the daughter of a previous prime minister who happened to steal money from the government. Paying off the media to cover it up along with other infidelities in his reign, and who now happens to be in jail. The other candidate is your 'silver spoon', privately educated option, who most detest due to the hardship many go through. Even his past, is complex – and incest to contend with – all of which makes the Peruvian voters' choice a difficult one.

The neighbourhood, Miraflores, lined with cafes and bars like a Parisian neighbourhood, is full of noise that the uncertainty of the election brings. Latino people are usually so assured and fiery, its awkward to sense Peruvians being jittery. It's not like I have much to say in the way of comfort or advice on politics; I'm occupied enough with my own thoughts of what's coming up for me the next two weeks, with the imminent arrival of the GBH.

The girl back home who I left, trying to leave all the things I hated in my old humdrum routine of life, getting to know her the last few months before I left, made the things I resented less important to me. Even in the tougher times away, keeping in touch with her, neither of us being able to move on, even with new jobs, meeting new people, and, for me, all the beaches, cities, jungle and food of six months. She's a distraction for me from my travelling world. Having been in her shoes of working for the man, to come out and visit, the situation is worse for her, and more guilt and responsibility for me.

The emotional discomfort of travel, of which there is plenty, has been epitomised by the GBH being in my mind. What if we've changed when we are together and this two-week vacation for her that she's sacrificed so much for, ruins what we had? Should we go to shit, how would it be for me carrying on here? I'm not even sure what kind of relationship this is or isn't.

I can't pick and choose what I want and when. To be the solo explorer who gets a boat down the Amazon for months, who treks for months solo and carefree without the GBH is unrealistic. It's not only because the practicality of those are hard, (hiking is tiring, and I don't have a never-ending bank account), but the support I guess I think I want from those things is actually the support of the GBH.

Tough moments for me coincide with tough moments for her, but they can also be opposites. Playing football on deserted islands is amazing, but for her grey rain in London, working a rubbish job is agonising. Whatever the distance, wherever your heart is, distance means little, you'll always have that pain and joy. I am starting to try and accept I can't do everything, and that's not a fault. I am becoming nervous and cluttering my brain to find a solution for something I don't need to be.

This is all going to be OK, right? She is coming all this way, she'll be great and after all we're still talking after all this time. Should small travelling peeves of hers pop up for me, I think I'm patient enough and calm enough to cope. I'm in Peru. For fuck's sake, get a grip. Even if it is shit, I'm in Peru – we're both old enough to survive. We have plenty lined up for her two-week trip. The worst that could happen is I'll end up going to hang out with lamas for two weeks and she'll hate me forever. I'm excited really. I hope she doesn't mind a bit of football; the football tournament, the Copa America, has just begun. Girls love football and beer, right?

I have found a tiny ceviche restaurant for us to eat in tomorrow away from the crowds so we can have an authentic taster (which usually means no English menus and the price being closer to one dollar than ten dollars in Lima). The national dish of the country, I can't remember if she likes ceviche, but what's not to like? Sat waiting and watching a flickering airport arrivals board, I have to distract myself and dive straight in to what could be incredible, or torture.

Cusco – best served with the GBH and some Churros 6.6.16.

She hates ceviche, even the best possible place we could have gone to, by the sea, made freshly in front of us in a tiny kitchenette restaurant, it was romantic, quaint and perfect, but she hates it. However, you know when you over think something and there was never a need to worry, you just pick things up where you left it with someone – that's the GBH.

We have a night in Lima before flying to Cusco which we have chosen as a base before venturing to the southern corner of Peru. Fresh off the plane with months of saving, the GBH is full of enthusiasm to explore and make the most of being here. I adore the enthusiasm and having someone I know for companionship, and realising how easy it is to travel with someone you know really well. The GBH is a historian at heart, so exploring the centre of Cusco and its Incas wasn't just an option but something that was going to happen no matter what. I was completely ignorant about my surroundings as I know so little of the Incas' history, the resemblance to the Peruvian culture and people. I learn from museums and the GBH's encyclopaedic knowledge that Incas weren't actually 'people' – people – a term easily used to pigeonhole a stigma or belonging, however, they're actually personnel who were elected to be Incas.

Cusco and its endlessly sloping cobbled streets follow the paths of beautifully carved boulders which took hundreds of years to build by the Incas with Spanish colonialism. The Spanish smeared the Incas' history; they wrote a lot of the evidence from their perspective or destroyed their literature (it's still to this day unclear how many Incas there actually were). It was a cruel action to arrive in the country and destroy their architecture, and their lives. Saying that, tourists idiotically deface sites too, I guess they've inspired people in a strange way. As the Spanish rebuilt artefacts, they destroyed with their Spanish colonial buildings, earthquake tremors resulted in Spanish architecture requiring restructuring. Meanwhile, the Incas' foundations stood strong compared with their invaders' efforts, never yielding to natural disasters which Peruvians relate with a modestly proud smile.

The area surrounding Cusco is known as the Sacred Valley, a sacred land, an area which historians are still unsure of, so I feel a bit less ignorant regarding my lack of knowledge now. Rolling valleys of once farm-land offer plenty to do around Cusco, with ruins galore for the GBH and I slow down our exploring with a long walk around various ruins. All infrastructure was smoothed by hand or other stones. The enormous boulders which were carried and lifted onto the walls, took apparently nearly a hundred years to build – but how smooth they were. The GBH, being new to the terrain, took it in her stride and fell down a boulder path. Much to my amusement...

The highlight being Sasayhuaman – pronounced 'sexy woman' – lightened any potential overdose of exploring serious ruins. Fair play to the Incas, they laid their houses out immaculately and even had a spring supplying fresh water despite obvious, basic living as they appeared to eat nothing but potatoes. The Incas were the first to grow potatoes on their farms as corn can't grow in the highlands of Peru. Their reliance on eating them came from originally feeding spuds to their livestock; then the Spanish fed it as their slavery meal.

Cusco is the perfect place to catch up with the GBH – coffee shops and park benches in the beautiful plaza with its steep cobbled paths for getting lost in – it is painfully romantic for a reunion. This being the gateway for Machu Picchu makes Cusco a touristy hellhole. There are tour sellers on every corner begging you to take an excursion, and enough western restaurants to compete with a US city. Even the GBH loses patience as her dreams of Colonial-Inca buildings melt into happy hour cocktail bars, McDonald's and Irish bars subtly hidden inside the old buildings. I begrudgingly laugh at her enthusiasm for perfection when travelling and seeing something new, compared to my scepticism, and acceptance that this cringeworthy practice is the norm across the world, taking in the painful fact that a McDonald's is on the main plaza of Cusco. I try to remind her that the authenticity of the city is still alive, buying her churros with dulce de leche from a street vendor for twenty cents keeps her happy and distracts me from her globalisation rant. It's a double-edged sword that I feel I've now seen so many places that I shouldn't have on my route.

Tourist trinket shops become annoying; the repetitive 'nonsense', as the GBH puts it, of being offered tours and 'massages' encourages us to find an attraction out of Cusco, an alpaca farm called Awana Kancha a short drive away. It's a farm where the animals look content compared to ones being forced into selfies, wearing sombreros with cringe outfits. The Third World isn't known for holding many ethical values, especially with animals, but there's authentic weaving of the animal wool which is all sold at modest prices in the farm's shop. The items on sale are described as expressions of life experiences, moods, memories, stories, knowledge and cultural values to Andean families, a far cry from a lama wearing fake Oakley sunglasses. It's enticing to spend knowing the value and quality of where the money I spend is going to be ending up.

The adventure out of Cusco reignites faith that even on the gringo trail, non-tacky tourism in Peru exists. The enjoyment helps to pile up the fun of my current company, removing doubts I'd previously had. When travelling backpacking style, the overwhelming adjustment doesn't give a second's respite. You sink or swim straight away, adapting to the rough and readiness whilst being absorbed and allowing yourself to be exposed to the different situations at every moment. The GBH, on an adrenaline overload, jumps at the idea of a lunch in the San Pedro market. Somewhere to eat anything Peruvian possible is followed by a night sat on a plastic stool in Cusco's square eating fried chicken. No moaning, she loved every second – I could do whatever I wanted and feel completely comfortable with my travel companion, and I was convinced that she was too.

In an attempt to go more upmarket, as it turns out the GBH is getting tired of plain rice with everything, more accustomed to luxury on holiday it seems, we ate at a Peruvian folklorico show in a restaurant, this instantly backfiring with an overpriced, noisy and posh dinner, the highlight being dismayed by the folk dancing and laughing about expensive wine. I'm glad it wasn't for either of us. Shuffling in the cold back to our room, curiously looking at street food vendors who are selling kebab sticks, the GBH grabs my hand to take me over there and have a taste, to feed my curiosity. I used to judge or think travelling as a couple would never work, they always seemed to argue. The GBH and I have bickered, to only laugh about it minutes later. We only have two weeks together; it's too short a time to argue, but, when isn't it? Travelling with someone totally in sync with you, a couple or not, is perfect.

Lake Titicaca – best served with reeds 9.6.16.

The GBH's first night bus travelling from Cusco to Puno which is the destination to get to Lake Titicaca was a cold, loud, bumpy experience. Patience thin, the GBH's early discovery with loving travel is dwindling at the first taste of brutal discomfort which some buses can be. A stopover in a freezing cold bus terminal at five a.m. was precisely the romance she'd dreamt of when visiting the highest lake in the world. Fortunately, with a spectacular sunrise we warmed up and boarded our narrow boat to the islands of Uros to stay with a family on their own island, made entirely out of reeds.

Greeted warmly by our host – the mother of the family, walking across the small 20m square island was bouncy, as if wearing gravitational shoes to sink into the reeds beneath us as we walked across to our cabin. Bags down, our surreal first impression of this remote island of reeds goes further as we are turned around to go back with the husband of the family onto a gondola-like boat, which is again made of reeds from the lake to go fishing for their source of protein.

Lake Titicaca stretches across the border into Bolivia. The island we are on is within a cluster of inhabited islands, floating within a mini-forest of reeds growing out of the lake water. Weaving layer upon layer of reeds into mounds of floating roots in the water, they are then anchored into the lake to avoid 'drifting off to Bolivia', as the husband puts it, in the windy conditions. When the family feels like drifting off to somewhere, they lift up the anchor and allow the wind to take them wherever they want. The layers of the reeds go as deep as ten to fifteen metres and are built in blocks. The explanation of this engineering process, whilst sat in a boat made of the same material which is all around us, convinces me how solid and reliable the material is. Even his sombrero is made from reeds as he explains how this island requires an adaptation to the modern world with a sustainable approach.

At first the reeds were chewed for nutritional value, but they're also used for kindling as they cook over fire. This is still the case for their kitchen routine, although, as time developed, the chances of surviving on reeds alone wasn't going to get them very far. Trips to the mainland town of Puno happen once a week for essentials such as rice and fresh soil, allowing them to grow their own fruit and veg on their islands. The water supply varies in certain parts of the lake; the area they're anchored in at the moment isn't suitable for drinking, so bottled water is brought from Puno too.

Plastic bottles make me think this isn't the sustainable island life that I'd initially thought, to then be told how waste and plastic is separated into what goes back to Puno, and what can be used on the island for infrastructure. It adds four to five years life when the plastic is stuffed inside the boat. Speaking passionately about sustainability, which he has learnt from his mainland-educated daughter, for a sheltered existence he's well aware of the environmental responsibility of his and other islands. No bleaches or cleaning products are used on the land which could potentially contaminate the water. Their awareness and motivation to keep up with trends has allowed them to successfully run their guest house business, using modern and traditional techniques. The honesty is refreshing in not covering up how they actually live as the family now continue their lives but run a tourism business.

Other than reed hats, their clothes catch my eye being so bright and radiant. In the First World they'd look strange, so it was good timing to be taken through how they're made, and a chance to 'dress like an islander' alarms the GBH. The husband had been wearing a big baggy jumper which I was tempted to buy off him in the first instance. Trying it on as the freezing cold night began, it brought a welcome warmth. The comedy of our host's clothes was strangely entertaining. With only six other inhabitants on the island, it felt that we had the whole island to ourselves.

Leaving the island the next day was sad after only one night. Even though it wasn't an island that required much exploring, being on this beautiful, remote, peaceful and freezing cold island with the GBH dressed in multi-coloured wool was paradise. The family who live here tell us in their boat that they feel homesick away from their island even when running errands. The isolation and charm, and their enthusiasm for how the reeds are their everything – food, clothes, fuel, transport – instantly attached this place to me. The love they share is contagious, and the simplicity of their life to have that happiness makes life seem so easy.

What's My Age Again? 9.6.16.

Amidst the charm and delight of Uros, the family didn't miss a trick when trying to make more money from selling their souvenirs made on the island. I was happy to support their sustainable approach and know that with this family the money went straight to them and not via a travel agency; they are renowned for being crooked around here. This seemed like a good point to send the GBH home with a souvenir from this favourite spot of ours; she can take it home so I don't have to carry it too.

The GBH loves to talk about the future, not knowing at all what that might entail, while being wrapped up in the moment of the island, curious for what's next. Adjusting to my new travel companion with half my head thinking about home as it's where we met, the GBH was a big draw on that for me.

Still riding the wave of enjoying the island and wanting to give something back, there was no material possession that I wanted, the best of the bunch being a pillow case. Of course the GBH decides she now wants a pillow case, and with only enough cash between us, I swing between enthusiastic and awkwardly silent in suggesting we buy it together. The man who ran away to avoid his life back home, be independent and free, has just bought a fucking pillow case with a girl who lives on the other side of the world.

It's a pillow case that suggests, 'who knows what'll happen in the future?'. This is now a symbol for us. A pillow case. Not sure where I'm going next week, but I know there's a pillow case for me in London one day. What must the GBH think of me? I can't focus on me so no point guessing her right now. Could this be a jinx, a symbolic 'yes' a good omen? Was that panic in fact what I really wanted to say and do? I do like the pillow case; I just didn't realise I've turned into something I never thought I would.

The Colca Canyon – best served with a pisco sour, disappointing the GBH 11.6.16.

Exhausted from hiking and being with the more delicate GBH, we opt for a tour as opposed to a hike to the Colca Canyon from nearby town, Chivay. Another so called destination and tour on the gringo trail – what have I become…

Arriving at Chivay, which is in the middle of nowhere, two hours late for our tour, due to bus delays meant a day in a town that's similar to a building site recovering from an earthquake ten years ago. This would be the perfect place to have an argument with a disappointed GBH. Having not seen each other in so long, to going into a very intense few days together, intensified squabbles amidst the fun and face of it all I guess would be inevitable.

The worst enemy for a traveller is money, an entity that needs to be managed, while for a holiday-goer in employment, it's something that can be earned back quickly upon return. The GBH has much looser purse strings than I do and I have to say no to spending more than I want. The appeal of a western home cooked meal, when I'm sick of rice, is strong, but it can't be done when the price of western food is so high in comparison to local cuisine. The compromise: homemade sandwiches with cheese and ham sat on a dusty floor by the bus stop. The result: Peru is not well known for its cheese and ham for that reason, a disappointed GBH and a guilty feeling me.

These arguments, as we adjust to being together again, build up and make things feel a bit shitty, when really everything is fine. An hour or so of awkward silence and one-word conversations lead us on a walk on the roadside to the opening of the stunning canyon. As we walk to the Andean Springs thermal baths for some expensive R and R, we salvage a day of being sat arguing with nothing to do. Pisco sours in the baths turned out to be the perfect cocktail. Again, realising that the petty squabbles really aren't worth the fuss; it's more a fear of growing up and having to deal with someone as part of me as opposed to not looking after anyone apart from myself, which is all I do when travelling.

The tour being booked up proved too easy and convenient to be true. Latinos' punctuality is not something to be admired, especially in comparison to the efficient GBH. Waiting for our tour bus for nearly an hour, concern that something is wrong sets in. A few calls at the crack of dawn and our tour has left without us, driving past our accommodation to the pick-up point. This is why I hate tours. A taxi ride to chase after our tour, which had waited for us to look at a church, similar to the other churches I've seen, but the GBH missing out one church creates more disappointment – I'm great at this disappointment lark. The church however allows us to catch up and relax; we make the tour a day later than planned and are finally heading to the canyon.

The canyon itself is in view along the bus journey, driving uphill to a viewing point named Cruz del Condor. This was a hangout where condors up to five metres in wingspan fly around hawking the area. That comfortably makes me bait for these birds...

The view at the point is spectacular, away from the road and scraggy dirt paths along the ridge with different views. It gave the overcrowded view some sense of solitude and peacefulness, while in awe at the enormous depth going to three thousand metres. An elderly woman lugging her supplies on her back, can be seen on the other side of the canyon going to a small settlement. No marathon running or fitness gurus could prepare you for such harsh inclines and altitude. Only a local, who knows it like the back of her hand and has the mindset of mind over matter, could cope, keeping her strength and feet moving forwards and upwards in what must be a daily routine for the location she's in.

Areas of the canyon go to five thousand metres deep and there's a four to five-hour vertical climb on foot for hikers. A condor is relatively a smudge in the landscape and the flock near us made me a speck on the scale of the situation here. It's a canyon with a mix of Quilotoa's green crater fields and the Grand Canyon's desert. This is certainly an attraction but, as everywhere, everyday life carries on. It's the farmland here, amidst the desert cacti at the peaks of the canyon, where Peruvian workers ply their trade. The sancayo cactus is mixed with pisco for tourists to taste the Chuquibamba sours drink, all part of the farming process that supplies most jobs in this area. Two hours of gazing at condors and the never-ending, intimidating scenery in dry, thin, cold, dusty air – it was time to jump back on the stuffy, smelly air-conditioned old folks' tour bus for a rickety ride to Arequipa.

Arequipa – best served with an alpaca 13.6.16.

Cusco, Lima and Arequipa – the major cities I've visited in Peru – all have their own style. Lima – a cosmopolitan western hub for the country. Cusco – with its Inca charm that hasn't yet been overly spoilt with modern infrastructure. Arequipa – the one somewhere in between: cobbled streets and colonial buildings with a European-style square and restaurants. Mixing an essence of classy Peruvian cuisine with its local rough around the edges pockets, this was the perfect place to slow down and enjoy some good food and sit in the square watching a 'mixed' city pass by after a few busy days.

I love how the GBH adjusts to the tempos of travelling, not wanting to exhaustingly cram everything in. Arequipa is a great place to sit in the sun with great cafes and restaurants, from budget to expensive (even for those not on a traveller budget). The GBH and I treat ourselves and eat some more pricey delicious food than my budget would let me deal with; I've been strict in Peru and it seems easier to prevent an argument to spend a bit more. Every day is a treat when travelling as it's continuously being somewhere you want to be, your choice and decision, but forking out money on something I don't usually do is fulfilling, especially as eating has become our main excursion here so it doesn't feel so bad!

From the farming bedrock that Peruvian living is built on to Incas starting the farming revolution by taking advantage of the vast land everywhere, the Spaniards' intrusion turned farming into labour without changing the interpretation of how the national treasure, the alpaca, is farmed. A cuddly pet to the western world, for Peruvians it's an expensively farmed cut of meat. Just how their processes of labour out-lived the Spanish methods with their building techniques (evident again in Arequipa), their farming methods could be out-lived too. A wincing GBH reluctantly watched me devour a steak from the animal, expensive but tasty.

A whole day of eating and drinking pisco sours ended with a decisive Copa America football game – minnows Peru against the mighty Brazil. The GBH, sporting her new fake Peruvian football shirt, (another token purchase along the gringo trail), and I join locals in a small back alley bar away from the clean tables and cutlery, next to a churros stand with hot oil wafting through the door of the sticky floor bar. An insight into the shy Peruvians' sense of humour – knowing full well their place as an underdog, their pride and positivity to make a stamp on the game, while enjoying themselves, is all they cared about. Winning late on, they didn't quite know how to react, apart from celebrate wildly amidst being in hysterical laughter.

Bragging to Brazilian fans in the bar with good taste, pisco sours being thrown everywhere, they danced on tables and chairs; they seemed so reserved until now. They even got the GBH excited about football; maybe she was coming around to the random antics of travel after all...

Wonders of the world and their price – best served on a credit card 15.6.16.

Machu Picchu, the main draw to Peru and arguably the continent, was saved as a 'best till last' excursion for the GBH and me, also allowing time to acclimatise to the altitude. With many options on how to get to Machu Picchu, it becomes a logistical investigation, especially when time and budget restraints are taking their toll.

Conscious that hiking to the site was overpriced, over-done and paths were worn out, we opted for the budget option of an expensive train journey taking us back from Machu Picchu to Cusco for our last night, confident enough that our journey to Machu Picchu the day before our assigned ticketed entry would be enough. Our plan was to take a bus or train, which I had read and learned from travellers was a safe bet, to the base town Aguas Calientes before the site.

Stopping to change vehicles half way between Cusco and Aguas Calientes, trailing off in conversation with a local while asking for directions to the bus or train to Aguas Calientes, we learn that the train was in fact another expensive train, not a local hop on and off. It was a train that sold out in advance, and the short bus journey in my mind to take is a seven-hour night bus, leaving once a day, had also sold out in advance and wouldn't get us to Machu Picchu in time. Suddenly we were up against time, stranded and in risk of missing out on the one attraction that the GBH had wanted to do forever and ending our trip together, which had been an emotional battering to redemption. It's now on the brink of ending in the most disappointing fashion.

My heart frantically pounding I start to look where it was possible to buy more tickets for the next train which was due shortly; the bus won't work for us. Nervous, and as the more experienced backpacker between us, I'm responsible for this balls-up. I sprint to the ticket booth without warning, leaving the GBH behind me to carry my bag, so I could try and salvage something somehow. I see a queue at the ticket booth was closed for a 'late lunch' – is there even such a thing in Peru?

I shamelessly queue-jumped to the front as the booth reopens and with no option, paid for another extortionate train journey on my back-up credit card. It's the card I never wanted to bring with me but it was now a necessary utility for me from here on and being used – a lot. I buy the last two tickets and leave an angry mob of tourists behind me in the queue. The guilt in comparison with how I would have felt if I had not got the tickets for the GBH is incomparable. Now I just have to remember where I left the GBH with all of the bags before the train leaves in ten minutes – an easy task compared to the previous hour.

With taking the last two seats, it meant we're sat in separate carriages for the train journey; the three hours was the longest that we have spent apart in the last two weeks. Moving along the old tracks, my heart rate eventually slows down, accepting that I've managed to resolve the problem. Staring up at the clear ceiling of the train designed to take in the views of the mountains and enjoy the spectacular views, the sun begins to set behind the canyon which our train line goes through. I painfully remember how this is so horrifically out of my budget (that I once had), and has been such an ordeal, falling heavily into the 'pay this off when I get home one day' category.

The GBH doesn't have expensive taste. I feel like I'm almost hosting the GBH as a guest on my adventure tour when it's both of ours; adding that responsibility to myself meant I couldn't not deliver. Time on my own allowed me to think for myself and remember how memorable the last two weeks had been with the GBH. I have found my perfect travel companion; she has the best flaws and when she leaves it'll be the first time in a while that I'm exploring solo again, which I normally love, but I feel lonely at the idea of it. What spectacularly crap timing this all is. I'm so glad I did this trip when I could, and perhaps I would have done things differently with the GBH had I never gone – but I'd have found an excuse to go.

I'm adamant that even with all the hype that Machu Picchu brings, it'll be worth the fuss. I put it on myself to make this good for the GBH. How, I'm not sure – it could be rubbish and an expensive, overpriced tourist trap like a lot of the other attractions that people claim are highlights around the world. All I know is, once the GBH has gone, and whenever I can get some cash together again, I'll be paying this off for a while but the questions of pain I have over my present dilemma of the GBH will carry on even longer.

Machu Pichu – best served being shouted at 17.6.16.

Aguas Calientes hasn't filled me with optimism that Machu Picchu won't be anything but one of those 'highlights' that are horribly touristy and over the top. Greeted by sombrero-wearing llamas posing for photos with gringos, I understand the need for making the most of the tourism opportunity, but the town renamed 'Machu Picchu Town' is like a ski-resort mixed with Disney and Vegas. I feel queasy drowning in tack. I wasn't expecting abandonment and a hub of archaeologists, but it's a small step away from 'It's a small world after all' being played in the background whilst an American wearing a paper-mache Inca outfit offering to take your selfies for you with a selfie-stick – cringe. Arriving late and wanting to get up to the top of Machu Picchu for sunrise, meant it was a welcome early night to avoid the town.

A cold four a.m. start with just the noise of our footsteps marching frantically to the walking point entrance, we're greeted by several hundred others in a queue to get in. Patiently waiting till five a.m., the line hasn't moved and with at least an hour of trekking uphill to go, the gate finally opens to the realisation that a speedy hike is necessary for the GBH and myself to make sunrise.

Setting off quickly, the pace drops as the density of the people walking the same steep, paved path uphill, all holding small flashlights creates a congested motorway of headlights in slow-moving traffic. I am itching to overtake people and make it up to the top and see sunrise, the GBH by my side as the air starts to warm up with the sun creeping up, the ascent becomes tougher with the altitude. Two weeks of acclimatising and being in good shape haven't done the GBH any favours. Stopping for a breather too many times, people are overtaking us and creating more congestion ahead, their backpacks pressed against our faces as we crawled up behind them. The sky is turning from a pitch black to a dark blue, the sun is definitely rising, it's not waiting for our moment at the top.

The GBH is adamant that I should go on ahead without her as she struggles to adjust but I can't leave her now – the pinnacle of our time together. Determined to help, I encourage her to 'just try your best' which results in an angry foot stamp and an appalled look as she gears up for her rant. The wrong thing to say, we're now wasting even more time and, unless the top is close, we're missing the sunrise.

I walk next to her and we slowly take it step by step. For all the touristy slagging off I've done, this was something I wanted to see and do. Should we have left earlier? Taken the bus? At this point I'm so pissed off I just want to turn around and storm off home like a child as the GBH snaps at me for a second time. Missing sunrise, our last day together and we're arguing at five a.m., Machu Picchu so far – you are expensive and shit.

Even with the slow pace, the crowds and the altitude, we do the walk on the time we anticipated. Queues at the start of the climb and the final entrance kill our chances. We would have needed to be the first people through the gate to make sunrise or have run up there which would have prompted the third 'shouting at Matt' session in the two hours I've been awake. This can't even be a lesson learnt; I probably won't ever be back here; it's a hard one to swallow.

Held at another queue for final ticket inspection, I'm bitter that this expensive attraction has let the masses of queues crush my chance of perfection, as swarms of groups from ten to thirty people are cattle-herded through with their guides it's over congested, slow and not enjoyable. My patience is thin and we go for a walk away from the main view, after we have taken the standard photos that you see on all traveller photo albums which look towards Mountaina Picchu. The view I've seen but struggle to be excited about in the flesh.

I have to accept it for what it is, a wonder of the world which was never going to be abandoned. It's just a shame, that being such a popular destination in my head, never allowed me to think it would be how it is: overcrowded. As we start to explore my mood improves and I suddenly realise this is in fact another amazing moment, and when away from the crowds, this place is special. High up against the peaks and tops of mountains, the infrastructure that was somehow attached to a mountainside with nothing but thousands of feet worth of gaping drop next to our feet, follows perfectly smoothed Incan rocks, just how it is in Cusco.

With the awesomeness of this experience, and the fact that the GBH has forgiven me for her arduous climb, my mood improves drastically and, despite the main area of the site being something I've seen a thousand times on photos, it's spectacular and I appreciate it. The postcards and tacky paintings people try to sell in Cusco don't do this justice. The Incas who built this were geniuses, but like all geniuses that follow, to build it how and where they did – geniuses are crazy! The smaller ruins and tombs on the site are their own diminutive adventures within the area. Some even have their own water systems; the Incas knew what they were doing!

At Machu Picchu I still feel ignorant, not knowing much about the Incas, especially compared to the GBH, although it's nice to learn more – another bonus to travelling. Learning from the GBH it's even nicer, as I don't feel obliged to make small talk with a tour guide, more inquisitive. To some historians and archaeologists this place must be porn. I enjoy it but I'll be 'ruined-out' by the end of Peru for a while.

Approaching midday with the sun at its hottest and groups of Chinese tourists taking photos of every rock in the site, we find a quiet spot to ourselves and sit down to relax with our feet over the edge. I began ignoring the continuous, mesmerising, rolling mountains that we looked down on of green forestation, enjoying one another's company for the last day and just look around at this amazing site from our view.

My time with the GBH is coming to an end. At times, while keeping in touch, I've felt she's known a lot about the journey. Now she's had a taste of it and leaving we'll go back to keeping in touch via phones. I doubt I will keep it at the bottom of my bag now. We can sit together and both feel proud we've done it, as I think we're actually, somehow, whatever this is – we've made it work. The GBH was able to save, to make it out here for a guy, when the odds were stacked against us, and I guess, less spectacularly, for me carrying on. Why am I carrying on without her? I don't understand why, and if she can, then she must be worth keeping hold of, even if it's thousands of miles away. One more night in Cusco will be bittersweet. The happiness I went out looking for here came out to me, and now it's leaving.

Leaving Peru – best served torn 18.6.16.

Three weeks in Peru and I'm barely a fraction wiser on the history of the Incas, but then again, I'm the same as most Peruvians. The best and worst thing about the country is their tourism, the most inundated place with visitors since Costa Rica; this isn't always a bad thing. Machu Picchu, Colca Canyon, the north's mountains are all spectacular. Ceviche is part of Lima's lifestyle that can't be missed. The western-style café culture in Lima is lapped up by the locals and tourists alike. It's not the stool and ladle serving out of a mesh tin on the streets in the quieter areas but a classier affair – they know what to do and charge for it according to their western clientele.

Then there is the other end, the poorer less attractive side, always peeping through to tourists, which feels like it's deliberately hidden away, covered up and even a bit unknown. For example, the horses' heads in the markets that are on show, what's done with them? Their food is an entertainment attraction in itself; the colourful markets, the reverse western logic of cuddly guinea pigs and alpaca meat which are hung out to showcase their touristic dining opportunities, the chicharrones fried in oil in the mesh tin on the street. Yet it's always 'glammed up' to be lean and clean in restaurants, and the guinea pig isn't even the best thing here. It seems that amongst travellers few who visit here really see the side of Peru that made it what it's known for today – a destination for all who came from agricultural living from their farms and the Incas.

The Inca signs of positivity and negativity, the 'P' sign 'swirls' on Peru's tourism logo, mirror the pros and cons of tourism in the country. Promoting yet spoiling any opportunities for tourism that they can offer. The Spanish influence here really fucked them up, but still had a positive influence in the long-term from their infrastructure being made to look far superior.

The price of things in Peru is grating, ignoring the fact my financial situation has been self-violated, but where does the money outside Lima go? – not to the desert concrete block housing which makes up the majority of the country's residential builds, or to the farmers using mud and reeds for warmth in their homes or to the craftsmen and cloth makers. The tourism money feels a bit disheartening when it's spent and shared so badly for these lovely people who get exploited in their trades for tourism. It's rare to find sustainable ecotourism which Costa Rica excels in, and only at Awana Kancha did I see it in full view.

My time with the GBH and her fresh-faced zest for learning the culture here, has pushed me to keep a promise to learn about how history intertwines with itself. I have started thinking about home life more after this trip as I approach the last bend of my time away. My biggest challenge will be to not fall back into the negative habits but to make time for things that are positive and enjoyable for me.

For the first time since Costa Rica, I head off on my own, knowing that I won't see a familiar face for a few months. I am learning to travel solo again – something I love but have adjusted to moving on and appreciating different things, while no longer having the GBH by my side, the best of all travel companions. I have started to get flu in the last few days. Knowing that she's leaving I'm ill and upset which is a first for both of us since I left her in London six months ago.

I leave the GBH at the airport and it's completely emotional. After her plane takes off, I go to meet Fergus for a quick bite, a fond farewell to a different kind of travel companion. It's unlikely our paths will cross again – no more football chats or endless food discussions, or dreaming of luxury on our tight travel budgets. I take the long walk to the bus terminal as a packed Cusco celebrates a festival. Busy, congested, chaotic, it's not the quaint, peaceful square I sat in with the GBH two weeks earlier, watching her drink copious amounts of coca tea to fight altitude sickness.

Peru and Cusco still look spectacular; fireworks are going off behind me for the festival and I see Peru getting knocked out of the Copa America on penalties as I stand outside a bar with my bag on. This is all very dramatic as everything around me feels like it's ending. I've been gutted ever since coming back to Cusco to take the GBH to the airport this morning – the most saddening of goodbyes as Peru ends what for me was no doubt, a love story I wasn't expecting, with a heart-breaking separation at the end that I wasn't prepared for.

Bolivia

Bolivia – Best served eating Rellenos.
- 500g potatoes
- 200g minced beef
- 1 chopped onion
- 1 tomato
- 2 garlic cloves
- 1 boiled egg
- 2 tbsp. plain flour

Peel and boil the potatoes until they are soft, drain and mash them into a smooth texture. Meanwhile, slowly cook the minced beef with the chopped onion, tomato and garlic all together. Let it cook for 10 minutes, seasoning to taste, and then allow the pan to cool. Mould the potato into round balls and creating a small hole inside of the potato ball for the meat mix along with a slice of boiled egg to go into. Seal the hole with potato again, lightly cover the outside with flour and fry in boiling oil until golden all over.

Into La Paz – best served in the markets with a Cholita 20.6.16.

During the lonely night bus journey around Lake Titicaca which joins Peru and Bolivia, I'm woken by the same sunrise I shared with the GBH a few days ago. The sunlight turns everything orange in my sight; there's total nothingness on the horizon which feels empty and strange. Only hours since the GBH and I separated, I'm unfairly apathetic to Bolivia.

The border crossing is cold and, like most border towns, run down. Although it's early and no one is around, the depressing nature of the town and my mood, it doesn't seem it would be any different on the best of days. Cold and waiting at customs, I am definitely hung up on the GBH situation. There is nothing here, it's just a battered town where people are passing through. I don't even know really where I am, near a lake on a road with a border control hut. Don't care either, frankly.

A frail young girl, who must be about seven-years-old, walks slowly from a distance on the road with an arched back, puffing her rosy cheeks heavily like a marathon runner, or how the GBH was walking up to Machu Picchu. As she approached I saw her wheeling a cart filled with bricks, with more strapped to her back like a mule. Struggling with the weight, the bricks were about to crush her and I looked around for some assistance. The bus driver, who is passing through the border, waves dismissively that it's normal, as a man appears next to her to share the load of the cart with her. It's seven a.m., it's freezing, I miss the GBH, I'm tired, and brutally awoken to an introduction to the working lives here. A setting of brutal poverty, surrounded by wasteland, it's another border crossing, another stamp in the passport, a procedure that happens every couple of weeks.

The journey, crawling towards the highest capital city in the world, La Paz, doesn't improve aesthetically. It's a run-down city and for the first time on my trip I start feeling depressed and my mood to explore is dampened further. I miss the GBH and feel winded from it. Fortunately, arriving on a Sunday, most of the city is closed down so walking around aimlessly and staring at more cobbled walls, more colonial churches and feeling glum is an easy option to occupy my misery. There are some parts prettier than others, but a lot is dirty and miserable. Have I mentioned that I miss the GBH?

One site that I wanted to see here was the San Pedro prison. I read a book a few years ago that put La Paz on the map for me. A prison which inside has communities and businesses, where money is needed to buy a cell and food, just like a normal world of restaurants, politics, but inside a prison. In the 1990s an Englishman was arrested and imprisoned for drug trafficking, sent to San Pedro prison and resultantly set up a tour agency as his business to survive in an environment where making cocaine is the predominant source of income. Dealers throw nappies out of the windows to the school next door, where children of the prisoners attend, to pass to their families to sell for income. A crazy world inside a jail, these obscure tours became popular so additional bribes to the police force for allowing drug deals to go on with the need for more necessary security – the tours got out of hand with tourists entering the prison then falling victim to crime, as such, the tours have ended.

I was interested to see inside San Pedro but when it came to bribing my way in and needing to pay the same amount that I'd spent on a week in the Galapagos, it wasn't happening. The police are underpaid and undervalued by the government; their best income is from taking advantage of tourists trying to bribe their way in, and from turning a blind eye to the deals out of the prison, a broken system that runs too smoothly.

Bolivians love their food, however unhealthy, and an attractive characteristic for men here is a plump girl – one who can bear children to allow the man to retire early and the children to take over the family business. Their love of food points directly to one dish – fried chicken. Shops on every corner selling unhealthy foods are common practice and in restaurants here, with little understanding of healthy alternatives. The four hundred varieties of potatoes the country have makes me laugh – I didn't know there were even that many potatoes in the world! This created the nickname across the continent – Potato Heads. Their heads are so big, women traditionally wear men's hats. The way they position them is a sign of their marital status and if they want to flirt or not – like a traffic light disco party for hats!

Despite feeling weak and fragile, a stroll around the market, Mercado Lanza, for some food showcases the Bolivian love for spuds. Mountains of potato sacks everywhere, the possibility to buy them in any shape or form is bizarre, yet it's endearing to see their cooking creativity with little money, or access, it seems, to much else. For a country not renowned for its food at all, the market dish of rellenos – a ball of mashed potato with butter which has minced meat and vegetables inside – for a short while makes me adore Bolivians. It's an unconscious attempt to make me feel better from my slump post-GBH and illness with their take of an English shepherd's pie-ball!

Bolivians appear open-hearted and genuine, even in the mad rush of La Paz – a chaotic city of traffic, which fuels the intense overcrowding and congestion all over, noise, dirt, crime and with the obvious poverty, despair. There are homeless and disabled people all over the streets begging in complete desperation, more so than anywhere else I've been. While trying to buy something healthy and get some vitamins for my feeble self, for a country that loves vendors who sell fast food, surprisingly they sell a lot of half-pint-sized fruit cocktails which was just what I needed. Munching away I eavesdrop on a young girl pouring her heart out to a vendor, the female stall trader called a 'cholita'. The translation is to be like a second mother, an agony aunt, their favourite vendor or market stall traders, who listen in return for their loyal custom at their stall. Renowned gossips across the market, they're loved and always able to throw in a few extra portions of fruit and veg upon purchase for them. I had a regular fruit stand by my old place of work. Goran, the Siberian in Kentish Town, was lovely but wouldn't care if I'd shared my life problems with him.

The market isn't only a stop-off for those seeking their agony aunt, but for city workers of all kinds looking for a meal. A menu del dia of a rice dish and soup is of course available, but there's also the popular Multivitaminico Drink – 'The Workers' Drink' – which is all the fruit their cholita can get hold of blended together with oats. No pretence or messing around, it's a source of goodness to help workers, be it at the bottom or top of the food chain, get through the day! – all served with a smile, by a cholita who has got her five-year-old child helping her out to cut the fruit! Their loyalty to their cholita, and the cholita's to her customers is obvious as it is to their own recipes amongst other traders, even traders overseas who tried to buy the ingredients of a famous chorizo seller, Dona Goitia. The best sandwich in town doesn't have a sale price to the franchises of the world she ferociously defends.

While exploring it's a shame not to be able to see all parts of the city including the witches' market which is open on Sundays. There are rituals and bizarre objects including shrunken llamas and sex stimulant potions. The witches are hard bargainers which makes me worried they'll try to sacrifice me or cast a spell when taking advantage of cheap souvenir shopping!

A week day is a working day, although in La Paz it's a day to protest about working. It's a politically unstable country which changes presidents more often than any other. A previous president fled Bolivia having robbed the people – since then, they've changed leader almost monthly in an attempt to find stability again. A love for protesting, if there's no daily protest in Bolivia, it is not a normal day. The government recently cut disability allowances and support to an equivalent of thirty dollars a month; the city was out in force to fight for more money – meaning more places were cornered off to control the crowds.

The culture of sticking up for each other amongst Bolivians is obvious, as is their good sense of humour. When TV networks threatened to cut off *The Simpsons* from daily viewing recently, of course there was a protest, as there is most days about something in La Paz and protestors dressed up as Simpsons characters to march the streets. The result: the Simpsons is now on twice a day.

The Amazon Rainforest – best served not in the rainforest 22.6.16.

There is a list of things I wanted to do, or attempt to achieve, in Latin America. An authentic, non-touristic experience of the Amazon was top of my list. The size of the Amazon is absurd, and almost every country on the continent offers the opportunity to visit it, yet Bolivia offers the most bio-diverse, as well as the cheapest – by far.

After a seven-hour flight delay at La Paz airport for maintenance work, the sixteen-seater plane looked as if it could be a wind-up plane and thrown to my Amazonian destination of Rurrenabaque – it was tiny! The short flight there, for someone who isn't a keen flyer, wasn't comfortable, but it was real. The plane shook and bounced the whole way as we quickly started to fly above the Amazon. The dream was happening and, amidst the nausea of the flight, seeing the huge murky brown river meander through the green jungle a short way out of La Paz was exhilarating. *This is it*, everything I'd imagined the Amazon to look like, I want to be in the thick of it all right now! One of the things I'd dreamt of doing since I was young, and I was about to do it – one of the reasons people travel is to fulfil ambitions and go to places they always wanted to – this is it! Soon enough I almost have my wish; our plane feels like it's falling apart as the duct-taped wing skims tree-tops coming into land and I start to think of my own jungle survival story: 'tiny passenger plane goes down in the Amazon as gringos fight for survival, Englishman moans about a girl back home'.

Stepping off the plane (alive, after a skid landing) to a wall of humidity – it's instant sweat and heat I haven't felt since the Lost City. The town of Rurrenabaque isn't quite what I expected it to be. Having landed on a dusty runway in the thick of the jungle, I dreamt the town would be a dirt track with a few huts offering tours, like some kind of romantic jungle movie. Alas, what's on offer is a small town of buildings with pedestrianized town squares, goading gringos into their businesses for authorised and certified, immaculate-looking tours. Many national parks like this have bad practice of how animals are treated and where they go, so despite the anal routine of going with a certified tour, it seemed the best way.

Amazonian experiences are offered two-fold – the Pampas, seeing the Amazon by boat down the river, or the jungle which offers fewer chances to see wildlife, but was a more rugged option. As the itineraries were explained, the repetitiveness of my previous excursions in the jungle and rainforests, in Nicaragua, Colombia, Costa Rica come screaming to me. The Amazon is an entity of adventure in itself, like no other surely? Why does this feel so repetitive to me? The tours sound great as my hand is forced into the Pampas. I don't have the time to shop around for what I really want, and this tour leaves for the jungle first thing in the morning. I feel like a rat race-drained, spoilt brat who isn't as excited about something that he is fortunate enough to do when he should be. My dream of going through the jungle, living off the land in the hard conditions, eating bugs in the dark and scary Amazon has gone. This is it – again, just less exciting.

So as a group of six (having coincidentally been on the same delayed flight who scrambled for the last available tour), we file into a handmade wooden long boat and set off down to the Pampas as a pink dolphin pops up not far from our boat but in a flash it's gone. Excitement levels rise. With the sun creeping out, laid back in a chair and enjoying a boat ride wiggling around bends and shrubbery, it's not a bad life!

I didn't consider the changes of landscape in wet-dry season (why would I, as I try and convince myself after an hour I'm a jungle expert). However, now being made aware how the landscape is completely different, the water line on trees next to us goes up another three metres higher. Rainforest flooding is evident, but fortunately not damaging my trip. The benefit of missing rain is that the river feels more alive, the river banks are tighter together and closer to our boat's course, making it easier to spot caimans and crocodiles on the river banks. Animals I have seen before, but also, it's a bird watcher's paradise – the variety of shapes, colours, sizes, noises and behaviours sharing trees with monkeys reminded me of how closely the animals mix together and was wonderfully entertaining. With there only being one way up the river, unfortunately it was the route for all of the other boat tours too, as swarms of people crowd around animals to take photos which scared them off, even in their natural habitat.

A few hours cruising the river and animal spotting, we dropped our boat off at our base, a basic wooden hut with mosquito netting and a dining room for dinner. I've stayed in worse hostels for double the money on my way here. This was starting to feel like the kind of tour I don't like; I don't know what I quite expected but this was turning into a retreat in an Amazon hotel. A short walk away was a big playing field surrounded by mangrove bushes, with the sun setting on the flat horizon over the shrubs. I was easily entertained playing football but this wasn't anything I'd hoped or expected it to be, despite having enjoyed the day. Spoilt so far by my experiences, this wasn't the savage Amazon experience I'd dreamt of. The animals were great but, as can happen when animal spotting, we didn't see tons. Perhaps I'd over-elaborated my imagination as a character in the Jungle Book – befriending jaguars or swinging from vines. This was underwhelming in comparison to other journeys. Perhaps I've seen too much so that I'm spoilt by making comparisons.

I went to bed satisfied and content, but knowing that this was the kind of place and tour which could change with some persuasion. I had to be selfish, again, and see if there was a chance that I could taste the real Amazon. I had a few conversations with the guide to see what was possible and there was a chance, only after the slight suggestion of offering some gringo American dollars… finally a more ethical bribe! I had to hold out on logistics their end with guides; a chance was good enough for now.

The next day, I was instructed first thing to join another group who were finishing their tour today, giving me a better chance of getting into the jungle somehow via other means of transport. Off we went, in a boat again, but this time pulling into pockets of water in mangroves to jump into the water with the pink dolphins. The brown river water that I saw from the plane was exactly how it looked to be – thick, gross, smelly water that was clammy on the skin, within an instant. The pretty pink dolphins I imagined to be beautiful and friendly, turned out to be ugly looking, unfriendly and shy, swimming away at any chance of interaction. Again, not quite how I'd imagined their persona to be as we shivered in the cold water after a freezing night as the temperature dropped in the cool of darkness. Perhaps I'd been presumptuous, and over-excited for my 'this is it' moment as I crawled back into the boat awkwardly from the water – I stank of the river and desperately waited for the sun to break through in full to warm me up. Shivering away, it was peaceful and I was totally unreachable from the chaos of the real world. This was it and it was pretty good.

I was longing for the perfect picture I had in my head though – moments torn between, this was it – and was this it? I would have loved to do a trip down the whole of this river but the dream I'd created back home never quite came to fruition when put it into practice, be it financially, logistically or even having the nous on how. I was in the Amazon, somewhere I'd always wanted to go, and I wanted something else. The GBH was part of it, but now I had to make sure I got into the jungle.

The Jungle – best served chewing bark 24.6.16.

Money talks in Bolivia, and although I don't like to take advantage of it, I know I won't be back here in this moment. I felt this was my last chance to do it and that I had to do all I could to make this happen; slipping the guy on the Pampas a small fee I hoped would achieve that.

After the dolphins, the boat steered down the river to the mainland. A man wearing a shirt of the tour company asked for me. Unclear of what he said in mumbled Spanish, I jumped into his old battered truck and we bounced along in the suspension-less dirt road back to the nearest town. I was introduced to a friend of his and was told that I would go with him on his boat towards the jungle. Now we're talking.

I boarded another narrow long boat that seemed more used for locals, given the lack of padded seats. In fact there were no seats. Just me, with the friend of the guide who was dressed as a regular civilian but with an Indiana Jones-esque hat who I'd only met five minutes before. A pool of water floated down the boat up to my ankles. Sat on the floor of the boat looking up at crumbling, orange-brown clay river banks of thick jungle. This part of the river was different; wider, dirtier, it was clear how enormous and intimidating the Amazon is. Armed with a satchel which included a sleeping bag and mosquito net, all we had between us was a litre of water and a flashlight; there wasn't going to be any eating. I knew straight away this would be memorable. Out of the boat, we pull it onto dry land and walk towards the dark green jungle canopy as the sun began to set.

After a forty-five-minute walk through the trees, we arrived at a steel-roofed, skinny, wooden, gazebo-shaped house, held up by bamboo and rope. With no walls we approached the house to a warm welcome and small talk with the father of the hut. He was insistent that I swapped shoes with him as my hiking boots weren't appropriate for the giant ants that lay ahead. I had to take his gumboots with no choice or question, a kind gesture to delay potentially being eaten alive by ants which the idea of seeing strangely enthralled me.

As darkness came, I was still so excited to be in the thick of the jungle and have no idea what's in front of me. This was my last point of interaction with civilisation, if this stand-alone hut in the middle of nowhere could be called civilisation, that is. The young boy of the family, being unfamiliar with a white man, was desperate to interact with me and introduced me to the pigs and chickens which freely scuttled around their open-walled living quarters which the family had built themselves under their tin roof. Animals lived amongst the family, the boy threw food scraps to the pigs to scavenge beneath the communal table that's next to their bunk beds.

The flashlights go on as mosquitos and bugs dance in our light and begin to nibble me. Well beyond the point of insect repellent being able to help me, I casually accepted my fate of being eaten alive. My guide pulled me away from the family to sit me down for what was building up to be a father-son conversation to explain what was ahead. Snapping a piece of tree bark into each of our hands, could this be the start of some strange jungle ritual. Will we rub bark on our heads like Rafiki in the Lion King? No, we started to chew the bark and it doesn't taste good, and my facial reactions amused him no end. The next instructions – spit the bark into my hand and mix together with a palm full of cocoa leaves; this wasn't the sweetener I was hoping for which then arrived in the form of baking soda. All mixed together in my mouth I started to chew it like gum. The most abnormal of tastes, sucking the bitter juices from the concoction was an unpleasant effort as the erosive baking soda dripped down my throat. This would clear up any lingering illnesses, and the vapour from my breath would be an insect repellent, along with chain-smoking a pack of twenty cigarettes for good measure. Choking on the tenth cigarette inhaled in nearly as many minutes, I was drastically prompted to grab my satchel and we go, not on a path but into pitch black jungle. Now *this was it*.

Walking in silence so we can listen for animals, occasionally the guide would pause sharply, but subtly to raise his hand like an officer bringing his battalion to a halt. This was all very dramatic as he tilted his head upwards to make an animal call in an attempt to tease an animal closer to us. The idea, he said is to entice a jaguar closer; I chose to ignore the thought that the jaguar may come looking for food to discover us. The first creature we saw was an enormous snake, inches from our feet. Harmless, yet beautiful, and surreal to be so close to such an intense animal. I almost go over on my ankle in the dark down an armadillo hole whilst I kept my head pointed dorkishly upward searching for monkey movement in the tree tops. Flicking our lights on and off we remained silent to try and hear them. There was no path, just fresh animal footprints guiding us through the jungle. It was relaxed, with no sense of feeling forced, yet is immensely intense and my heart is racing.

We walked for four hours up and down hills in the thick dark jungle. I still had the cocoa-bark-baking soda creation in my mouth; we arrived at a small flat area on a hillside and make camp. Clearing fallen leaves and sticks to check for insects, fresh leaves are cut down and laid as a flooring. We attached our mosquito nets to hanging trees for protection, our beds were made. We light a small fire for warmth and to repel bugs. I learned the biggest threat to the Amazon now was not deforestation, but bush fires. A few years ago, thirty kilometres of Bolivian Amazon was destroyed in rapid wildfire after a careless pit fire by visitors. Well done, world.

After a couple of hours' sleep, a morning stroll was up a mountain for sunrise to an incredible explosion of colour with no one for miles but ourselves. Almost romantically, were it not for his hat and stench of tobacco, it was the most brilliant sunrise I'd experienced and an observation point for the damage through the mountains of jungle the fire had caused. It was so dry and the trees are so close, it was fortunate there wasn't more damage.

The morning was spent walking through trees that hadn't been destroyed, hearing of the medicinal cures and plants that were suitable for living and eating survival. While drinking from logs and leaves from the stream water, and chewing bark was appetising and replenishing, we walked past oranges, coconuts and grapefruit trees for a more accustomed and welcomed source of energy as we carried on hiking. This was it – I was loving it. Being miserable in a London office, I had a feeling of what I'd imagined and hoped for behind that desk, and now I was even happier than I'd expected this part of the journey could make me.

This area of the Amazon was sporadically inhabited by tribal families. Despite walking a good twelve hours I didn't come across any. An amazing opportunity missed, but, for tourists to start peeving into their lives could be intrusive and some things on some ventures needed to be left alone. Returning to the family I'd met yesterday for our boat (which was still safely left untouched on dry land), I returned the gumboots and accepted this was as close to an Amazon family as I'd ever be. Just as remote as the tribes, they insisted we stayed for food and eat one of the family's free range, well-cared-for chickens – the same one the boy played with the day before.

Despite their isolation, they became fascinated to know all about me, and their social interaction seemed incredibly similar to normal society which I didn't expect from their isolation – if not friendlier and kinder than your average man! Totally relaxed you would never expect them to have the fear that their home which had no walls, runs the risk of being washed away every wet season from river flooding, or that they hold no prejudices or resentment to the rest of the world. They were completely happy and contented with their remote lives, the opposite to my London.

I left them and jumped onto the boat for one last time. I'd miss getting into boats! Totally fulfilled and more reassured that the things that I had dreamt about when I was at home, were in fact possible. I returned to normality in Rurrenabaque to the news that Britain had voted to leave the EU, questioning the positivity wave I was riding. Having had such simple surroundings in the jungle, not thinking about money, just enjoyment, suddenly my exchange rate had plummeted as a result of this political vote. I was relieved there's a life of innocence somewhere, however remote that may be.

Sucre – best served in a café 27.6.16.

I had planned to go to Central America, from there I would wing it. I knew of places I wanted to visit, destinations that I'd read about over the years but plans were loose other than to attempt to learn the language in Guatemala as soon as I could. Since then, the cheapest and most renowned place to scrub up my Spanish was in the UNESCO heritage city of Sucre. A relaxed, pretty and welcoming city, like a posher Xela, made it easy to take to heart.

Taking on a new language felt like déjà vu after my dislike of uninspired language learning in high school. An enthusiasm for it to aid my travel experience and leave me with an accomplishment would put closure to that disappointment. Months after my first day in Xela, there was still a recurring daily theme – being talked at in Spanish at a million miles an hour, sometimes only picking up a few words, and sheepishly replying with a slow nod, and from there hoping for the best. A third of the Spanish vocabulary is similar to its English equivalent, guess work isn't always a bad option, but grammar is totally different and requires studying.

My time in Granada with a family of young children proved a great learning experience as children's vocabulary isn't complex, so their questions and answers make learning easier and quicker because there are no complicated surprises, other than their cheekiness! However, the father of the home stay in Granada, Juan Carlos's favourite English expression of, 'I am horny' in broken English gave the kids a comical close run! Asking a question even slightly incorrectly can lead to a confused look and humour but it can help you to learn. Saying that I have three wives as opposed to sisters paved the way for me into Juan Carlos' heart along with my attempts to learn new home recipes in the kitchen in Spanish.

Demoralising moments – the anguish of travel which happened a lot when starting out. I hated my school in Granada, it was too quick for me to keep up and being in a group I found it hard to learn and be able to practise. Trying to re-join a conversation when not processing the language quickly enough was like stepping out of a car on a highway; it passed you by and won't wait for you to catch up. A slow week was a long week when pouring money into something that you haven't enjoyed and are alone, especially when your brain was being overloaded with foreign information. It can be exhausting too. I wanted to give up so much but never admitted it to myself. Although, when the information sticks and the phrases you practise lead you to where you want to be, and you learn about a place from a Spanish speaker as I had in the Amazon, the sense of accomplishment was a real ego-boost adding to the adventure. My Indiana Jones-esq tour guide, and me, the plucky non-bilingual sidekick going through the Amazon! To think your language fluency was improving can easily come crashing back down to earth in a moment of utter confusion moments later. In Colombia Duncan, Marius and I spent two hours in Medellin trying to find the right place to buy football tickets in the pouring rain by misunderstanding instructions, while not having a strong knowledge of numbers consistently has led to overpaying for things at times. For the joyfulness of travelling, being misunderstood, or misunderstanding is annoying.

The atmosphere of learning made it fun, just like at school with your mates, if it was going well it helped. Sucre and Xela have so many cafes that after classes, going for a coffee to do homework, it was sociable and fun to meet other students there (who stood out for their pigeon pronunciation before their skin complexion) and practise with them. That was exactly how I met Fiona in Xela. The gringo look was a light bulb for locals to try their luck at practising their English but also to show their willingness to be patient and kind to those who were showing an interest in their country.

Latinos are keen to boast their ability to roll their r's. Even after a day of tutoring from a local, I sounded like an internet dial-up tone. I was certainly more suited to the Guatemalan and Bolivians' slow and clear pronunciation, which made Bolivia an ideal place to learn. Comfort and practicality in gringo trail hostels had made me lazy at times; the essence of 'use it or lose it' kicks in if there's no need to speak Spanish with English help available. I have tried to take every opportunity to learn where I can, say a tour in Spanish when I'll ask them to speak slowly. Often still not being able to understand it, and relying on hand gestures as a way to learn a new word or phrase here and there, an added dimension to the entertainment of a tour! In the jungle for a few days of speaking nothing but Spanish, I picked up loads of new words from such gestures; for animals it was a kindergarten-like session, the result of total immersion which had been the key to sustaining and improving my language skills. I'm not quite sure how people survive here without any basics at all, ignoring ideologies that it's rude not to be able to say 'thank you' or 'please'.

The most enjoyable part of learning Spanish had been the experience of meeting people through the café culture of learning abroad, be it socialising with class mates, tour guides or teachers after excursions, our struggle and achievement. I started without knowing how to order a drink or what certain dishes were; the first attempts were awful but I improved from being around those who do and don't know. Reading menus, trial and error in ordering the wrong food and making a fool of myself had been that learning curve. I spent my last evening in Sucre watching football with a Bolivian I met in the coffee shop whilst I was doing homework that afternoon, who invited me to join him for a beer and a game to practise our English and Spanish. Language is often a barrier and people can be mocked for it, sometimes maliciously. However good my Spanish will get, I would always have a pigeon dialect, meaning I'd sound like an outsider when immersing myself. My teacher for two days in Sucre said I was fluent – I felt it was like my mum telling me I was the real winner at sports day when I finished last, although it was nice to hear a white lie now and then. More often than not with the way Latinos are, I'd found it more of a bridge than a barrier.

Potosi – best served in the mines with soda and dust 28.6.16.

Wealth from the mining industry once placed Potosi as one of the richest cities in South America. It doesn't take a genius, with the poverty here, to figure out that that's no longer the case as Bolivia's mining reserves have fallen behind other global resources. Even though the mines are still fully operational, they're a landmark to understand how they helped the city and Bolivia develop. Having never visited a mine before, I knew it wasn't going to be a comfortable day out.

With a view over the city of Potosi, surrounded by scattered, semi-abandoned rusty equipment like an old Western movie set, it was obvious mining work still goes on in the ghostly location from the huge crater holes where mining work has started. A slow, clogging sound in the background to occasional thundering explosions, I'd invited myself onto a building site for leisure as part of a one-man tour which was awkward, especially as I gawp at the vast operation here.

Entering the mine through a covered hole in the ground, I stepped down an old wooden ladder where the legs split more and more with each step into darkness. Work helmets on, the lack of air and dust made it harder to breathe as if being back up at extreme altitude. The initial danger was the ladder's descending steps only to be followed by crossing over bottomless drops from mining digs which the headlights couldn't see through the old wooden planks; it was a potential death trap.

The claustrophobic experience continued as the mine morphs into an underground maze; the guide and I crawl through the small holes which are created each day by the miners' explosive work. There is no sense of escape or knowing how to get out, pitch dark other than our flashlights and the only sense of direction was by being able to hear the thud of dynamite explosions above us. Dust from the mines falls into our eyes with each eruption. I'd had no idea of where they'd be or how I could get out.

My sensitivity to the surroundings made it an uncomfortable day. Even crawling the tunnels, which felt like exploring were tainted with anxiety; it put into perspective working conditions and how the whole city at one point did this for their whole lives. Only ten years ago, children were banned from working in the mines after an accident when a mine shaft collapsed, killing those inside it. Now it is law to be over eighteen but, as fiercely as people stand by this, there are definitely some people who look, very, very young working in the mine, with or without being covered in soot from head to toe!

Nonetheless, the workers seemed happy and content as they sat with us in the cubbyholes built for their break time, chatting away about everyday topics. I took some sodas to help bridge a gap in the awkwardness of being a tourist visiting their difficult work place, but they were more than content to eat the same cocoa leaf concoction I had in the Amazon for their fuel and to suppress their hunger. Every gulp or bite was taken with a mouthful of dust.

There is no doubt that the miners and Bolivians have it tough. Albeit a 'tourist attraction' this was an extreme situation, but it's so rough, however crucial the mining minerals are for the country. Enjoying their ninety-six per cent alcohol fuel in breaks which tastes like petrol, they put to shame the First World's self-proclaimed hard-working culture. This brings a whole new meaning to it and certainly confirms that, there's always someone else worse off.

Uyuni Salt Flats – best served with salt 29.6.16.

The travel photos of envy seen almost weekly are usually identical but rarely identifiable as to the location. If taken from Bolivia the chances are they're of the salt flats of Uyuni.

Greeted to Uyuni with melted snow, it was the first time it had ever snowed out of season (six months later than expected) and was bitterly cold. A blunt reminder that South American winters are horrid when they want to be. Uyuni, similar to a lot of Bolivian towns, was famous for exporting its resources. Here it's twenty-five thousand tonnes a year of salt to Chile for commercial use (at a ludicrously cheap rate) towards housing and food usage.

Piercingly white, the dense salt floor reflected the bright sun in the bright cold blue sky. The biggest salt flat in the world is a blue and white horizontal landscape as far as can be seen for an area of twelve thousand square kilometres. The day was broken into sections as our first tour stop was the train cemetery. A graveyard for retired eighty-year-old steam trains that were transporters in the past, it's now a deserted playground with climbing frames for tourists to clamber on. Pressed for time I had only taken a one-day tour. I hadn't had a chance to meet people for a while and to be honest, I couldn't be bothered to either. Everyone seems a bit rubbish in comparison to travelling with the GBH. Not really helping myself with my loneliness, sometimes at a big attraction like this, it would be nice to have some company.

Companionship did develop in our group of six during the day as we began to bond at how uninformative and unfriendly our guide was. Our day seemed to be interrupting his 'alone' time as he dropped us at the famous 'Salt Hotel', built entirely of condensed salt to create a solid brick-like structure in the middle of the desert abyss that we stood in. Inside, our Bolivian meal of rice and beans, which I'd had almost every day, was served on a salt-made table; it was a well-insulated room for such a unique building, even if it did smell like a factory. For a tourist destination, it was so cheap here I stocked up on souvenirs, buying bags of salt for my family to then step outside and realise I'm surrounded by twelve thousand kilometres of the stuff, the equivalent of buying sand from the beach.

Then came the part all tourists flock for. By flock – I mean like a zoo. How a salt flat this big can be crowded I was not sure. The salt flats hold a mirror effect, making size seem irrelevant for objects, allowing photographers to try to out-do each other with unique photos. I have carried with me my friend's PG Tips toy chimp since I saw him over a year ago, and chose to send him a photo of the toy chimp towering over me. Sizing up a six-inch monkey to look like it's towering over me, wasn't easy, nor was avoiding other tourists getting in my shot. With the help of my short-term lunch companions from the tour, we struggled to get the right dimensions as we rolled around in salt trying to perfect our pose whilst trying to hold a smile for thirty minutes, while our guide watched our feeble attempts, from the warmth of his car. My teeth were ready to freeze off in the wind chill to match my cracked face in the sun, all for a photograph that everyone had already seen.

These disorienting salt flats suggestively looked as if they go on for hours and hours into nothingness. I was uncertain how our useless driver would find his way back to the town of Uyuni. The sun set with small Andean peaks in the distance. We stopped in the white-salt abyss to watch as the flats reflected the sun, into flowing changing colours around us, creating an iMAX three hundred and sixty degree, breath-taking colour show experience. It was an incredibly intense spectacle to end the day as the colours dimmed; it was time to continue driving through nowhere towards Uyuni with the small collection of friends I'd made in the jeep, through the common ground of it being freezing cold. Making friends on a short tour like today was like meeting people at a staff training day. You became friends for a few hours and then never ever spoke to them again; you moved on. Only a few people really stuck with you emotionally, and time showed who they were and who you wanted them to be. As it got darker, it got colder and I was moving on myself, onto a four a.m. bus to Chile.

Goodbye to Bolivia – best served alone but in good company 30.6.16.

Amidst the varying landscape and with plenty to do there, the people were what I'd recall the most. The importance that the culture of agriculture and mining have to Bolivia could never be ignored. I hardly scratched the surface of the rainforest, where various tribes offer an anthropological world to Amazonian living. The family I met there I wouldn't classify as indigenous by any means, yet they hold an unwavering affection and pride for Bolivia despite being so secluded, especially in comparison with the chaos of La Paz. There are a collection of people living in a type of everyday poverty which was more obvious than any isolation that I saw in the Amazon. A city which was home to the country's first indigenous president, Evo Morales, from rags to riches, he runs the country to a bipolar swing of calamity and calmness.

Popular with the poor because of his roots and plans to nationalise larger corporations, along with his investments for further education, his tendency to take a bribe or imprison anyone against his rule is border-line dictatorship, causing daily protests in the capital. The dictatorship turned many against him as he tried to introduce an extension of his time in office (usually two terms, he's now on his third) to a fourth term. A narrow referendum result backfired with the outcome to 'leave office'. Bolivians love their food without the country being renowned at all for its cuisine. The president's remarks of how eating their beloved fried chicken dinner can turn you into a homosexual or cause baldness created a philosophy of negativity, and stupidity. From a man of humble roots to create that atmosphere brought a sense of being closer to home than I wanted to be. People elected into positions of power have a responsibility to create positivity. The rage and bitterness from the media into people's heads over Britain leaving the EU travelled to

Bolivians asking me my opinion, picking up on how a toxic environment can stick with you for a long, long time in a country. The British were once known for being polite, gentle people which had been turned upside down it seems. I was glad to be thousands of miles away, bullshit like this was why I wanted to leave in the first place. It was only the GBH who turned my head back home.

The kindness and loyalty of Bolivians was what I wished I could take back home, an attribute from travelling I must hold onto – their loyalty to a lunatic president, to holding onto their cholitas for groceries and emotional rants. Even Dona Goitia of the chorizo stand in the market won't sell her legendary recipe to commercial chains. 'Coca-Cola won't sell their recipe so why should I?' she claimed with pride, and a dismissive tone as if it was not even a conversation worth having, for all the money in the world. Staff aren't even allowed to know the recipe, she only allows them to know how to cook it, preserving its unique value and taste.

Their social element and willingness to help was lovely, be it being lost, sorting a tour or learning Spanish in Sucre. They filled my void and willingness to be anti-social as I travelled through Bolivia quicker than I wanted to. Distracting myself from wanting to be alone after Peru, I was lonely and bored, having been in company for three months almost constantly. A change of scenery to a new country could be the kick start for me, especially as it would be so much more developed, potentially easier.

Feeling down post-GBH, the sight of poverty around me in Bolivia had been hard to take. What a brat I was to have complained about my 'hard' life in London and earning my money when it was another stratosphere here, it was my own attitude and those of others that created our own indignation, changing that, was down to ourselves alone. Now it was time to take on the rest of South America, it'd be tough to find more genuine and interesting people than the Bolivians.

Chile

Chile – Best served eating Chorrillana.
- 1 frying steak
- A portion of fries
- 1 egg
- ½ a diced white onion

Oven bake the fries at 200°C for 20 minutes. Cook the onion in butter and flash fry the thinly sliced steak, all in the same pan for 2 minutes either side. Once the fries are cooked, scramble the egg in the same pan as the onion and steak and pour all of the pans content over the portion of fries. Best eaten listening to self-proclaimed injustices in Valparaiso.

Suffering to San Pedro – best served cold 1.7.16.

Heading to the north of Chile, the old bus I took with its windows and doors open throughout as people frequently piled on, was chilly to start with. An evening where the salt flats were having snow again, and travelling through one of the highest deserts in the world at night, made all of these elements unbearably cold.

The steel bus became a fridge, as twenty or so other Bolivians and I wriggled for hours to keep warm. With no chance of sleep, our breath could be seen throughout the night like a mist or fog floating around the bus; condensation quickly froze on the windows. The only moments of warmth on the bus was going for a piss. Painfully cold, the sting of normally having frozen toes became frozen feet which crept up my shins, as I started to believe that I was slowly freezing to death.

The darker it got the more unbearable it was. As the black of night began to change colour to sunrise, our bus dropped us by a single three by three metre brick hut in the middle of nowhere in the ice-dry desert with nothing to see but an unattended lift gate and no fencing – the border. Stepping off the bus with no sense of feeling, my feet weighed like cinder blocks. I had no movement in my joints as I tried to take the steps off the bus. An old lady fell in front of me as she couldn't walk from what must be the same pain. No one was able to help with any speed, as I begged all the layers of clothes I was wearing to try and somehow become warmer. Was it possible to be this cold? What happened to all the lush comfortable buses I'd heard of around South America? This was a living, frozen hell and I now had to wait for this unattended lift gate to open, and from there – I had no idea what was awaiting me on the other side, albeit five metres but a never-ending stare into the cold abyss past the gate which didn't fill me with hope.

My water bottle in my bag had frozen; I'd held the bag all night in desperation for extra warmth. The sun was rising faster now. A lady wrapped from head to toe appeared from the hut and set up a picnic table with a cloth. I couldn't seem to edge to get closer, still frozen to the spot and confused as to whether this was an illusion of warmth as a coffee flask appeared. The crowd from the bus scuttled towards her slowly and paid her for the instant coffee from the flask. An angel had appeared with warmth and been rewarded with a month's trade in five minutes from freezing passers-by!

I knew this bus ride had to end; something must be coming to collect us on the Chilean side of the border. Chile holding 'second-world development' gave me hope of something that wasn't always guaranteed – a hot shower, a warm bed, warmth, please, just any warmth. The sun was painfully rising on the horizon, and this being a desert gave me cruel hope. The salt trains from Uyuni ran all the way to this border; there was life here! So still, so eerie, it felt closer to death than anything else as hours later the border control hut still was unattended, and I'd no more money to pay for instant coffee. Resigned to the cold and hoping it would be over soon, warmth was no better on or off of the bus. Hope was fading and I was not sure what fate I was expecting.

The rusty train track morphed into a gas pipe, a reminder that a more developed world was close and hopefully had warmth.

A moment of salvation, the immigration hut opened! I scuttled to the hut to create a distraction from the freezing cold pain, clinging to the hope that warmth is closer with this movement. Two hours in a customs queue later, which was still freezing cold, formalities get completed and I was back on the bus to the fully risen sun. Transport while travelling can be a chance to see and experience, meet and enjoy amazing things – this journey was torture and something that would stay with me forever. I could never possibly be this cold again.

Arriving at my destination in the late afternoon, the entirety of my remaining journey was in view of scorching desert outside the bus but I was still shivering cold. I walked through San Pedro, a warm, sandy, desert town head to toe in thermals and a coat, looking like I was going on an Arctic exhibition, not to the desert of Atacama.

Atacama – best served with a sandwich 2.7.16.

San Pedro couldn't be less Latino if it tried. With tourists flooding in and out of the one-tiered, flat-roofed housing and tour agency shops which occupied every single allotment, strolling dusty San Pedro's narrow roads was more like an Arabian desert.

Lately I'd been exhausted and after my journey here I was in no mood for thinking for myself so opted out from independent travel. I was willing to pay for some comfort and warmth. Flute players busked on the streets to the tune of tourists buying excursions, to their tune I bought a tour to see the Atacama Desert. Albeit tacky, this totally different bubble was a welcome new experience, but I assumed that Chile was an easier country to travel. A go-to meal of a sandwich was popular here, and sandwich cafes were as frequent as tour operators in San Pedro. A quick bite in, or to be taken away, it was ideal for the working-culture which the area lived off, and for tourism, and ideal for me to grab a quick meal before I headed off to Valle de la Luna, a short journey from San Pedro.

In Valle de la Luna (The Valley of the Moon) I went from being in a bubble to a different planet. The vast, orange dusk of never-ending spiky varying desert landscape, as far as could be seen, overlooked a towering grey volcano that pumped out sulphur. Only the volcano offered any similarity to the deserted sense of living here. I had seen a lot of desert and barren land lately, and here was the ultimate sense of everlasting nothingness. Gazing into a visual chasm, our outing involved crawling, scrambling and sliding through multi-mineral cracks and craters, some a few metres, others up to three-hundred-metres-deep, seemingly endless on the horizon but vertically deep into the abyss. The surrounding landscape was constantly changing from the wind blowing sand and dust, but the materials that made up the rock had constant chemical reactions in the wind, rain, heat and sun bringing salt crystals to the top, creating 'snow cap' looks on the peaks – the illogicality on top of dusty, bone dry peaks of heat.

Despite no sign of wildlife or civilisation in the desert, the sight of cyclists riding through was terrifying and bonkers; watching people riding into nowhere, covered in sand and dust, was mad to me but strangely inspiring. The Pan-American highway was a popular route for cyclists; with destinations such as this, creating an interesting way to travel. Travelling a lot on buses takes its toll physically and is unexpectedly draining; this was a new level of adventure. I met one cyclist here who had started in Alaska and would end in Patagonia to raise money for charity. The dry heat was brutal on the skin and the constant need to drink was overwhelming. I was not even on a bike.

Climbing a sand dune for a view of the sunset was a nice way to end the afternoon. Sat on the rim of a dune on my own, away from the noise of tour crowds, was quiet. I could see people a hundred metres away but could barely hear my own voice in the deafening unknown silence of desert. There was just noise ringing in my ears from being on so many consecutive buses. Too much moving around can take the fun out of travelling from place to place. Looking out at a desert to see every angle of my view changing and know it always would be in the climate which consumes Atacama. I was tired but happy and felt that when I did have to return to London, I'd be mentally in a better place, in part from knowing that I'd learnt the importance of slowing down.

Science and Stars – best served with reflection 2.7.16.

The Southern Hemisphere is established as the better half of the world to stargaze. Whether I'd been told a lie and was easily persuaded or not, San Pedro seemed one of the best areas with several space stations to view stars. The multiple stations offered different options for viewing.

Not knowing what to expect, if I could've imagined a professional stargazers image, the 'comic book guy' from the show *The Simpsons* would have been a guess, and that's who I got. An enthusiastic, nerdy, obese Chilean, whose passion and enthusiasm for something I knew absolutely nothing about, must have made him feel that his time and efforts were wasted. I trip over his twelve thousand dollar, six-foot tall telescope – his pride and joy on the brink of being damaged did open up an opportunity for us to bond, albeit for a short time, he probably wanted to kill me. I failed to convince him that with hindsight there was a funny side to the episode.

Openly and comically explaining how girls don't find 'star-nerds' impressive, I was inundated with his knowledge, although perhaps my lack of knowledge, made that easy for him. Seeing a star with the naked eye, then looking through his equipment to see a sky of glitter, a milky way comparable to a rainbow above us, and planets of all colours, lines and glory as if from a pamphlet was amazing. It was humbling to learn of how far away they are in year's worth of travel, just a spec on the eye and significantly bigger than planet Earth. Today had put our size and significance into perspective for me. This hilarious star genius had accidently convinced me about ideas I have had in the back of my mind, scrambled in the rest of its confusion, and cleared their way to the surface for me.

Our size and significance to the universe are so small – desert or sky. As the world makes its best attempt to environmentally and politically self-implode, we are all comparatively just small specks of shit spinning around on a rock. The level of science is all so far over my head, how there are equations for it, I'll never know. That evening was another new experience for me, which for many is what spurs people on to travel. Some new experiences, like feeling I may die of cold on a bus are not great experiences, yet the collective emotion in my head is that this journey, now that I'd slowed down, is a positive one.

Having been away for over six months, I'd enjoyed myself when looking ahead to this trip, when it seemed so hard to accomplish, when feeling sorry for myself; with hindsight that was a laughable thought process. I was not racing to get to the GBH, or keeping busy to try and distract myself; this trip had probably restored my faith in the world. This fucked-up world which drove me insane, where my sizeable significance to this universe is hysterically insignificant.

I think that we'd all be a lot better off if we tried to get along and act on things that we actually want to be part of. Had I not come away or done this as I have, both through logic and gut, I'm convinced I would have resigned myself to be forever miserable and to chase something I didn't have. I would have found a poor excuse to not carry on with the GBH, as a way of hurting myself too.

The charity cyclist who was in my room and his bike have gone. Just like the feeling from staff training day, easy come easy go. I didn't bat an eyelid. Perhaps I was controlling my thoughts better; I was not looking for something I thought I needed or wanted any more – I was content.

Valparaiso – best served admiring houses with a plate of Chorrillana 5.7.16.

The twenty-four-hour bus ride from San Pedro to Valparaiso via Santiago, through even more desert on one road, was close to a new, albeit an uninspiring and unwelcome record for me of time spent on a bus. The straight Pan-American highway runs down the length of the country, the proverbial 'spine' of the continent. One long road.

Valparaiso is a shipping city, the port of the city's bay is shaped like a shoehorn with ships, containers and cranes. There are forty-three hills in Valparaiso with buildings (all of which are homes or once were) squeezed together at the most impossible of angles. Hillsides of varying heights and degrees, are accessible by steep walking or taking the picturesque cable cars which have accidently led them to be a touristic excursion, providing panoramic views over the centre.

The city grew from the docks, further and further up the hills, with no urban planning, allowing houses and neighbourhoods to develop very unique characteristics. People built them exactly how they wanted; creating a multi-coloured, French bohemian cartoon with crooked windows and steel walls. Squeezing in between what seemed, on reflection, impossibly small gaps, at impossible stilt-supported angles, on the hills piled on top of one another. Some are even built in a ship-shape as a tribute to the city's port which holds the history as to why these settlements came to Valparaiso in the first instance.

The dockyard prior to the Panama Canal was a shipping hub for South America with Europeans coming to Valparaiso and Chile. This is why Chileans, especially central Chile to the south, have paler skin compared to the north which reflects neighbouring Bolivia and Peru. The varied European-bohemian housing reputation that it built for itself makes Valparaiso unique and a destination for immigrants. It's multicultural, so easy to settle in with friendly people who naturally create a welcome atmosphere. Naturally it's developed as an enticing tourist spot and place to live. Not long ago it was made a UNESCO heritage site, to safeguard the style of the housing and their layout, which are the prominent visual characteristics of the city and stand out compared to other cities I'd ever visited.

Valparaiso is certainly a worthwhile destination for tourists, usually a sign that it'll be easy to meet people, but here it doesn't seem so. Sat in my hostel and having not spent much time with anyone other than myself or people passing on tours, I sat with a bottle of Chilean wine and a book in the communal area to meet people. The change of dynamic in travelling from previous experiences was the accessibility of having a phone, a tool to bring people together. The culture of relying on and using a phone, as opposed to socialising, was new to me travelling. It was a boring habit in comparison to meeting new people from all over the world, making friendships, exploring, let alone drinking the amazing wine, the best alcohol so far on the continent. There is only so much effort someone can make to be sociable with people who only want to stare at their phones; it's a bottle of wine for one in Valparaiso, I was happy to avoid being so obviously anti-social.

Valparaiso was a key line for the growth of Chile as its exporting of minerals has helped the country become rich, only for the brutal dictatorships of the 1970s–90s to crush any fair distribution in Valparaiso and Chile. Many locals feel this is still the case today. Local frustration during this time was creatively expressed with artistic paintings, similar to Bogota; as a period of political demonstration in a positive and creative manner. Resultantly, after the dictatorship, the city cemented its artistic and bohemian identity globally, and the money from both UNESCO and the flourishing tourism is a result of that which helps them to live a life beyond their reliance on shipping.

This is a beautiful city with its enticing architecture and culture crying out to be explored. Walking through its steep undulating hills, no road, house or building was the same; it was impossible to be bored when there was a view in each corner of the eye. I would certainly live here: the people, the food, the views. The freethinking locals were so friendly as the abundance of independent cafes and handicraft shops always resulted in long, welcoming conversations with locals who were keen to make a genuine impression on the tourists.

There is still so much history here and a stroll by the port into a dockhand's bar for a traditional feed of chorrillana and music was entertaining and insightful. The chorrillana is a pile of chips served with onion and scrambled egg, mixed together with a steak on top – a hearty meal, what every worker wants at the end of the day. The local dish doesn't try to hide that this is still unquestionably a workers' city. It was served with a beer in a smoky, sticky-floored bar with no light. Photos of workers from decades gone by and beer coasters plaster the walls. A stench of mouldy beer and oil from the workers' clothes wafted around the room, and an accordion played a slow, sad tune of cynicism about their home and country.

Grieving about the lack of fair distribution of wealth outside of their nation's capital, it was obvious as the infrastructure needs reinforcing and more jobs need creating off the back of a very poor quality of education – a catalyst for negative knock-on effects. The sense of self-entitlement, albeit to a legitimate argument, struck a chord for me. Moaning about the number of stray dogs everywhere walking the streets (stepping in dog shit is standard whilst looking up at rickety housing), the habitants of the city are culpable for their mating as they feed them. Building homes illegally on unstable land causes accidents. A government benefits system, which is constantly exploited, gave me an unhealthy reminder that not only are the UK and First World lacking in a sense of responsibility for themselves, but the Second World is too. The grass when looking abroad maybe wasn't as green on the other side as I'd first thought.

Santiago – best served being cultural after a fish market 9.7.16.

The snow-covered Andes surround the city, engulfing everything in the intense pocket of action which Santiago breathes.

The viewpoint, Carrera Santa Lucia in the city centre, has a three-hundred-and-sixty-degree viewpoint of the city, showing how intense the fog is from the lack of climate shift available due to the city's position by the mountains. I hated the cold and grey English winters: they were depressing and draining while the Chilean winter is crisp yet sunny and dry during the day. The city's huge reliance on cars drives the fog into a smog and into the top five of the most polluted cities in the world. With low key governmental plans to tackle this, Chileans are encouraged by the authorities to have fewer BBQ parties at their homes during the Copa America tournament. A tradition which echoes the Super Bowl parties in America, the opposite then happens, to be topped off by the country winning the cup resulting in more parties than ever before in their wild celebrations.

From neighbouring Valparaiso, Santiago boasts admirably similar characteristics with its multi-cultural and cosmopolitan infrastructure with its immigrants and of course the Spanish heading inland from the port town. Walking down all the quieter streets of the city where a French-styled chateau would stand next door to a Spanish-colonial styled house. Santiago is the power house and epicentre of Chile, a South American heavyweight with regards to economic impact without any hesitancy to be diverse, but pride to maintain their cultural heritage and not showing any need to change that.

Central Market, aptly in the middle of the city, boasts the best seafood to eat in or take away. The paila marina, seafood soup, is the most popular dish, showcasing their quality seafood all mixed together into a soup, as a meal for any occasion, served in restaurants for the more elegant or on a bar stool next to the fishmongers for those who want the smell of fish behind them to add to the spicy aroma of the dish.

The fruit markets offered a global variety of fruit, most of which is imported as Chileans thrive off the south of the country's agriculture, predominantly potatoes. Yes, the Incas made it to Chile! With the Asian and American restaurants being everywhere, it was no surprise that the rat race of self-titled, 'Sanhattan' (from Manhattan) finance district, flowed into the bars at night where the atmosphere was unusually lively midweek, yet relaxed with a feel of togetherness as strangers happily sat and mix with other groups of partyers and joke with one another. Sharing Chilean wine, which I was falling in love with more and more each day, there was no turning back from here as I looked ahead to my next stop Argentina.

The Chilean's unshakeable spirit was thrust in front of me in Santiago with impressive historical landmarks of their triumphs through adversity. A national dictatorship from 1973–1990 which I knew nothing about prompted me to visit a museum, something I could often be bored of doing before I gave it a go. The timescale mirrored the generation that I was born into, the horror they lived through made it stupidly obvious as to why Chileans are so tough. Political leadership crushing culture and civilisation which made the culture of the Valparaiso era more inspiring, manipulating the media and murdering innocent people on top of those who were outspoken, mixed with thousands of disappearances – the harrowing memories are very real and fresh for Chileans and will no doubt create a precedent as to how they hold themselves out to others for generations to come. Missing notes and letters from children pleading to find their parents, lovers begging for help to find each other, were only a small taste of the cruelty of the dictatorship and the media enforcement to create fear and lies which brought a country to its knees.

I thanked my ignorance for having zero knowledge about this before visiting Chile. Following the news back home and the goings-on was a guilty pleasure, a self-sabotage for bad news. Here, not quite knowing where to look and a language barrier, meant that it could be followed in snippets. It was easy to avoid and easy not to get sucked into, unlike at home where it feels all-pervading and suffocating, especially when it's news you don't want to hear. As a guest in their country, I took an interest but enjoyed being able to switch off from the never-ending drum-bashing of negativity and factual lies that so much media is based on, and the dictatorship here thrived off.

Even the celebrity-craving people thrive on so much is insufferable. I finished writing this anecdote as a man walked into the café and sat on the stool next to me. Suddenly every set of eyes in the restaurant were on us and we were overwhelmed by gasps and flashes from phone cameras. They couldn't be taking pictures of me. I was no longer the white man who was a shock to most people, although it seemed that it helped to get me served a lot more quickly. While I had absolutely no idea who the guy sat next to me was, I could enjoy my wine next to someone who was apparently famous.

Leaving Chile – best served looking forward 11.7.16.

Latinos on the continent don't hold flattering opinions of Chileans – arrogant, rude, self-entitled. Bolivians have a fair crack at them (and rightly so even according to Chileans) after Chile 'stole' post-war Bolivia's access to the coast limiting their exportation opportunities. This still limits Bolivia today but it was the manner that irks them most, even Peruvians feel they stole the claim of inventing the famous pisco sour drink. As a result, Chileans don't have many friends, yet from the moment I arrived I had nothing but the opposite. My time here was far too short but each day I only felt Chileans' positivity, warmth and kindness, not in a desperate way. People are glad to meet you in a way that isn't cringe: they meet you, accept you affectionately and carry on.

Although in just that manner Chile is not a country that *needs* you – as an individual or a tourist, they can survive just fine without you. Their tenacity to go through awful events such as the dictatorship, which was long enough ago now that the country is no longer recognised as a dangerous, unstable place. Being back on their feet they can hold their own and more. Proud and boastful (a fine line that brands them arrogant) they celebrate what they've come through from the mining accident in 2010 when the workers showed their immeasurable resilience, to their Copa America heroics. Their star player, born into poverty during the dictatorship, never owned a pair of shoes as a child, yet helped his country win back-to-back titles, as the underdogs. Examples of herculean efforts and strength, and they have every reason to be proud and let you know all about it – especially when modern First World countries continue their sense of entitlement from living off pioneering achievements hundreds of years ago.

Chile is now in fantastic shape after their troubles. Intelligent infrastructural designs have proved worthwhile, while within recent years, new architectural builds withstood an earthquake of 8.8 on the Richter scale. (One Richter more than Ecuador was hit by in the spring.) This small change to their old buildings has saved the city millions, and their drink, the terremoto, the earthquake cocktail, is to celebrate this. Mixing ice cream, grenadine and cheap white wine together, after one or two your legs feel wobbly like there's an earthquake!

The demand for marijuana has been recognised and now it's legal to hold possession of a small amount and smoke it privately – strengthening the economy and limiting drug cartels. This is a recent idea adopted in certain American states as well, with much success and support. Willingness to adapt and modernise laws and culture responsibly as rebuilds from a dictatorship is inspiring as the country now sits on the brink of holding First World status.

The multicultural food is excellent and merits the First World, first-class status that's pending. With a variety on every corner Chile is open-minded and it's an attractive trait for a country to have. Proud of their market traditions, traders in Santiago bring in almost any fruit from every corner of the world, yet, true to their roots, refused to upgrade the market hall last year to maintain its authenticity and avoid any potential toxicity of a corrupt investment.

The cosmopolitan vibe here, mixed with Latino fire and spirit was so enticing, with small similarities to England – especially London and Santiago. There was a natural pull for me here with their forward thinking: the government recently introduced an entrepreneurship scheme called 'start-up Chile' to encourage more businesses to grow in the city, boosting the economy further. The food suits that culture of working, be it the on-the-go café-style of pick up a sandwich or hot dog, or feeding the dockyard men with a hearty feast, they work hard and eat what suits them. They are proud of their markets and what they stand for. The financial hub of the country, the city-slicker, rat race types, still go out and mix together to get along. They are friendlier here; testament to my peeve of why can't everyone try and get along a bit more? It's a testimony to their character of using their negative experiences in a positive way to make their lives better.

The length of Chile is almost geographically exactly what I'd previously travelled since December. From what I'd seen in Latin America, and to then go from the deserts, the star gazing, to see the Andes surrounding the huge capital city was energising. Chile was now what I imagined Colombia may well be in fifteen years' time. Venezuela is a country I missed. Dogged by brutal and violent troubles at the moment it could hopefully follow Chile's path too, should the timeline of history on the continent be anything to go by as a judge.

The first Chilean I met in the country (after having met several charming residents on my travels) was the customs official at the cold border of Bolivia. He could see I was freezing cold, and he pulled me aside to question me over accidently having an apple in my bag to add tension to the physical state I was in. As customs officials go, he compared having the piece of fruit in my possession as the same as holding a bomb. A serious but unnecessary statement, his line of duty still allowed him to squeeze in his opinions on football in Chile to me. Polite throughout, he shared his love of Chilean wine, while casually mentioning, in between asking me about Brexit, how the apple would be 'destroyed'. As I left he gave me a big bear hug in sympathy for how cold I was and in appreciation for our small talk. As he squeezed me in his arms, he whispered in my ear, 'Fuck Europe, come to Chile where the people and money is strong'. Chile is a lot like home, strong, vulnerable – his advice is very tempting.

Argentina

Argentina – Best served eating a Malbec-infused meat stew.
- 1 carrot
- handful of green beans
- ½ a white onion
- Mixed herbs
- 220g stewing steak
- 2 large glasses of red wine
- a chunk of crusty bread

Slice the onion and carrots and take the tips off the green beans, cut the meat into 2" chunks and throw into a casserole dish whilst pouring in the wine. Cook for 5 hours at 220°C and serve with the bread. Eaten after a wine tour hangover in Mendoza.

Ushuaia – best served at the end of the world 13.7.16.

After a day killing time in Buenos Aires following a twenty-four-hour bus ride from Santiago (every bus journey now approaches the 24-hour time frame), I flew down to Ushuaia in Patagonia – the end of the world. Winter there made land travel slower and more difficult logistically; it would take five days to get the bus there and neither time nor money was on my side. Ushuaia is the most southern city in the world and a departure point for expensive cruises to Antarctica. More commonly this is a gateway to hikes, of which there are plenty in the area, as well as being a stone's throw away from the border with Chile, which the region of Patagonia crosses into.

The Martial Glacier was one of those accessible hikes nearby while a lot of hiking routes were closed, due to the heavy snow and ice this winter. Hiking up the ski slope which leads to our destination, the crunchy thick snowed path was our route as the peaks peeping over the horizon were the huge glacier; the black and white and grey sketched into the white slopes was our icy eye line. Through the snow I continually sank in up to my shins; a step forward was a step back as the snow sledged you backwards down the hill, through the frosted trees. It was a winter wonderland. Cold breath from climbing the hill was perhaps not a fair reflection that, although it's cold, the Antarctica climate I'd expected in being so close to the south pole in reality wasn't so bad.

The viewpoint as the glacier plateaus was amazing, a gorgeous panoramic view over Ushuaia. Looking down over where I had walked up to, the glacier looked over the city and into the bay of Ushuaia from the mountains. The port's bay water was flat, shining with colours from the ice; a small city continuing its normal life. A blur of movement and in front of calm waters, the view of the end of the world was special. Taking in the view, despite having walked further away from the most southern point, I had again ticked off something from the bucket list – to have reached the bottom of the world and travelled the length of Latin America, and now I was looking over it. The passport stamp for 'Puerto de embarcacion Antarctica – fin del mundo' was my documented proof!

An obvious tourist destination, it was exuberantly expensive as my money was now running out, the currency exchange was now awful and my thoughts go back to how the countries before Chile were so cheap. Here I was paying over five dollars for a coffee as opposed to a couple of cents. Wealthy, adventurous tourists who visit here are leaving for the Arctic, the monopoly of the remote excursion business and location means there was not a lot that could be done to avoid paying through the nose. When looking at a world map, let alone of South America, the isolation, despite its accessibility it's obvious how remote this part of the world is, and how far it is from other large cities. The extortionate price of a postage stamp to send a postcard highlights this for me, yet it's actually a fair price due to the isolated location costings.

Exploring affordable options in Ushuaia and around was my only option for pricing myself out of a trip to the Antarctic; even trying to get on a cargo boat was overpriced, being thousands of dollars, regardless Ushuaia has plenty on offer. Looking at the bay it's the array of naval carriers harboured up at the end of the world that holds great importance today as well as in the past. Boats as early as 1520 sailed here and the Spanish invaded in 1888. They would crash on exploratory voyages to the Antarctic and around the Peninsula Mitre just off Ushuaia. Locals share stories of heroics and tragedy in attempts to save victims in the freezing waters. The prison in Ushuaia was first created with cruel intentions through the punishing cold winters, the idea being, to colonise convicts in abandonment and well out of the way of the rest of society. Darwin's crusade on HMS Beagle passed through these waters; the Beagle Channel is now named after the vessel; it's a good job there was no accident that time. There are stories of other explorers and geniuses who these waters may have consumed.

The boats which float in the water now, in comparison with the antique photos of the ships that used to sail these shores, are incomparable. From weakly-built wooden boats with sails, to the steel monsters harboured now – these look like they could plough through anything of potential destruction in comparison. It is incredible what was discovered on the old vessels and how their recordings were so accurate without today's modern technology. The sacrifice and audacity of such voyages in the conditions faced perhaps stand as the most undervalued and unappreciated pieces of discovery I came across.

National Park Tierra del Fuego – best served eating an asado 14.7.16.

The national park is a gem of Argentina and one of the most famous in the world. Free entry was a welcome surprise to my wallet that was now scraping the barrel and made it all the more appealing. The time lapse here meant that daylight hours are limited. I left at nine a.m. in the dark and arrived at the park to the white snow and frost-covered woodland in a beautiful dawn-breaking light.

I paused in the shade with the sun breaking through the mist, I was engulfed by the snowy mountainous landscape and it was freezing; finally, the climate I'd expected had arrived. Prepared for the cold, taking layers of clothes off to put more on, was a cold and lonely experience. After a few hours of walking solo in the park I still hadn't seen anyone else in the wintry woodland. The park's lakes are a spectacular channel crossing, most of which are frozen over and several paths are paved out to explore. Walking at pace seems a logical option to try and keep warm, more haste less speed soon rings true as I discarded my unreliable and undetailed map to find myself lost in the thick forest and I hit a fence which stretched a long distance with clear marking of 'no trespassing'. The path had disappeared. Caught up in magnificence and enjoying the sparkle of frost, I was cold and well aware that being lost and alone here would result in abandonment and not being able to get the last bus back. The paranoia about freezing to death crept in. At least it would be in some kind of beautiful woodland paradise.

Historical tribal communities referred to as the Yamons showed evidence of bodily abnormalities and sheer tribal instincts. Hunting deer and geese for food, I missed out on seeing geese as I tried to make the best of being lost. I found a path and walked aimlessly, and hoped I'd get my bearings again at some point. How the Amazon and jungle provide so much opportunity for sustainable and living for tribes, how they survived the winters with their cave-man lifestyles with nearly no clothing when everything is frozen, even the dung and manure – I don't know.

The Yamon people and their hunting skills offer the region one of its most traditional feasts – the lamb asado, when a lamb is gutted and spread on stakes standing upright over coals to cook for hours while gathering around the fire for warmth. That warmth could have come into good use. While becoming a little more anxious the more I thought of the Yamons, I came across the single lane road that ran through the park and I was able to vaguely orientate myself to hitch-hike a lift back to Ushuaia just as the sun began to set and it got even colder. I was relieved to be leaving before I froze, despite having perhaps not been able to make the most of the day, from my mistake of getting lost.

My last evening at the end of the world was spent with a bottle of wine and an 'all you can eat' lamb asado (BBQ grill) which the Yamons made legendary across the world. It was my first proper chance to have Argentine red meat, which the country is famous for, and I was certainly not disappointed. I could now imagine how tribal families would huddle around the tipi shaped grilling stands for heat whilst they ate. The imagery of simmering coals in a background of snow is a symbol of strength for survival in the cold conditions.

The end of the world was a destination I had desperately wanted to visit, and travelling the length of the continent, I felt, was my own satisfying accomplishment for my travel bug. A bug that I will never get rid of. Having been so close, I wanted to get to the bottom of the world one day, to Antarctica. As I headed back north, to leave one of the most spectacular places I'd ever been, out of the plane window were the enormously intimidating, spectacular Andes. I had seen the Andes a lot on my route here but the view from above was incredible, another view and another moment that I'd been blown away by over the last week. Back to the 'real world' of city life in the capital, Buenos Aires.

Buenos Aires – best served till the morning 20.7.16.

Stepping off the bus to the hostel from the airport, I was thrown into sneaky city tricks. As I walked to my hostel, dirty water was sprayed from above onto my hat, trickling down my neck and all over my bag. It smelt of mouldy vinegar and looked like ink. Not knowing what had happened, I stopped to clean myself as two women insisted on helping me. Whilst one lady started talking to me, the other was on her phone to what must have been a friend, their conversation in Spanish developed and they were trying to organise to rob me.

Unbeknown that I understand Spanish, they claimed a bird had shat on me and they wanted to help clean me up. I pushed my way out from them as they stood together to block my path in the main road of Buenos Aires' shopping district. I angrily stormed towards a café over the road. There was not a lot I could have done to avoid the situation, but grateful the draining Spanish lessons had been useful to some degree to navigate this issue. Those tedious days, working in the class room, that I didn't think would pay off, have done, for this occasion at the very least.

I had planned to arrive in Buenos Aires in time to meet a friend from SBA, Duncan, so we could travel Argentina together before going to Brazil. With friends being reunited, a couple of beers are never far away, and excellent wine was taken full and heavy advantage of. Buenos Aires' nightlife is renowned for being lively. We arrived at our hostel's drinks party already well inebriated at ten p.m. to find out that clubs didn't open till two a.m., – our deterioration had begun. The slippery slope of continuing to get more and more trashed on the best cheap wine I'd ever had, resulted in a heavy night of partying and crawling home at eight a.m. The next day, it was a day wasted being wasted, but worth it. The cliché of a city never sleeps, was completely accurate for Buenos Aires. Even at seven a.m. there were bars to go to for a drink, a bite to eat, tango and theatre shows; it was endless and made it the best nightlife scene in the world for me.

Cycling a hire bike to explore the city the next day still hungover was a wobbly idea but having craved a bit more First World development and comfort, cycling around Buenos Aires was similar to a major European city. Wide roads and safe cycle lanes, Latin America had been fast forwarded to modern day Europe while it kept its air of personality and Latino identity. The Parisian-style tall buildings and architecture and the large Italian population living here, most restaurants are Italian, as opposed to the stereotypical steak houses. Italian migrants mixed their pizza dishes with the nationals' love of cheese creating the Fugazzeta pizza – a local favourite of a cheese and onion stuffed pizza crust, with no tomato base, just cheese. Even more cheese is layered like a pie, adding another heavy and rich dish to the Buenos Aires cuisine philosophy they have and share with Europeans.

Peddling through all the pricey districts of Buenos Aires, glittered with lavish and grand government buildings, the cold spring weather shook off my hangover. A strange remedy for a hangover perhaps wasn't the main attraction on the Northern part of the city, the Recoleta Cemetery. A graveyard where aristocrats spend up to five hundred thousand dollars buying grave plots to then have architects design tombs for their deceased loved ones. Some tombs are bigger than dorm rooms I'd stayed in and even have elevators, designed like a model village it's creepily eerie for this 'attraction' to be a spot where people mourn, but also celebrate, as is the case with Argentina's beloved Evita being memorialised here.

A heroine of Argentina and the world, Evita is only out-shone by football god, Diego Maradona. The old stomping ground for El Diego in the Boca district is the home for this football-fanatic country's biggest football team, Boca Juniors. The adoration in Boca for the club is painted in broad daylight with the striking blue and yellow club colours on tin housing in the district. Tango dance classes take place on the cobbled streets as collages line the walls and the club souvenir sellers trade hats, shirts and scarves on the shady roads which lead up to their coliseum-like stadium that the team play in, their mecca and focal point of Boca. There wasn't a game on, yet there was still a relaxed and sociable atmosphere in the streets with locals enjoying the endless meat grill restaurants available throughout the coloured streets of Boca that provide their social meeting point.

With no football on, there was the chance to watch Argentina's only professional rugby team, the Jaguars, play as our 'pre-nightclub' entertainment. Recently turning professional, the sport is finding its feet amongst the fickle population of Argentina. The premier Southern Hemisphere competition of the Super18 in the empty stadium was a silent atmosphere in comparison with the energy in Boca for football. The public announcement system awkwardly booming out Jaguar roars in an attempt to create an atmosphere but punters are more interested in the 'hot dog at the ball game' like atmosphere and food offering runs all over the world. Delicious choripan-sausage sandwiches with chimichurri sauce post-game create more excitement for locals in the cold than the sport. Stick to what you know best I guess!

The European behavioural influence of being fickle, grumpy and temperamental was obvious with the locals. The infrastructure, the mannerisms of the locals, all the way to the fashion sense is incredibly familiar, but their pessimistic outlook is the obvious European trait they have. The locals are disappointed with the recent change in government as they feel that further corruption holds the country back each day. Inflation is stuck at ten per cent at the moment, giving me little ground to complain about how much more expensive it was here or about my First World problems or moaning how much or little I felt I should have earned back home. There was an air of defeatism to the establishment already, tepid daily demonstrations look in vain.

A city which feels and looks like a superpower is in fact severely handicapped and deflated until night time, when it explodes with carefree energy, as if it could take on the world. A loyalty that can't be broken, for the parillo meat grills serving up juicy steaks and endless carvings of meat which host the traditional family Sunday meal. With the good food and wine, there's enough to keep the locals happy and occupied in a city declaring that 'God is Argentine, but he serves in Buenos Aires', a phrase coined from the centralisation of politics in the capital compared to the rest of the country, but for me it was about the steak.

Mendoza – best served with wine 23.7.16.

A region with some of the finest wine in the world wasn't the postcard picture of old Argentinian vineyards I'd imagined. There were no elderly couples romantically cycling around tasting wine out of their bicycle baskets through the Andean vineyards. Instead there was loud traffic that woke you to a gritty, dirty city that was aggressive on the eye: graffiti tags on incomplete construction work, open drainage which dropped six feet into the ground, potholes in the road were more like cement craters which are covered by freight pallets for walkways. In comparison to Buenos Aires' elegance, perhaps this was a more honest version of Argentina's cities.

There was a one-hour journey out of Mendoza to Maipu where bodegas (wine villas) and vineyard aisles line up towards the more scenic landscape of the Andes mountains on the horizon. There were overpriced tour options taking you from bodega to bodega, I opted instead for the more realistic and affordable backpacking version – I hired a worn out rusty bike with Duncan and two random travellers that we'd met in the dorm. With a fixed basket fastened to the bike, perhaps we were going to be that romantic Argentine image I had in my head. The four of us combining different routes and ways on how to do our own tour, with a lack of signage and overshooting our bus stop on the bus to start our tour, our day started late, lost, and more desperate for a glass of wine that wine tasting obliges. For all of the technology, advice you could take on board, things you could read about on how to do something, nothing could beat going and finding out yourself and just winging it. Glued to the gringo trail, being herded on a route or a way on how to do something can take away the adventure of going with your gut into the wild.

We stopped off in four different bodegas, from a five-star resort-come-winery experience, sampling any three wines we wanted for a very reasonable price, to sitting with an elderly, wine-shrivelled-faced Argentine on a wine barrel on the front porch of his tiny wine shop as he freely passed around free bottles of wine for us to swig from. All of this in between cycling around twenty-five kilometres during the day, getting lost, the day became a fun ordeal. My quintessential day bike riding, with my bottle of wine and sandwich in my basket, I was merrily peddling with wine legs along the loud, dirty highway of trucks driving past, holding on for dear life. Pulling into the vineyard I celebrated the achievement of not being killed, in wonderful silence. Looking at the vineyards growing, relaxed in a chair with the sun on my face, laughing awkwardly at who came closest to being hit by a van on the bypass that we had cycled along. I struggled amidst my drunken ways to digest whether the GBH would love this or not, drinking in the sunshine and a bike ride sounds lovely, drinking wine she probably wouldn't like, next to a motorway on an unstable bike was a reality she, along with others, may struggle with.

The suburban attitude was more hospitable compared to the rush of a city. They want you to stay and enjoy yourself. Of course we were paying for glass upon glass of Malbec, but offers of free, baked Argentine empanadas to line the stomach were a nice touch. Uniquely, locally reared beef marinated in chimichurri, sweet potato and cheese – I didn't mind cycling through traffic for. Their lifestyle motto in the Mendoza area that we were in is 'wake up, love life, love wine' – they love their lives and I may be drunk, but I love you. The two travellers accompanying us seemed to be having less love for each other as they start to drunkenly bicker, meanwhile Duncan and I seemed to be peddling slower and slower with each glass we drink, as our day boils to an end of swerving cars and trucks, in the dark, as we drunkenly pedalled as quickly as we could, to return the bikes – the glory of hiring bike.

With a hangover to boot, there was ample to see outside Mendoza and as ever the Andes are obviously available here for adventurous trips in this huge country. The lazy, therapeutic option of thermal pools in Cacheuta close to the city was the leading candidate. Wine tasting was fun, but drunk cycling was hard and I was now retiring in a drunken defeatist fashion from heavy excursions. Cacheuta is a tiny town buried in the mountains, the perfect place to sit and take in the beautiful views that surround Mendoza, nursing a follow-up glass of red with a Mendoza-Malbec meat stew. The baths were packed with screaming obese children (probably too much red meat) as it was the school holidays, in murky-gross waters; it was a steamy room of hell but awkwardly faultless before another long bus ride back to the capital and its pandemonium with a belly full of wine.

The Steaks of Argentina – best served medium rare 25.7.16.

A quick stop, two hours out of the capital, is the cowboy or Gauchos territory town of San Antonia. A town just too far to commute to the capital from, but close enough to be connected and hold its own ground built from its pride and joy – cattle. A slow-paced town, the occasional abrupt squealing through the town square from a moped engine with laughing passengers cheering affectionately as they pass by. Short takes of seeing people bond in such a way felt like the romantic image of Argentina I was trying to convince myself to see from the images I had in my head before I came here; a real scene from the Motorcycle Diaries. I felt a lot further away from Buenos Aires than the journey there reflected.

Even further away from the town, is the countryside of Gauchos racing their horses, breeding their cattle for beef in open free spaces, where the livestock live happily and with space, eating fresh grass. It is idyllic compared to the streams of city traffic disturbance. From the smiles on Gauchos' faces it was clear they were happier in an unrecognisable way to me from what I'd engrossed myself around in the past, how cynical I was but also encouraged to know and see how travelling could make you want to change. A slower pace of life and the outdoors creates a happier life in this country. Understandable from the natural beauty, but it's also the pride in their tradition of teaching generation upon generation, how to breed cattle to produce some of the best cuts of steak in the world.

Their secret to how they produce the best meat – simplicity. When it comes to cattle, allowing them to be free, not caged, feeding them grass as opposed to unnatural pellets, giving them plenty of exercise, result in cows being less fatty, and their meat being how it should be, natural and tasty. The more I saw of what are recognised as methods are often the oldest ways proving the most effective. Following the older methods and techniques for things that can be so complicated could be the future way forward. It still works today for Peruvians from the Incas!

Argentinians also use more of their meat too, producing more variety of cuts. Within a T-Bone steak, there may well be another cut of meat off the bone, so there are more good options to have available and, as ever, in an enormous portion! Restaurants offer dozens of cuts all over Argentina, with a map or cow diagram to explain them to the ambling, clueless gringo.

The skill (which it certainly is) to cook the meat on a parrilla-grill, strictly on wood or coals on a medium heat, is taught to the younger generation at family weekly gatherings. A whopping thirteen million cows are killed each year in Argentina for their cuts of beef, the best I'd ever had. I consider that all other food could be held up in comparison to – the Argentine steak. I was educated by Gauchos in a San Antonio bar, whilst waiting, writing, and for two whole days there was non-stop rain. The Gauchos were waiting in the bars to go out to race their stock so I could see it in action, they never did, and I never saw their cattle. They're not keen on the rain but, fortunately for me, keen to talk to me over a glass of wine and tell me about their pride in what they do, generation upon generation. Unshakeable belief in their common sense and love, it lightened my disappointment on missing out because of the weather, something I could do nothing about.

These nationals aren't the heaviest meat consumers in the world though; that would require a trip back to Buenos Aires (again) for a stop at the legendary steak house, Don Julio's, to make sure the hype of the best, is in fact the best. After that, I would need to go over the river to Uruguay and find out more there.

Uruguay

Best served being a carnivore 28.7.16.

A last-minute dash to the ferry port for the first boat of the day from Buenos Aires to the Uruguayan town of Colonia was frantic because of traffic and getting lost. The short one-hour journey felt a lot longer and more uncomfortable with bad weather making a stable boat weary in weather which was coming in sideways, and a one hundred per cent hike up on the normal fees from the last dash of purchasing the tickets. Tired and grumpy, the excitement of arriving in a new country was cold, wet, expensive and gloomy.

The port town of Colonia is known as a beautiful cobbled town, it is now practically underwater and the trees are bending from the strong winds. The safest and driest place to go was on a bus to the capital Montevideo and to come back when the weather was nicer. This wasn't a situation of there being nothing to see there, there is – but it looked grim right now.

It's the capital of the world's largest consumers of meat, allegedly eating over one hundred and twenty pounds per person a year. An enormous consistency when spread across the year to keep consuming such heavy food, that's true love and dedication! My dedication for travelling at this moment however was drenched. The weather was even worse in Montevideo; walking down the street in some of the most intense city weather I'd ever been in was far from my travelling dream. The love of travelling – winging a trip to a new country, a new city, to explore and take a chance – was backfiring right now. So far, it was cold, expensive and trying to find an affordable hostel, with no energy in awful weather for two hours wasn't fun. Again, whoever says 'you will love every minute of travelling', is lying. You won't. There are times you don't love your travel companion as Duncan and I started to bicker. There are times when you arrive somewhere with high expectations and it's not as pretty as you'd imagined, or hoped and that's disappointing, however fortunate it is, to be having that chance. No one loves every minute of travelling.

A love for travel doesn't really burn out, it can be replaced or diminished with experiences but it's always there, and the need to carry on, to fix a situation, is more in a mindset than about travel itself.

Agreeing to dive into the next bearable hostel with our soaked-heavy bags, drying off we headed back outside again, not to compound our misery, but to go for a parrilla grill at El Puerto Market, where grills were famous across the country. A mountain of cooked red meats, staked for individual portions or to share as a group on a portable grill was put in front of us as we sat on bar stools, after one waiter successfully ushered us in, amidst the competition. Tucking into what felt like the first bit of warmth in a long time was bliss, but even the view of simmering meat on a grill behind the counter couldn't perk up the atmosphere inside the market. There is no hope for someone who is vegan here, it would be an insult to the Uruguayan carnivores!

The market was a beautiful converted train station renowned for its feisty atmosphere of crowds and buskers entertaining diners as they enjoy all imaginable cuts of meat in a party atmosphere. Instead, impatient waiters who had wooed us into their restaurants grumbled on what must be a slow day of trade for them too because of the weather. Apparently, when the sun shines, the parrilla stands go onto the streets to entice passers-by with the smell of cooked meats too, a carnival atmosphere to the smell of food. I was starting to feel pathetically defeatist and sorry for myself from the fortune of being there and having to deal with some bad weather when I didn't deserve or need sympathy at all.

Slightly drier the next day, but just as windy, a walk along the famous coastline promenade was met by a number of cafes and bars being closed down for winter. This cold horrible walk offers no refuge. It would be a great city to visit on a weekend or at a warmer time as even strolling the centre, where I'd now seen my thousandth colonial church or historical building, everything was closed for the busier and more explosive holiday period. A missed opportunity but I couldn't have it all; I'd had my share of luck with turning up at places.

I felt I'd missed out on something here that I'd never known. I wanted to be able to blame Uruguay but perhaps I'd been travelling for too long. I loved to travel – the freedom, the adventure, the food, the culture, the experiences. I don't love every minute of travelling, but at least I was travelling. A bad day travelling was better than a bad day at work. This long trip, there were bound to be times like this, times of feeling down. Unless I shifted continents continually I would always have a cold season, and a time where the novelty of new things wore off.

Making the best of the situation, the remedy for being indoors though was food and beer, always. And that was exactly what we did as we stuffed ourselves on meat and the famous Chivito Sandwich before returning to Colonia. Uruguay had been slightly disappointing as a result of bad weather, but we were able to walk in dry and wind free Colonia for an afternoon freely and in fact, it was beautiful and worth more time than Montevideo for attractions – a realisation and imagery that home was soon. The days which were difficult were not enjoyable, more interesting than being sat in an office at home for sure, yet nothing that anyone would really envy. It was not necessarily a good or bad experience, just something that happened and which you take home and may or may not talk about. Just how good things I've experienced I won't talk about to people because they're hard to explain or for others to understand.

The approaching fear of home was the new novelty. The new country and city I visited here which perhaps a few months ago I would have enjoyed, was now dominated with the expectation of seeing old friends back home again. I will be skint when I get back, then do the rounds of seeing everyone and answering the same questions, confused about how to explain my 'experience'. Describing this would be a confusing and complex emotion, yet an emotion that I've taken on board. Something that I will have forever, something that some may envy, to have plunged into that change and escapism which will hopefully be the springboard to keep the clearer and more positive mindset I have now for back home, despite the last few days.

Iguazu Falls – best served impressed 30.7.16.

Another landmark of South America, a draw within itself; although I went in with low expectations to avoid any disappointment off the back of Uruguay, and the sense of a sad ending as I came to the end of the continent.

Expecting an attraction of a waterfall at Iguazu that for all the fuss – should be good. The norm would probably be me walking around it, then perhaps a quick swim in the pool at the bottom or even a viewpoint from afar. Iguazu is a national park amid thick jungle and occupies a whole day of walking and exploring two hundred and seventy-five different waterfalls. The humidity of walking in the thick jungle as small pathways led from small falls to the enormous main area of the falls, where there's a view over the falls to the noise of an eruption – water continuously pounds the pools below at the bottom of the fall. It was a monster of enormous amounts of water pouring down and spraying all around you. The intensity as you peered down, the magnitude of the oblivion from the top was nerve-wracking. The view alone made this a worthwhile landmark on the continent.

To enjoy the view from the top, to then go and take a high-powered speed boat into the falls itself, made the magnitude of this monster even more surreal. The largest fall, known as 'the Devil's Throat', is a fitting metaphorical name. The boat up to the water drop area made a terrifying noise and felt like a water park ride. I was drenched from head to toe in the open-roofed boat, having the perspective of this wonder's enormity from the top and the very bottom was a great moment of the power of water and nature that these natural falls share with Brazil.

The spray of water at the top and bottom of the falls creates a white cloud at both ends. With a closer look to the falls, the water has a green-red shade to it from where the deforestation of the jungle has led to soil displacement flowing through the river and down into the falls. The multicolours only add a depth to one of the most impressive natural wonders I'd seen in the world. Argentina is breathtakingly impressive.

The last evening in Argentina after the falls was spent watching the sun set over the Iguazu river which goes to the falls on Argentine soil; to the left is Paraguay but to the right is Brazil. All within one hundred metres of each other, it would be an easy morning crossing into Brazil from here.

Adios to Argentina – best served with red meat and wine 31.7.16.

When the riches of a good steak and great wine are good value, the best of the best comes in the world's most aristocratic price bracket. The disparity in wealth here is as clear as any country in Latin America. The worst quality food is cheaper, yet it's still expensive for the poor, creating the American-style eating culture of the poor eating poorly.

Football keeps Argentinians happy, but with the country's love for horses, the poshest sport of all – polo – isn't far behind, yet is so inaccessible financially for most of the country. The love of horses does have connecting ties across the socio-demographic. Even with horse racing pundits in the First World, it is a rare moment of the working and upper classes to mix and back each other's horses, just as they do in Gaucho territory, where, after the race, everyone enjoys a cut of steak from the well-cared-for livestock.

This class gap creates a culture of negativity while the European culture gives people a loose tongue. The Latinos are unafraid to show their fickle and stroppy side, with a negative tone underneath their friendly tone, especially the beautiful women whose Latino fire and European elegance set them apart from other Latinas.

The value of wine and steak being in the natives' favour keeps them appeased. I'd hate to see them priced out of that more than they already feel they are. A reason why Argentinians are no longer the world's highest consumers in beef is because of pricing; should it continue there'll be more than demonstrations. My love of wine in South America continued to flourish; the cheapest wine available even in supermarkets was still delicious and a lovely way to enjoy an evening after the chilly walks of Patagonia. The love of nature and determination not to alter their parks, or produce their wine or meat poorly, is admirable when so much of the world mass-produces to lower quality, but gain financially. Quality is the motivation here because it's their vanity on show to the world. The adoration for tango dancing in the country, their immodesty in showing how good they are at entertaining, yet the common theme of Latin American-inspired dancing, after all, is the illustration of their repression.

For all the beauty and pride, the gap in social classes and political, economic and social traits remains so great here, creating a cultural attitude of redundancy. ATMs churn out fake currency bills. A country that has a one of the worst fluctuating currency rates in the world is infuriating for travellers. I can't imagine how annoying it is for Argentines who then end up having to circulate fake bills themselves and the path to stability appears even more challenging. The new government has created minimal hope for Argentines as gas prices have risen dramatically since I'd been here in just three weeks. Along with inflation, I felt I'd had a soap opera of a country in economic collapse in just a short space of time.

The reputation Buenos Aires has, as a powerhouse, for all its beauty is a flawed representation, papering the cracks that the country has. A huge country of wonderful things, but there's a horrible cloud of apathy to problems which they can't seem to keep control of. All they can keep, it seems, is their pride in their wine and red meat.

Brazil

Brazil – best served eating a Mortadela sandwich.
- 10 layers of thinly sliced smoked ham
- Sliced white cheese
- Soft 6" subway baguette
- 5 sundried tomato slices

Spread butter onto the baguette and scatter the tomatoes across the length, layer the ham on top of each other and gently melt the cheese on top in a sandwich press or under a grill for 3-5 minutes. Eaten in the central market in Sao Paulo with an old friend.

Foz de Iguazu – best served in a different country 31.7.16.

Iguazu National Park stretches across the border, allowing sight of the Argentine falls on Brazilian soil, a reversal of the view from the previous day. A bus over the bridge of the river dropped us at the park entrance. With less to explore on this side, the park didn't have the open access to the multiple smaller falls like Argentina. The platform's vista was of the Devil's Throat alone; the raised land elevation allowed you to look down to the green fauna which Argentina's adventurous side offers, and the monster of yesterday looked significantly more peaceful. Only until a walkway path which stretched into the mouth from above did I remember the noise and density of water as I got soaked with splash back from Iguazu, albeit significantly less peaceful in a herded pen of travellers.

As far as border crossings go, this was without hesitation a favourite and the falls were worthy of a visit on both sides for different aspects of scenery. Into the welcome warmth and humidity of Brazil, moving away from the colder south's winter, my final country on this journey was ahead of me. Brazil is in a political mess at the moment. I hadn't tried to understand the full picture with the news in a second language but the current tensions would no doubt influence whatever was ahead, a more realistic Brazil to the glossy white beaches and cocktails I'd heard of, back home. Despite this, I was excited, maybe it was because the sun was out or I knew that the glorious idyllic-sounding stature that Brazil has across the world got me going. For once, I couldn't wait to get on a twenty-four-hour bus.

Florianopolis – best served with Havaianas 3.8.16.

Or so I thought... I was definitely bored of buses now, arriving in a huge city it was the first time I had to pretend to speak Portuguese. Arriving in new places with Spanish, trying to figure out how to do things was hard enough but here I was instantly out of my depth, despite similarities with Spanish. Trying to board a bus – the basic phrase you learn in school or a book doesn't have the response of: 'nah mate, not this entrance, walk to the back, hop on and pay the conductor.' – I had no chance of understanding simple instructions said unceremoniously robustly. I felt very, very small in a very big city for the first time, feeling the heat while digesting how enormous this country is as the city stretches long and narrow across ocean and lagoons.

   With an abundance of options of where to stay in this huge city, long bus journeys having taken their toll, Duncan and I unwound in the beach village of Barra da Lagoa. Welcomed by a clean, clear, endless white beach, with warmth I'd craved for weeks, with a one-track mind I got swept up in the therapeutic noise of the ocean which sent me to sleep. Like arriving on holiday when tired out from work, I was shattered from the amount of travel and journeys we'd done recently. No single journey lately had been less than a day, physically draining and ludicrously expensive for the most basic options. To lie down with my toes in the sand and a beer in the hand watching nothingness in the ocean was bliss, and the vision for keeping positive while cramped up on a bus, and what I definitely wanted to do when sat in an office in London – a pain so strong it's still with me months and months later.

A surfer's paradise and with that, sports are available everywhere. Perhaps the beach lifestyle is in the forefront of my mind, but the laid-back Brazilian approach hits you straight away – there is no rush at all. Surf culture dominates Florianopolis and the seafood and surf-style food is what you get. Eating in a surfer's trailer park-come-food court, the first sighting of Brazilian fashion was over the road – an havaianas store. Walking in, I now understood a girl's obsession with shoes; I love flip flops and havaianas have always been the best for me. The laid-back yet serious salesman must have been licking his lips seeing two gringos en route to the Olympics gazing at hundreds of different colours and patterns printed onto the footwear.

Among all the patterns, there was one design intentionally priced cheaper than the others, a white sole with a single baby-blue strap. Historically, a design for the working class to try and look more fashionable and wealthy, they would pop the strap and turn the sole upside down for a colourful and more attractive style and it worked. As a Brazilian supermodel at the time, was then photographed wearing the working-class number on the beach in Rio de Janeiro, making them suddenly a sexy, attractive, and an affordable commodity to have.

Sucked in, we eventually left with two bags of flip flops each that I'd neither needed nor could afford. Every time I opened my wallet now, it felt like something I couldn't afford, but I loved it as I packed up to head back to that very beach that made them famous, Copacabana, in Rio de Janeiro, for the Olympic Games.

Arriving to Rio de Janeiro – best served in a favela 5.8.16.

Arranging accommodation where the location was going to be busy with the Olympics was laborious and expensive. In Rio, the notorious favelas have over the last fifteen years started to become pacified during Rio's influx of global tourists who have increased in number due to hosting major sporting events. Staying in a home stay, in a favela, was therefore what I chose as a cheaper and more interesting Airbnb option.

The favela of choice, Santa Marta in Botafogo, is one of Rio's smaller favelas with five thousand residents. Arriving by cab, I was dropped at the turn-off from the main road, at what I recognised as normality. I couldn't look more out of place as gringo if I tried. I walked up to the noise coming from afar of what is the main epicentre of the favela, the basin of a very steep hill which looked exactly as I'd imagined, crammed with damaged and disturbed houses. Wearing two bulky rucksacks, I saw a party was building up. I started to sheepishly interrupt, asking for assistance on where I should be going in bad Portuguese (what was coming out of my mouth I couldn't even be sure was Portuguese). People were clearly waiting to party as they grilled food for their friends on their own portable BBQ drums, but they still seemed interested to help me out, the confused gringo that I was. Standing out like a sore thumb, dressed head to toe like an Olympic tourist in the wrong part of Rio, and Brazil were about to kick off a football match, the timing was so awkward but perfect.

The obsession with football here is obvious and crowds of people around small TVs insist on helping me find my way, but only after I watched the game with them. With no idea how to even begin to find my host in the favela, I conveniently had no choice but to join the party. Not long into the match I was greeted by a man who introduced himself as Gilson, who easily spotted me in a herd of green and gold coloured Brazilians wearing their team colours. In a fast-paced ramble of Portuguese, something about Airbnb was mentioned and I slowly responded 'sim' (yes) back. Gilson directed his hands for me to go with him, I hoped this was my host, otherwise I was following a random man into a favela, but what was the worst that could happen…?

A cable car-type system was installed here about twenty years ago, helping locals to climb the steep favela. Any fears of safety and security were quickly put to rest. Gilson insisted that while we waited for the lift up he would show me around the base of the favela in more detail, where fruit and vegetable traders in the base of the favela played the role of security guards for locals. I left my bags in a makeshift baggage hold (a vendor's shopping trolley). The tour continued and I returned to find the bag hadn't moved at all in half an hour. Guarded with integrity, it quashed my paranoia of accepting to come back to no bag. If there was going to be any crime here, that was the chance.

I ascended in the cable-car over the favela city built of cylinder bricks and tinned roof housing, a seemingly never ending vertical wall of houses going higher and higher, where at the top a small football pitch for kids was being played on. With a sense of authority, Christ the Redeemer overlooks the homes. To the right, Sugarloaf Mountain is behind white concrete high-rise flats which show the way to the beach beyond the favela. Having done a lot of hiking lately, the walk after the cable car to go further up was intense, steep and challenging as we weaved through a narrow, unlit maze of discarded rubble and dog shit which littered paths that smelt of sewage. The crumbling walls were sporadically coloured for aesthetics, but also for creative purposes to celebrate their favela's stories as well as offering an escapism and career path.

Recurring murals are of Michael Jackson; this is the favela where his video 'They Don't Care About Us' was filmed, raising the issues that the favela has to a mainstream audience making him their local hero.

The favela is equipped for residents like any other town: a church to pray, a local burger shack along with dozens of snack and soda stalls. Citizens of the favela have normal, day to day jobs, from builders to even a helicopter pilot. When they earn good money, those who've been raised here often still stay because despite the bedlam, this is their comfort zone, and their home. The favelas started to become pacified to try and reduce drug crime which still lingers today, in the hope of improving the image of the city ahead of hosting the World Cup 2014 and the Olympics, a popular move on the whole, when conducted in a respectful way. There are police who live in the favela and although daily patrols take place throughout the area, their permanent presence is deliberately restricted to the foot of the favela at the roadside, close enough, but far enough away to avoid antagonising.

Santa Marta felt like a happy place. Enthusiasm and energy in conversations amongst locals, a soundtrack of background noise and groups of cheers and commotion, cropped up every so often in response to the Olympics entertainment. I finally arrived at my small room, a basic four foot by four-foot room with a splintered bunk bed and no windows, making it hot and stuffy. The smell of dog piss is absorbed into the wallpaper and flooring. It was unglamorous but was a convincing introduction to what favela life was like, this was my home until I wanted to move on from Rio. The view from outside my room where the bedroom-kitchenette was, was a panoramic view of all the sites that Rio has to offer. Children are having a pool party in an inflatable paddling pool on their flat tin roof, hoisting makeshift kites made out of plastic bags in the wind of the favela's hill.

The history of the drug wars and fights which have taken place here was as baffling as it was curious; people are so kind and happy, all sat together enjoying one another's company. From the jovial atmosphere of now, it was hard to think how scary that must have been and then the sacrifices the peace movement had made. The idea of how these fights happened here was boggling; the place is a tight, confusing maze of a city with no structure or organisation; it would have been an incredibly tense guerrilla war for those who knew the paths, and those who didn't.

Coming back at night, after a couple of beers, having walked up the entire favela was a stab in the dark in terms of luck finding my way. Aimlessly I walked up-hill trying to recognise crumbled landmarks or a building that looked the same as all the others, a tattered poster or piece of graffiti that I hoped I hadn't seen before to avoid going around in circles. Locals in the favela shouted in Portuguese at me; I had no idea what they were saying or if they were trying to help or not. To them I was a foreigner in a place which was unrecognizable to a traveller at this time of night. It was intimidating and the motivation and tolerance for those situations was near the end, after eight months, now it was more annoying. After several dead ends, wrong turns, I made it home. For all the good will, this didn't feel like the kind of place to get lost in. The Olympics being held during a politically turbulent time for Brazil highlighted the story of 'how the other half live'; in the favela world, the real Rio, and the bubble of the Games, it was an exciting mix to be with and see.

Meeting the neighbours – best served next to Christ the Redeemer 6.8.16.

With the favela kicking into life, the sun breaking through the panels of my room woke me up. The musky smell of dog piss in the sweltering heat was suffocating – it made me want to get up and out, and see the mayhem I had heard across the hill. The view of Christ the Redeemer was misty from the heat of Rio awakening, but the landmark of Rio enticed me to explore.

After a cold shower with a towel wrapped around my waist, to see a towering six-foot four-inch black man I'd never seen before, being the only one in the house, standing blocking the door staring aggressively at me, square in the eyes. As far as first encounters go, this was odd. My pigeon pronunciation of 'Hola', was greeted in response by his stare continuing to be more and more intense into my eyes. This wasn't all the Portuguese that I knew but I wasn't going to be able to elaborate on my thoughts of: 'What the hell is going on right now? Where has this guy come from, and what is he doing here watching me shower?' We continued to stare blankly at each other as I waited for him to say something, anything! I tried not to laugh with awkwardness, as I subconsciously thought I might need to protect myself with a skimpy travel towel – the only defence I had which covered my modesty.

Our stand-off ends after what felt like five minutes of blankly staring at each other, when finally he turned his body allowing me to squeeze past him to the tiny washing area that barely fits one of us, let alone two of us and I was allowed to get changed in privacy, still without any words being said. Standing in my underwear as I rummaged through my bag, he burst open the bedroom door with a smile from ear to ear. Energetically shaking my hand, he then walked out. Relieved that the tension had been broken, but I had no idea who he was or what was going on as not a word was spoken.

Walking to collect my Olympic tickets from a ticket hub in the city, I bumped into Gilson who informed me that this was the local nutter who is completely harmless, but just likes being friendly and seeing people, which in hindsight was exactly how he was, just the 'seeing people' part had been pressed against my face in the shower. Walking around the favela to try and get my bearings, it was incomparable to the working cities I'd been to, from suits and glum faces of workers to generations of friends playing cards together, football together, laughing with each other in their confined community.

I hadn't had a haircut in a few months, so a visit to the favela barbershop was the life admin part of the day that I had to do. Four old gentlemen were sat outside playing chequers on a makeshift crate-pallet; they waved me in with a welcome hand movement. A relaxed attempt at getting business into the shop, more concerned about continuing their game, but it worked.

Not speaking Portuguese at all had to change for me and I had to try and improve. A young teenager cut my hair while his group of friends sat next to us talking about chasing girls, playing cards and football; I was able to piece together a few phrases and questions (albeit from the similarities of Spanish in his response). Using google to translate on my phone (one of the perks of having a smartphone), I was now becoming a fan of the anti-social traveller with their eyes glued to their phone as it helped me communicate again, having not met any English speakers yet. Trying to get a haircut is a gamble when you don't speak the language. I had no right to feel disappointed with how it turned out, but the young man who cut it looked very proud to have cut a curly haired gringo, who was obviously not a regular client for him. With a big smile, I said 'sim' to him in polite approval at which I was greeted by 'noooooo, no, no, no – we love Jesus'. With no religious opinions, I politely nodded in confusion as the group of friends in this small barbers stood up slowly. I was still holding onto a bit of cynicism on my surroundings – was I about to get kidnapped? This could have turned out to be an expensive haircut. They raised their hands level with their heads and the six teenagers broke into a loud, hysterical fast-paced prayer. One of the lads had placed his toddler on the barber's chair and the baby began screaming from the noise. My hands were up in unison with them. I thought I was either praying or about to get noisily robbed.

The frenzy stopped; amid their screaming exhaustion I picked out a word I understood – Amen – my cue to thank them and leave. I set off to sit on the beach to meet Duncan who was staying on Copacabana Beach, to have some drinks before we checked out the nightlife of the Lapa region. An interesting first day in the favela, I was surrounded by beauty and chaos after all.

Let the Games Begin – best served awkwardly 7.8.16.

Lapa is an area of downtown Rio with a reputation, amongst its packed-out bars and street parties, of a lively and artistic night out. Artist Jorge Selarón's efforts to make the area more aesthetic was to add tiles to create a mosaic along a staircase known as 'the Lapa Steps', for every gringo in Rio poses on steps you've already seen. Locals are referred to as Carocas here, and they love art. The tacky art sold most commonly isn't a fair reflection on the work Selarón did as a community project in Lapa which has spread over the city and other virtuosos have created since in Lapa. Selarón's work of goodwill has inspired those in the favelas to be artistically creative with their own murals. A lot of street art has been cleaned up for the Olympics to give it a nicer image, but its reputation for free-flowing caipirinhas is still strong as the night escalates ahead of our ten a.m. session for beach volleyball tickets that I'd brought for the next day.

Again, woken by the sunlight through my door, I saw forty missed calls from Duncan who was waiting for me at the arena; it was twelve noon and I'd overslept. I leapt out of bed, grabbed a shirt and ran barefoot down the favela. Unsure where I was going, I just ran as fast as I could downhill, hurdling dog shit as I sprinted to Copacabana. Today is also the GBH's birthday. What excuse could I use to say why I'd forgotten? What excuse could I use to say to Duncan why I was three hours late?

Other than some casual football on the beach, this was the first time I'd done any running since my foot injury and it hurts, not just from the injury but the scorching tarmac in the midday sun as I ran in between Copa's white, over-priced high-rise flats to the most famous beach in the world where a temporary arena had been constructed for volleyball.

A thousand apologies and another dash through the turnstiles later, we sat down as I gasped for air and water in a desperately hungover state. The realisation of being sat in a unique sports arena was joined by the realisation that I definitely owed Duncan a few beers at least from the kiosk bars that stretched along Copacabana beach. The post-exhaustion energy boost that I had and sunburn had made me feel rejuvenated in Rio, with Copacabana being a much nicer beach than I'd expected. With the scenic shallow mountains behind the beach, there was an assertive energy and excitement on the streets. With gym-exercise machine frames on the street promenades, I'd started to think that I should really do some more exercise and be healthier, just in time for temptation from a caipirinha vendor who walked past and sold me a fresh cocktail as we sat on the sand, fuelling the festival atmosphere to beachgoers as the festivities seemed to carry on in the city.

The build-up to the games came with sour coverage for Brazil. Reported fears over the zika virus which had been prominent in Brazil has put people off coming to Rio and the rest of the continent. As a consequence, Rio was quiet. It was nice not to feel over crowded at a peak time, the stigma attached to the country was now magnified by an event showcased around the world. The image of a disease in people's minds and in a country is a dampener. During my travels people have false fears of virus or diseases when people don't seem to know much about them. Zika has been used as an excuse to stay within a comfort zone and not to travel, tarnishing a country's ability to protect itself against unknown illnesses. Should something you know nothing about be off-putting then chances are you are never going at all. Apparently, they have not handled the situation very well, Brazil has been mocked for their efforts and questioned – should they be hosting the Olympic Games?

In 2009 when Rio's bid for the Olympics was successful, the city promised to 'clear up' its nastier image. 'Clear up' is what they did, their choice of words apt and damaging, not 'improve', 'help', but 'clear up', as if junk would be thrown away and the junk being lives. A wall was built to hide the favelas which lie by the airport, to hide them from the first impressions of visitors as they arrived. Humiliating for those habitants who, I imagine, like the residents in the Santa Marta favela, take pride in their improvements to then be shunned as if their own city is embarrassed of them. Making up such a sizeable amount of the population here, authorities don't want them to be seen as the world turns its attention to Rio. The original promises of tickets left spare for the poorer seem to have fallen away. If my session was anything to go by there were a lot of empty seats. Surely not everyone was as hungover or asleep as I was?

Football is the number one sport in Brazil but a few mutters that Cariocas don't want to go are untrue. Walking back to the favela a young boy screamed at the top of his lungs: 'Judooooooooooooo'. His voice echoed down the narrow favela walls. Half my size he ran at me and attempted to throw me on the ground with a judo move as he giggled with enjoyment at recreating an event he'd just seen on the TV. Hungover, confused and tired from the heat and cocktails, Brazil had just reached the final of a judo round, and the favela had a spring in its step. I found another gear from their positive energy which I found so inspiring in comparison to the materialistic ways that happiness was portrayed by in the First World. In reality – all it does is clutter the mind with having too many unimportant objects around you.

There may well be an apathy and other reasons why the locals aren't attending or engrossed in the Olympics, but there was an opportunity to at least feel a part of the games which had the potential to positively engage and inspire in a country which could benefit from a lift in morale as they enter their second successive year of an economic recession. The event feels a little awkward to be held right now. The northern part of Rio seems to be having a favela war where trickles of news on the troubles seem to contradict themselves constantly. A strong army presence on the streets and military campaign posters at all metro stations sit uncomfortably for those who remember their heavy involvement during the dictatorship. Something doesn't feel normal; is this the real Rio that I'm seeing? Whatever the games are supposed to be about, it doesn't feel like today was quite it. Despite the sunshine and cocktails on the beach, the stuffy smell of piss was hard to ignore.

The Olympic Tourist – watching sport with a beer and a brigadeiro 14.8.16.

While the games have been taking place, Rio was a city with a double purpose for me – to watch sport and to be an out-and-out tourist, sightseeing.

Ticket sales are low so Duncan and I bought some last-minute entries for cheap. Low-priced tickets are great for us, being able to sit anywhere was a perk, but a shame when attending a quiet, half empty athletics stadium. One event was Brazil's arch rivals Argentina (who have brought hundreds of supporters with them over the border), taking on Algeria in the football. In Brazil, religion is important, but unquestionably dwarfed by football. Brazilians occupy a half-full stadium acting as twelfth man for Algeria; there was a samba party going on in the stands as beer was handed around while watching the game – a carnival celebration for sport and Brazil.

Just as football is a love of mine as an Englishman, travelling with New Zealander, Duncan, his passion for rugby led us to buying rugby sevens tickets. We brought tickets through an overpriced agency, borderline ticket touting making it expensively priced in comparison to the now last minute cheap deals.

A new hobby had started to develop during the Games, collecting individual and unique Olympic cups that drinks were poured into. So, drinking as many beers as possible became the name of the game to try to get as many different cups as possible. Drunkenly enjoying an underdog's win as Great Britain overcame one of the favourites, New Zealand, collecting cups like a childhood hobby the Olympics were turning out to be a boozy sports day in the sun, which was fine by me.

So good was the previous day that we decided to return for the final day as Great Britain reached the finals against Fiji. Despite a number of empty seats, with this being the best chance Fiji had ever had to win a medal, the entire stadium got behind them. I was completely outnumbered as I saw my home nation at the end of a thumping on Fiji's way to winning gold. A worthwhile journey for their travelling support but the gold and green-coloured shirts of Brazil were becoming more and more noticeable. Cariocas were beginning to take up the Olympic spirit and don their colours as the home nation started winning medals and the hosts started to share an interest with the tourists. Those visitors who had felt uneasy about zika and the political tensions the country has, were able to relax and feel more comfortable being welcomed by Brazilians enjoying their own event.

Brazilians' love of sport hadn't gone far enough to attend and fill the stadiums. Spending time in bars on nights of competitive events for dominant travelling supporters, the channel on the TV would change at key points of a race for a Brazilian football game. 'If Brazil can't win and it's not football, we don't care' was the general take of the Olympics. Trying to watch some key events in a packed bar, if there was a football game on, it was football or nothing.

With coverage of sport limited unless it was Brazil, visiting the postcard sites of Rio was a way to do something other than cocktails, sport and the beach. A cable car up three hundred and ninety-six metres to Sugarloaf Mountain puts a geographic distance between the mainland's congestion and myself. A packed, elbow shoving, sweaty and nauseatingly steep viewing platform for sunset at the top wasn't so tranquil, albeit a special view of the city, as the lighting along Copacabana came on. The volleyball stadium, beach and nightlife all started to turn on. It was an exciting time to be here, despite the negative press wanting Brazil to fail.

I visited the beach of Ipanema, a prettier and less busy beach, south of Copacabana, where beach and foot volleyball are played, tourists provided entertainment for onlookers by joining in the Brazilian beach sport, looking amateurish in comparison to locals' Olympian standard.

As the Games went on, it was clear that this was good in the short term for Rio. As Brazil succeeded in events, cheers rang out all over the favela and when golds were won, the city erupted with noise that could be heard from the top of the favela where I was staying and the lights below flickered from disruption. Car horns were going off, people samba danced on the streets and in the restaurants, the bars were packed, short-term gratification peaks. The famously rough parts downtown had been regenerated with a modern 'Olympic Boulevard'. Ambitions to turn the area into a cultural hub that locals could be proud of, had been met apathetically by the Cariocas. Almost tired of meeting new people continuously, with the same repetitive small talk to other travellers, it was nice to be introduced to a friend of my sister who was working at the Olympics, Robyn, a new face but a familiar home comfort to link up with and explore the classier side of downtown and try the classic Brazilian treat, a Brigadeiro. Originally made from condensed milk and chocolate as a quick go-to snack when rations and supplies are low at home, it's adored across the country by the rich and poor. However, in this part of the city it was more

250

of a gourmet snack with multiple variations available in the stylish patisserie style cafés that were new to the once rough part of Rio.

This wasn't the time to see the real Rio, the Olympics, was a façade as to how the city normally was. The Olympics are on, it was not a normal situation for visitors to come here, nor was it normal for the city to be hosting such an influx of people. In a city where the gringo trail had warned me of its dangers (which every city in the world has), the favela had helped me to see an abnormal life through my First-World vision at a unique time.

The community was close and the open-door policy with neighbours could be a little startling as my first morning was. At times it could be concerning when returning home to an unknown man sitting on my bed, which wasn't the norm in hostels for instance. 'What's mine is yours'; the churrascaria buffet of everyone helping themselves to everything was normal. In Rio it was delicious, eating every cut of meat available as a treat from cooking for myself in the favela, as my credit card spending, the back-up card, now reached its twilight zone. The 'pay it off when I'm home' card was being used, hard and fast as an expensive city in Rio, with the addition of an expensive event in the Olympics equalled spending more than I could afford to.

Having been away so long, my spending restraint had now been exhausted, and while feeling a little lonely from the language barrier on my own in the favela, I was spending to be sociable. Be that a meal out, or a beer at a favela party at the base of the hill. There was a realisation that this trip was coming to an end, and had to, partly because of money; the bearer of evil in the First World was depressing. In a bar I watched the Brazilian ladies' football team crash out of the tournament; you could hear a pin drop in the silence. The excitement for the Olympics was dying, and as I was starting to feel more limited in what I could go and explore here; it was becoming apparent that it was time to move on, maybe not even just from Rio but Brazil and Latin America. I heard a cheesy quote this week, which rubs a solo traveller's ego, that 'if your journey is made from the opinion of others, you're going to run out of gas'. This trip certainly wasn't built on others' opinions, but there was someone in my head back home that I didn't want to let go of, and subconsciously I think I'd emptied the tank deliberately for that reason.

With Rio having provided me with some revitalisation, it also came with the never-ending need to do and see attractions and a sense of needing to be busy to see all of them. Cattled in a herd like group up to the Christ the Redeemer, for a final dose of congested carnage. There was a viewpoint with enough heads and arms of people posing at the monument to fill the empty stadiums with attendees. The site was too hot and overcrowded to be enjoyed making it an overpriced view in my eyes, but a view nonetheless of a city with an obviously better standard of life compared to other cities in Brazil. With its weather, beautiful beaches, botanical gardens and mountains nearby.

The glory of the good life increases the gap between rich and poor. My favela of Santa Marta sits in one of the nicest districts of Rio to live in, where manor houses and mansions aren't out of place. With the local government having spent so much money to host the games, Rio has now run out of money, and the austerity gap outside the Olympic bubble is on track to worsen.

The final morning I have in Rio was spent again in a crowd of course. Myself among other non-ticket buyers watched the marathon along the beach, again it was blisteringly hot and uncomfortably crowded. I walked to the metro accompanied by a whore insisting on buying me a drink. Caraocas' reputation amongst Brazilians, I have been told is, 'they will invite you into their home, but they won't give you their address', a backhanded compliment as to how they treat their visitors. Well this lady definitely wanted my address, whatever her means were, as I left Rio against the crowd of enthusiastic yellow-wearing tourists going to the final events.

Paraty People – best served with Cachaça 23.8.16.

The Bay of Paraty, once the stomping ground for pirates who did their trade with the Portuguese here, is a half-way point between Rio and Sao Paulo. An untroubled and undeveloped pretty town, with the pirates' presence, a main road was never built to stop by here, in order to avoid the looters. Perfectly close but far enough out of the way of the cities to slow down and relax.

Introduced to Paraty by overcast clouds which quickly turned to rain, beautiful cobbled streets didn't feel as cute when walking and slipping on them, making the need to concentrate a priority as opposed to taking it all in. My injured foot had been as sore ever since I ran as I was late for beach volleyball; losing balance in Paraty's beautiful stoned paths was bitter-sweet.

With no overstated ugly buildings to spoil the landscape, the artistic and pretty culture obsession here felt perfectly unspoilt. Upon meeting a group of travellers over a beer in the hostel, we walked to Paraty's cultural festival which took place under a big gazebo. The whole town crowded around delicious food truck vendors to escape the rain and dance the samba, the nation's favourite form of music and dance.

Beer vendors strolled in-between dancers on the makeshift dance floor, selling cans of beer so cold that ice formed at the top of the drinks, so there was never a need to go the bar. Even as the music stopped and the party migrated to the beach, cachaça was then passed around freely and swigged from the bottle. This was Brazil out of the city, just as fun but perhaps more my scene, there was none of the pretence or intensity that a city brings.

As the rain kept coming down the next day, Paraty's cobbled roads began to flood and the boat ramps from the sea allowed water to come into the town. This created a Venice feel of a flooded town where you walked the streets with water-covered feet.

The surrounding areas of a town could be just as interesting as the destination itself. Forests close to Paraty hide cachaça distilleries in the hills, an opportune getaway from a damp cobbled town. Brazil and its abundance of coffee plantations being at the forefront of beverage production, I hadn't considered the nations other popular drink, cachaça, that was created nearby and pours into the parties in Paraty.

Hidden around distilleries, waterfalls ran through the forests. I went with a new group of what I felt would be temporary friends I'd made at the festival. This wasn't pessimism, just a reality of my trip coming to an end with the knowledge of travellers I'd met so far. I had tried to convince myself I should keep in touch and hadn't, these people would be no different. Any waterfalls after Iguazu were always going to be a squib by comparison, but amid the rain being able to slide down water rapids into a freezing cold plunge pool, a new way of riding a waterfall proved to be an entertaining day.

Refusing to Countdown – best served with acai 25.8.16.

The real world was starting to creep into my head. I knew it wouldn't be long till I left South America but I refused to count the days down. I didn't want to, and thinking about changing to a different yet awkward comfort zone made me nervous. The sun was now out in Paraty after a couple of wash-out days of rain, and the town had sprung into a new lease of life. Breakfast was no longer sat on a stool in a hostel, but taken outside to sit on the beach eating acai, the healthy Brazilian sorbet-like treat for breakfast. The smell of wet roads drying, there was now an anticipation that Paraty had more to offer.

Aspiring painters joined watercolour classes on the street as they brushed onto canvas their surroundings of pristine white buildings with tropical coloured window and door frames. Bohemian jewellers, who'd run away themselves from the overwhelming, expensive lifestyle of Rio, sat in the sun making sales. This felt like one of the happiest places in the world to be. Artistic fishermen have taken their lives on the water to their art store, shops were filled with retired boatmen painting their hand-made sculptures. They created miniature versions of their own boats that once supplied food to the town but now ran boat tours to cruise around the islands off Paraty which house beachside retreats.

Drinking caipirinhas in the sun, I tried to convince myself that I was not distracted by the inevitable return home. Accepting I'd be back in London soon enough, perhaps part of leaving something you didn't like is to return and make it better a second time around. Certain things I was looking forward to being over: no longer being in a dorm, some healthier food, the GBH... But the weather? Sat on a quiet beach, listening to waves in complete tranquillity, the adjustment to how people are with their negativity, could be a killer, but also in my head, of how I may feel again, when nothing has changed. Not that I want things to change for me, but the outlook I have to the rest of the world has developed, while I feel paranoid the world hasn't changed with me. But why should it have? I need to feel revitalised and not squashed by a return. I can't count down to a return just yet; I need to make the most of being here, enjoying now, instead of thinking about something that I don't think I want, or am ready for.

To Sao Paulo, To Old Friends – best served learning how to make cocktails at a BBQ 28.8.16.

Tiago and Fernanda were two Paulistas I worked with in London who travelled, returning to Brazil, coincidentally timing in with my journey to Sao Paulo. Inviting me to stay with them in their family home, I was gifted with a chance to see a city with a local, and live with a Brazilian family, which is more entertaining and comfortable. Usually pleasantries are the norm but I was now tired of snoring hostel dorm mates, obnoxious gringos and repeatedly having to be friendly. With little money left, and knowing my trip was going to be ending soon, seeing familiar faces was something to be excited about.

Welcomed into their flat with a home-cooked dinner, home luxuries included a comfy bed and a warm shower, a comfort I had forgotten existed. Travelling solo and being around people you know you won't see again, suddenly being with a family I realised how selfish travelling solo was. My surroundings and discomfort weren't all about me any more. I couldn't just throw my bag down and go out; being treated like family I was obliged to help with household tasks and wait for Tiago to do what he needed to do before we explored. It was nice to have humility forced upon me, having felt that I had it hard when nothing was difficult at all. I had got carried away being in my own bubble and this had made me feel uncomfortable for no reason prior to the fortune of being in a family home.

Sao Paulo is Brazil's most important city for politics. A recent right-wing coup means a presidential change is ongoing – the city's tense. Tiago showed me the heart of Sao Paulo where Avenue Paulista was much prettier and greener, with trees lining the road which drive through the centre, in contrast to the ugly concrete mess, as travellers had described the city. Perhaps I hadn't seen the worst. Now I was away from the gringo bubble, where negative opinions get thrown around at ease with tourists' own home comforts being their benchmark, I could judge for myself with more clarity. I was becoming a travel martyr, judging others by their opinions and thoughts. Now I'd become what I never wanted to be, a cynical and judgemental traveller!

Once having a reputation for drug trafficking and crime, one of the two most notorious Brazilian gangs is from Sao Paulo. Areas which were once violent hangouts and no-go places, have been converted to parks for teenagers to meet each other for skateboarding with community areas of bars and restaurants on the fringes. Protests against the government's current situation have been violent, media coverage and demonstrations are now twenty-four hours a day. I was relaxed as Tiago and I caught up, discussing a love of Brazil, our travels diluting any political tension in the air. Overdue beers with friends were interrupted by chicken coxinhas, the go-to quick bar-snack, a chicken croquette, which was ideal to munch on while sipping on beer. Long catch-ups led to a good bye, as Duncan popped by before he left Brazil. The length of our travels felt significant to our trips and a farewell was met with genuine optimism that our travel paths would cross over again. News of a birthday party, where I'd be the only 'gringo' as I was branded by a new group of friends of Tiago's, eased the travel-companion transition and motion of moving from place to place, and pragmatically from friend to friend.

Nearly all forms of housing are flats in the city. Tiago and his family's block of flats has a basement with a small community football pitch as the garden, the location for the birthday party BBQ. Valiant efforts in Portuguese with arriving guests are in vain. Knowing I was badly interpreting the language and not getting a lot out of it, I perched myself next to the BBQ chef, a big fat smiley man who was covered in coal dust and seemed to find my language efforts endearing. Next to him with a bucket of beer. I hoped that the more drunk I got, the better my Portuguese would get. We talked football, food and beer, becoming friends who somehow understood each other despite a couple of awkward pauses and nods pretending we knew what was being said via single Portuguese, Spanish and English words. The slow cooking of beef sirloin over the coals was therapeutic and a nice talking point. When the language barrier got in the way, we always manage to drift back to his love for getting loved ones together for a BBQ which seemed the most important part of the day for him. We bonded through that common ground in our comically bad attempted phrases of each other's languages as we made our way through our bucket of beer together inhaling BBQ fumes.

Two friends of Tiago's, a man nicknamed Sunshine and Tiaginho, recognised my feeble Portuguese as some kind of Spanglish and helped me out as I learned more about the cooking, our backgrounds and with the help of football chants, I learned some more Portuguese. The only thing that could perhaps make the day more Brazilian for me, than a BBQ on a football pitch, would be a caipirinha, and, just like that, as I went for another drink I was having my very own one-to-one class on how to make the famous cocktail.

Not really sure on how to offer a drink in Portuguese without some help, having had a few beers, my offer to Tiago and Fernanda's family and friends was more of a yelp with my hand in the air as I pointed at people offering a drink. Confused looks by some sympathetic takers who took pity on my attempts at being the lone and unfamiliar face trying to make their drink.

As knowing and remembering names goes, it got harder and harder as the speed of the pronunciation and drunk slurring added to an already difficult situation of trying to understand. I can use the excuse of being drowned out by drunk samba music being played by family and friends, as they passed instruments around on the football pitch, as to why I didn't understand.

My jolly chef friend had left as does my lesson on the infusion of a BBQ, football, cocktail, language lesson which all intertwined here – the loves and essentials to Brazilian culture. To other guests I was now just 'the gringo'. Never said with malice, but as I didn't know many people here, the gringo was the outsider. The surplus extra of the party, despite the event still being entertaining, I was the boy who didn't speak their language, that they don't want or need to get to know. Danny, in Guatemala had taught me that gringo wasn't an insult, but it wasn't a compliment either, and while sheepishly making a big effort with language it didn't feel it was quite good enough for the people here. Even if I'd stayed here after all, I'd always be the gringo, something I'd accept, but when feeling more comfortable with people, it was isolating to be branded something that represented negativity.

With London on the horizon, there was a realisation that going out of the comfort zone and feeling isolated was at times utterly exhilarating. Feeling like an outsider, when my sense of entitlement to feel like one of them, was demoralising, and patronising when you were working hard on something. Feeling home comforts with a nice family was amazing to have while away, but your own home comforts were perhaps something I'd underestimated what they meant, probably because I don't know myself.

The State of Sao Paulo – best served with a Mortadela, understanding the country 1.9.16.

The city of Sao Paulo, the capital of the namesake state, is as diverse with people as I'd seen within a state or region thus far. A historical hub for Brazil, when war broke out in Europe during the 1900s, a huge Italian migration entered the country. The migration has altered since, now Brazilians move to Europe with an Italian or Portuguese passport, passed on from older generations, along with the claim of Brazilians making the best Italian pizza in the world. Sao Paolo has boroughs within the city which are full of Italians. It can be hard to identify a Brazilian aesthetically. With a European influx the typical Latino look is pastier than normal, let alone the concoction of the Japanese population who are here as well. Little Venice, a nickname for an area with a high proportion of Italians, doesn't quite do it justice.

The area next to Little Venice in the city called Liberdade is part of Sao Paulo which hosts authentic Japanese market food, trading each Sunday. The rodizio-style all-you-can-eat service, traditionally for Brazilian BBQ food, is available for Japanese sushi in restaurants too, catering to the population here while keeping up the Brazilian style of being and eating together.

Spending more time exploring the city with a local, the more well-known side of Sao Paulo as an ugly, business focused city comes to light as Tiago and I hired bikes to go around the city's business district. There were times when we consciously, and subconsciously, pedalled a little faster, and intentionally didn't stop, in surroundings which felt like a place easy to forget but an incident could happen very quickly and easily, to make it memorable for the wrong reasons. The city's business district had, however, one of Latin America's best food markets, Central Mercado. Notorious for the quality of food on offer, setting it apart from other markets, a grand building design with stained glass windows. The beauty of the city was the blend of a little bit of everything from around the world in one place. The infrastructure of the main train station was built from structural pieces of London's Waterloo Station, to now house the Brazilian-European-Asian market and there were all kinds of high quality food on offer. The legendary mortadela sandwich, an interpretation of immigrants' Italian ham sandwich but bulked up to be a stack of ham and cheese, was a perfect hangover antidote for people watching in the market hall.

A strong Catholic city, named after Saint Paul, religious differences are ignored in a city that's intensely diverse. Nowhere I'd travelled before has homosexuality been open enough for same sexes to be able to hold hands; even nightlife entertainment is openly advertised which I hadn't seen since London. This liberal approach sets Paulistas apart from the rest of Brazil and the continent in a refreshing way.

Although this is not a pretty city, it is a city that looks after each other and people don't turn their noses up at each other. They are respectful and conversational with each other, be that the man in a business suit or a beggar. This was evident from the surroundings of the market where both ends of a demographic congregate. The financial capital of the country stands proud of its wealth, as so many live in comfortable, nice apartments here. The polar opposite is unavoidable in the heart of the centre at the landmark Patio do Colegio. A homeless epicentre forms around an electronic billboard which lights up the government's tax income to date for the year, a sum of money which increases each second as beggars lie without shoes in the winter on a cold marble floor that suits and bankers walk over each day. Abandoned by their government's benefits system, now choosing a self-punishment of having the wealthy rub it in their faces.

The political tension gets worse over the week as the president's impeachment means Brazil has a new president, Temer. Recognised as a right-wing coup, almost every time people sit together, there's an intense, bordering on aggressive debate on the matter, even among those who are the best placed and relaxed people. Tiago's family are incredibly kind and warm with each other, family is number one, yet daily political developments strain them. Of course, it's soon disregarded in laughter as they talk about football to cheer themselves up. I loved the home environment with no dorm room nuisances, varied food, not having to make the boring small talk, and being able to learn more about an area that wasn't much of a destination other than for its food, having once been the food capital of South America.

I took a night trip to visit new friend, Sunshine (from the BBQ), in the coastal city of Guaruja. It is a very ordinary city with a selection of beaches but worth the while. Brazil is so spoilt for beaches and I hadn't even seen the best of them in the north of the country. Time in Brazil, and a samba and beer session was never far away. Sat on the beach with a few kegs of beer to keep us company, we listened to music on the beach at night. Away from other tourists, the simplicity and comfort of mutual pleasures being with friends was something that was memorable and taken for granted.

The car journey back with Tiago and Fernanda was through the industrial heartland of the state. Ugly factories churning out fumes and emissions which are unregulated illegally, to the government's knowledge, were now being sold off to foreign countries. The new president was quick on this and another discussion based on fear from poor decisions from the elite, comes up in the car. Industrialisation wasn't a forte of mine, but a decision to sell off a country that only ten years ago was on the brink of becoming a superpower seemed a poor one. Those in power should be educated, always. They often are but how can their decisions seem and be so wrong?

I could concede these were my own limitations and thoughts and the radicalisation in the news doesn't help. All the great things to be seen in the world were so often spoilt by individuals' inability to take responsibility to make those things to be experienced better, more enjoyable, happier, healthier, fairer, more equal.

The Home of Food and Football – best served together 8.9.16.

Every country in Latin America loves football; Brazil is beyond obsessed. The romantic image of Brazilians playing variations of beach football, and foot volleyball, on Copacabana beach, with the beauty of Rio surrounding the stage, kids in the favela playing and scoring as they then scream their heroes' names that they dream to emulate one day. Children, barefoot, play as a pair of football boots or trainers would cost closer to what you would pay for a top-end pair in the UK; boots are simply unaffordable.

The perk to the Brazilian football machine is that when kids start their footballing education shoeless, they perform and progress to the point of 'earning shoes', with the luxury of earning money. The toughest days are behind them and their motivation to excel is there as they can only get better. This misfortune has been a blessing in disguise and will continue to be a cycle for generations that's unlikely to change. Brazil, has the most football World Cup titles to their name. Most players from those teams have come from such backgrounds. The highest profile team in the world, with all its grandeur, loses its way as the corruption in the governing body (the CBF) has allowed money to spoil their structure by building stadiums that are now unused. Giving their star players too much money, too soon, has at times been a hindrance.

This makes it easier for Brazilians to affectionately remember the older generation who share a love of the game as opposed to the stereotype of loving money which modern players have now. I visited Fernanda's family in the city of Ribeirao Preto where Brazilian legend, Socrates, is from. Corinthians, the biggest club, has a plaque where he used to sit each time with the fans, at his favourite local bar.

In typical Paulista fashion, Palmeiras is traditionally an Italian club known as 'The Pigs'. Fortunately, there was a big Sao Paulo derby game when I was in the city against local rivals, Sao Paulo, who are known condescendingly as 'bambi', translated from slang as faggots. Going to the game with Sunshine and Tiaginho, a late evening kick-off allowed fans to have three to four hours of build-up on the streets after the working day. Streets packed in club colours of green and white as a street party kicked off with singing and beers were passed between street vendors with the purpose of serving you to boost the adrenaline that was in the air in beating their rivals, along with the green flare smoke going off around us, of course. A big day for the city's football teams, a carnival finale as fireworks shoot down the streets to drunken cheers as the fan groups lead the bouncing crowd with chants.

The game opens to a deafening chant as the national anthem was drowned out by Palmeiras fans singing their team name along to the tune of their country's chorus. Brazilian's flair and pace set the tempo of the game, attack, attack, attack! Here, with far less logical or tactical build-up their aim was to show off and entertain their fans and themselves, on point with their good time lifestyle. An early lead for the opposing Sao Paulo against the run of play to the disgust and devastation of Palmeiras supporters as their fickle nature came to the fore. Two quick goals back from Palmeiras sends the adrenaline into overload and the ecstasy that sport gives Brazilians. A rocking stadium and the noise of cheering and more firework rockets and chanting outside was a love for the current moment and the joy on peoples' faces was a level of happiness I hadn't seen in one place before, there was no sign of pessimism or negativity at all. Love for football in Brazil is totally indisputable. Being asked if you like football, the only reply was a definitive yes, as if to answer otherwise would be absurd, bordering on insulting.

The adoring necessity for playing the game is so distinct and not just on the beaches or favelas. In Sao Paulo they have converted unused space across the city for people to use as pitches. Tiago and his friends invited me to their pitch that they hired weekly, inside a converted warehouse. With rolling teams of six a side, while not playing it was a big social catch-up with beers and a BBQ of meat on the sidelines. Living in a city where the cost of living prioritises their chances to socialise, football and a BBQ was their only chance to get together, as well as secondarily, their outlet for exercising, balanced out by going through case after case of ice-cold beer, as the only way they allowed the beer to be served.

Older generations create the same social connection with football which hasn't changed through the generations, be it kids or elders, as Tiago's father was invited by his friends and we filled in as extra players. Grown men were as competitive as I'd imagined they were when they were younger, desperately flying into tackles and achingly rattling their creaky bones, heckling each other to get the edge over one another to win. Comically surprised at how seriously they took the sport was wonderful to see, the two components of the nation's strongest loves, football and food, bring people together.

Whilst people drink more and more, I was thrown into my own Portuguese lesson of listening to their favourite football team's chants, and being made to recreate them in pigeon Portuguese as an initiation of being accepted into a group of friends. Not understanding what most of what I was saying meant, I was trusting the approval of Tiago, while being forced to down beer and insult Argentina, chanting to a samba tune, 'Gringo, gringo, Maradona is a whore', as booze seemed to help my linguistic skills in some shape or form. I knew what that song meant!

Football had been a way for me to learn the language, small traits picked up such as why 'inho' is added to words and names that I learnt from football: Ronaldo to Ronaldinho which translates as little. Speaking with Tiaginho I butchered my pronunciation to the enjoyment of our footballing group, who seemed to enjoy my pronunciation of this word more so than other mistakes I'd made in the past. It turned out my butchering of the language translated into me calling my friend, 'Little Vagina'. I realised that Portuguese wasn't my forte, but the social football and food combination was something Brazilians have mastered.

Goodbye Brazil– best served at the end 12.9.16

An enormous country with a sexy yet dismaying appeal to it. I was leaving with regret that despite having spent six weeks here I didn't see more, particularly in the north. Exhausted by the love of travel, energy and cash limitations slowed me down as well as a love of everywhere I visited, a desire to see more and more in each place, I was so comfortable and relaxed. From the outside Brazil seemed so different to neighbouring countries yet fits into Latin America better than it likes to portray itself.

Brazil's brilliance stands unconventionally with its mayhem. Infuriating stupidity can make things tedious here more so than other countries. The city of Rio was named incorrectly; founders of the city thought the bay was a river (translated as Rio), a 'namely' mistake which portrays stupidity and stays with them forever. There was a desperation in trying to get every penny out of travellers that they can, more than the rest of the continent. Every single street food vendor has a gringo price. It was tiresome and almost put you off the street food in comparison to the quality of food when you sat in to eat somewhere in Brazil. The culture of being together with loved ones is paramount in Brazil and a table or stool is their magnet to restaurants and diners which is a nice change from fast food chains being the dominant places to eat. Quality food, from every corner of the globe, eating and sharing big portions in their home is their style, sitting down together so the whole family can be there. The small bites you can buy when in a rush like a coxinha are rarely bought, 'to-go'; again it will be with the purpose of a sit down meal. After all, Brazilians don't rush anywhere, such is their nature. Punctuality in Brazil doesn't exist, so arranging to meet at a time probably means to meet a few hours later.

Spending time with people who know an area always makes things easier, quicker to see things that you would and wouldn't have seen, easier to learn, easier to adapt, the comfort of a home. The emotional and physical struggle that travel brings is softened and a different angle opens up, like a room you wouldn't have walked into, suddenly opening for you.

The irritation at not being able to contribute more than a football chat or small talk about cooking techniques at a BBQ I think soon passed. I absorbed it as a blessing of being able to be ignorant of heated political discussions and drift off to think of the things that Brazil does best: food, football and beaches. With every right to boast about these things which will remain Brazilian flagships forever. Brazilian-Portuguese is its own language anyway, it's Brazilian slang, abbreviations of the Portuguese language and spoken jovially at a rapid pace. They don't care, they've inherited phrases and a language from the metropolitan nature of the country and now it's theirs.

The government's turmoil (a theme that trickles through South America) and latest coup attracts global attention onto Brazil post-Olympics. Governing issues aside, how locals have been treated for the sake of hosting an event in Rio doesn't sit well. It's a bleak future for Rio which is about to declare bankruptcy as money hasn't been shared evenly, nor has it across the country.

A maliciously-toned media has now started drip-feeding the favela with news that occurred leading up to the Olympics – what happened in order to 'clear up' the city for the Games. The number of police-caused deaths from gunfire during the Games to keep disturbances under control for the event is coming out now. A perplexed situation of the Olympics being a double-edged sword for Brazil, but with a more painful than beneficial legacy.

A serious short-sightedness when seeing the homeless problems that Sao Paulo has, the north is allegedly much worse off economically and very different, perhaps more intriguing than the parts I'd seen in Brazil. I'm intrigued, as even at the end of my trip when I was broke and tired, I still had that urge to see all I could and to do more and more travelling.

So, to the end of a continent, I had one final low-key night in Rio, solo, before I flew home. As I took a cab to the airport, along the motorway the sun fittingly set like a perfect cliché ending with Rio behind me. I was attached and besotted with Latin America all over again, a well-travelled part of the world, there were so many popular and unpopular things to see and do.

My departure day had arrived uneventfully other than a final caipirinha on my own on Copacabana to try to get a final bit of tan. I hadn't counted down the days. I had tried to just enjoy the concluding days and moments and not overthink going back but now I felt lost and confused what was next. An unwelcome and awkward sense of familiarity to be lost and confused on what I would be doing next.

There was always something I'd have missed which I clutched at as an excuse to come back although knew I probably won't before I visited other places new to me. Every new place is exciting, the next thing – a new experience and travelling and cuisine can be that. The whole process of dreaming it, booking it, doing it, is a chance to figure out what you really do want to do and how you want to be.

As the drive to the airport continued, Rio got smaller and smaller. I was mentally distancing myself from my trip and wondered how different it would have been without a tie to home. Would I have explored in the same way? From all the things I saw and yet didn't see, or felt I'd missed as I longed for more, all of the planning and dreaming as I agonised back in London while being unhappy with what I was doing. This had been special, but if I was unable to remove parts of my life I previously hated then it was a trip of martyrdom, and pointless.

I was returning to London to be the limelight, the new shiny toy everyone wants to see. People hearing what you've been up to and saying 'oh I can imagine', but can they really? They will tell me how they'd love to do that; some are genuine, most are full of shit and they know when they are, because they feel the need to say something to connect with the enthusiasm of the story you've told. I am flattered but it's not what I want. I want to be able to feel comfortable somewhere.

A new sense of enrichment and enhancement has been taken on, but I don't know how I've changed otherwise. I've blended into a new comfort zone which has been learning new things in a foreign language to the point where a Portuguese-speaking country became a new place of discomfort; London seems an unrealistic transition to me.

To finally have done something productive and enjoyable with life while balancing them together with a passion for food, travel and culture, it's what I'll remember when I need that comfort and assurance for wherever I'll be next.

Acknowledgements

Pegasus gave a debut writer a chance and for that I'll always be grateful. When I was young, older generations made travelling and cooking so interesting and still do today, they are a genuine inspiration. Of equal importance are those who I met through Latin America, my direct inspiration for this book, by sharing their stories with me and creating new memories that are forever imprinted in my mind. To Oie's on Fenchurch Street, London for giving me a job that allowed me to work and write, while feeding me the best food London has to offer.

Thank you to those friends and family around me whose positive energy encouraged me to do something new.